MW01631960

Mark,
God bless you & our country!

MYTHS OF AMERICAN SLAVERY

Walter D. Kennedy

MYTHS OF AMERICAN SLAVERY

Walter D. Kennedy

Foreword by Bob Harrison

PELICAN PUBLISHING COMPANY
Gretna 2003

Library of Congress Cataloging-in-Publication Data

Kennedy, Walter Donald.
Myths of American slavery / Walter D. Kennedy ; foreword by Bob Harrison.
p. cm.
Includes bibliographical references and index.
ISBN 1-58980-047-8 (alk. paper)
1. Slavery—United States—History. 2. Slavery—United States—Public opinion. 3. Public opinion—United States. I. Title.
E441 .K46 2003
306.3'62'0973—dc21
2002007056

Scripture quotations marked *KJV* were taken from the *King James Version* of the Bible.

Printed in the United States of America

Published by Pelican Publishing Company, Inc.
1000 Burmaster Street, Gretna, Louisiana 70053

Contents

Foreword . . . 7
Introduction . . . 9
Chapter 1 Slavery: A Worldwide Phenomenon . . . 13
Chapter 2 Slavery Comes to the New World . . . 21
Chapter 3 Abolitionism Versus Christianity . . . 69
Chapter 4 African-Americans, Free Born and Slave . . . 101
Chapter 5 Slavery Versus Secession . . . 141
Chapter 6 Lincoln: The Un-Emancipator . . . 163
Chapter 7 Slavery and the Confederate States of America . . . 183
Chapter 8 The Flag of Slavery. . . . 195
Chapter 9 On the State of Slavery in Virginia . . . 211
Chapter 10 On Jordan's Stormy Banks . . . 221
Addendum I Abstract: On the State of Slavery in Virginia . . . 235
Addendum II Early Anti-Slavery Tract . . . 241
Addendum III Recommended Reading List . . . 247
Notes . . . 253
Bibliography . . . 269
Index . . . 275

Foreword

I met the author of this book, Walter D. ("Donnie") Kennedy, at the first annual Southern Party convention in Charleston, South Carolina. I was profoundly impressed by his knowledge of the *facts* of Southern history and the War of Northern Aggression. Even more so, he immediately gained my respect and admiration as a man willing to give anyone an opportunity to debate his views as stated in his books. Donnie and his twin brother Ron had already gained fame with their book, *The South Was Right!*, and subsequent titles, *Why Not Freedom!*, and *Was Jefferson Davis Right?* (a copy of which remains on my desk at work). His fiery spirit, a twin to my own, comes through in his speeches and writing and always manages to evoke thoughts, both pro and con, in those who hear or read his words.

When Donnie informed me of his decision to write a book on the *truth* about American slavery, I was immediately intrigued. After reading his manuscript, I guarantee that all who read this book will find evoked in them feelings regarding this issue that will still generate controversy and anger. As a first sergeant of Company B, Thirty-Seventh Texas Cavalry, C.S.A. (a historical reenactment unit), a Southern Party staff writer, a descendant of two Virginia slave families, a history scholar, and a modern black Confederate, I already possessed many of the same feelings and much of the same knowledge that Donnie displays in this book. However, since reading this well-written and well-documented work, I have been greatly inspired to look even deeper into the minds and experiences of the slaves (of all color and ethnicity) who endured that "peculiar institution." As a historian with a strong wealth of knowledge about Confederates of color, I already knew that much of what is being taught as "gospel" regarding slavery is highly suspect at best. The information provided in this book fills in many of the gaps that the "official texts" leave empty.

The introduction to this book is thought provoking and sure to "get under the skin" of mainstream liberal black leaders and members of civil-rights organizations. In the introduction, the author makes a strong and logical argument against slave reparations. He explains that, while injustices did occur throughout the history of American slavery, (1) slavery was *never* a regional issue confined to the South, (2) slavery was *not* condemned by the early Church, and (3) through the institution of slavery, blacks were given *real* freedom—freedom from the harsh realities of slavery and the slave trade which still exist in Africa to this very day! I am certain there will be those who will attempt to label Walter Kennedy's fine work as a document laden with racist diatribes. I am certain there will be those who will choose to ignore his acknowledgment of the horrible acts committed during the history of American slavery. Regardless of what they read, some people will choose to believe that he is saying that these horrible acts never occurred. The author makes it abundantly clear that these things did happen. However, those with the courage and the fortitude to allow themselves to ingest all of this book will discover that what they think they know about slavery and the "truth about the institution of slavery" are not one and the same. The author, my personal friend and Confederate brother, has put together a work drenched in true historical *fact* that will not only evoke emotion, but will also clearly indicate that the way this tender subject is taught must change immediately. I dare say, he is *right* yet again!

Bob Harrison
Southern Party Staff Writer
First Sergeant, Company B
Thirty-Seventh Texas Cavalry, C.S.A.

Introduction

No subject [slavery] *has been more generally misunderstood or more persistently misrepresented.*[1]

Jefferson Davis
The Rise and Fall of the Confederate Government

Few if any Americans would consider slavery as anything other than a curse on mankind. From the beginning to the end of this work, this author maintains that slavery in its various manifestations is nothing less than that very curse. Yet, understanding the "curse" of slavery and having a through understanding of that institution in American life is not one and the same.

In the history of these United States no subject has been more discussed, debated, and fought over than the issue of slavery. To modern minds, the idea of slavery is incomprehensible. Nothing appears more "self-evident" to modern Americans than the fact of individual freedom. This "self-evident" notion of freedom is so ensconced in the American psyche that even those who attempt to fairly discuss the subject of the institution of slavery are subjected to ridicule, being characterized as "defenders of slavery." Therefore, the point must be established that, telling the whole story (i.e., the complete truth) about the institution of slavery is not the same as defending the institution of slavery. Rather, it is those who refuse to make an unbiased study of the institution of slavery who are defending a lie, a myth, or at best, a half-truth; and, therefore, defending an evil institution. If the truth can make one free, then condemning those who are searching for the whole truth is an attack upon intellectual freedom.

As has been noted, the issue of slavery in America has deep historical roots. Since the end of the War for Southern Independence, the "party line" from the victors in Washington has asserted that the blame for all problems arising from the issue of slavery should reside preeminently in the South. An open-minded individual should notice that Northern heroes and symbols are seldom condemned for racist comments or for being involved with the African slave trade or even slavery itself. The brunt of condemnation for slavery is reserved for Southern heroes and Southern symbols. The victors assert that in the so-called Civil War,[2] the North fought for human freedom and equality while the South fought to maintain the institution of slavery, even if it meant the destruction of the United States. The party line, repeated by virtually every agent of information (that is, the media, academia, and theologians) is systematically enforced with the tyrannical effectiveness of George Orwell's Big Brother. Therefore, the average American today has only a superficial knowledge about the subject of slavery. For most modern Americans, slavery was (and is) a "Southern" problem.

In fostering this official view of the institution of slavery in America, the victors have subverted the truth into a myth. Unfortunately, this subversion has consequences far beyond academic discourse. Today, because of the acceptance of the myth of slavery, virtually everything Southern is under attack. The petty prejudice of the sycophants of the myth (those who flatter to gain favor) respects no limits when attacking those who hold views that differ from the accepted view of the institution of slavery. Even, as will be demonstrated, the lives of those who love the South have been placed at risk due to this slavery myth.

If you are intellectually courageous enough to be open-minded, you will come away from this work with a more complete understanding of the institution of slavery in America. Be assured that you will not be transformed into a defender of slavery. As will be demonstrated, you will join the ranks of some of America's most prominent leaders who advocated the end of slavery while defending the truth about American and Southern history. Yes indeed, the truth *will* set you free.

In the following text, we will look at the myths surrounding slavery in America. The myths of slavery, as maintained by the established order (i.e., the victors of the War for Southern Independence), are composed of several false allegations. Among the more prominent allegations are: (1) Slavery was an institution operated by white people for the oppression of black people; (2)

Slavery was a system organized by Christians; (3) Slavery was a Southern institution; (4) Slavery was a self-evident sin and so recognized by the Christian Church; (5) Slavery only existed in the North for a very short time and had little economic effect; (6) The North ended slavery because it was offensive to the moral character of Northerners; (7) The North offered the black man equality and brotherhood; and, (8) Racial discrimination and/or segregation is a legacy of Southern slavery. These mythical allegations that support the currently held view of slavery in America will be investigated. In investigating these allegations, the author intends to demonstrate not only that these myths are predicated upon a false premise, but also that in most cases the very opposite of what is stated is true.

If all this book does is to expose the myths of slavery to be a pernicious lie, that alone will distinguish it as a most unusual work. But more must be said about how the issue of slavery has been politicized, both in the past and in the present. As one Southern writer has noted, for far too long the issue of slavery has been used by unscrupulous politicians "led by fanatical hate and armed by all uncharitableness," to rally voters to their ticket. With little regard for the truth or the consequences of their rabble-rousing politicking, demagogues have taught several generations of black Americans that they are suffering today because of the legacy of past slavery. This then is the myth that must be dispelled. The questions that must be answered are: Is the legacy of antebellum slavery the cause of undue suffering for the present generation of African-Americans? Would they have fared better if their ancestors had never been forced out of Africa? Is there a land in Africa or any place upon *terra firma* where America's black population would fare better than here? Like driving a wooden stake into the heart of a vampire, dispelling this myth will destroy the demand for innumerous government-funded programs, multitudinous schemes for reparations, and countless calls for apologies from the descendants of the presumably offending class. After a long and hard look at the facts surrounding slavery and the African experience in Africa, the United States, and the western hemisphere today, the author is convinced that rather than charging all white Americans reparations for slavery, black Americans should focus on building with everyone together the kind of country that any American would be proud to live in. As will be demonstrated, nowhere in the world are black people better served and treated than here in the United States. Rather than demanding reparations, black Americans should be grateful to their ancestors for surviving the hideous passage to America; a passage that freed modern African-Americans from the ongoing slavery that still exists in Africa today; a passage that brought today's African-Americans to a higher standard of living than any Africans in the world; and a passage that eventually brought them real, lasting freedom. This is not to minimize the injustice done to any individual or group of Africans brought to America involuntarily. Injustice has been done, but it is here in America that injustice has been challenged and, more often than not, defeated. As will be demonstrated, no blacks in Africa have a longer life span, a higher literacy rate, a lower infant death rate, a higher per capita income, or more personal and civic security than black people in the United States. And even more shocking, even when compared to life in Mississippi (one of the poorest states in the Union since the close of the War for Southern Independence), the blacks of Africa are still far behind their African brothers in Mississippi! So the questions that must be asked are these: Are black Americans worse off because of slavery, or are they better off than any other black people in the world? Has American slavery been a curse or a blessing to African-Americans?

The time has come to look at the issue of slavery in America with composure and an open mind. Emotionalism and preconceived notions about slavery and its consequences must be set aside. This book is not a defense of slavery; it is a defense of the truth about the complete nature of slavery in America. In a free society, no one should be expected to examine only one side of an issue. How fair would a court proceeding be if only the prosecutor was allowed to present testimony in a case? This treatise sets before the reader a viewpoint that has heretofore been denied a hearing or has merely been scoffed at and gone unheard. In the market place of ideas, no one must ever be so sure of himself as to refuse to investigate ideas that may, on the surface, seem disagreeable. To investigate is not necessarily to embrace, but to refuse to investigate is to guarantee the death of truth and the birth of ignorance. Freedom will not survive a generation that allows the bliss of ignorance to obviate the search for and the acceptance of the truth.

CHAPTER 1

Slavery: A Worldwide Phenomenon

THE ANCIENT WORLD

The idea of slavery was so deeply ingrained that no one questioned its propriety. All nations either endured or enjoyed it.[1]

A. O. Sherrard
Freedom from Fear

For most Americans the term "slavery" evokes mental images of the antebellum South and hundreds of African-Americans toiling away in fields of cotton. Yet, slavery existed long before the American South was settled by Europeans. It should also be understood that slavery knows no racial or ethnic boundaries. Long before the advent of modern Western Civilization, various forms of slavery existed. There are few ancient cultures where slavery did not exist in some form. Historically, whenever one society conquered another society, any captives that were not slain were then considered trophies of war and disposed of as slaves. Ancient civilizations, like Egypt, Assyria, Babylon, Greece, and Rome, all practiced some form of slavery. Historians have noted that the foundational cultures of our present Western European civilization were the slaveholding cultures of Greece and Rome.[2] The ownership of slaves during this time was not restricted to the wealthy alone, for many common and even poor people owned slaves.[3] The ancient system of slavery, like its more modern American form, was based upon the economic necessity of providing a dependable and uniform system of labor. Ancient Athens, the cradle of our modern "democracy," had more than twenty thousand slaves by 413 B.C. Some historians have estimated the ratio of slave to free in Athens to be three to one at various times in its history. This ratio is even higher for Sparta.[4] As cruel as enslavement might have been, its benefits to the people of Athens and future generations of mankind cannot be overestimated. Then, in 272 B.C., after centuries of warfare, Rome conquered Greece and took tens of thousands of better educated, more sophisticated, and highly cultured Greek citizens as slaves. Through them, Rome experienced great advancements in art, science, literature, architecture, medicine, drama, and government. Even laudatory intellectuals such as Plato and Aristotle spoke favorably of the institution of slavery:

> [A]ll people who differ from one another by as much as the soul differs from the body or man from a wild beast . . . these people are slaves by nature. . . . For a man who is able to belong to another person is by nature a slave.[5]

Plato often spoke of the necessity in an advanced society of having a "subject people" for the flowering of civilization. As noted by O. A. Sherrard in his work on slaves, the idea of slavery was indeed deeply ingrained into the fabric of the ancient world.

Two important changes have been noted in the nature of slavery in ancient times and in modern times. In the earliest days of slavery, one nation would go to war with another and capture part or all of its population. These conquered peoples would then be made slaves of the victorious nation. Therefore, slaves were more likely to be owned by the state rather than by an individual. Slave labor was used for public works projects such as the building of temples, roads, and aqueducts and for other services deemed good for the victorious nation. As time progressed, this system of public ownership of slaves changed to the more common modern system of private ownership.[6] Another important change in the nature of slavery in ancient times was religious in nature. In the early days of slavery, slaves had their own religion but were seldom encouraged to become participants in the religion of their masters. Eventually, slaves were given back their "souls," that is, they were encouraged to adopt the religion of their masters. This was true both in Ancient Israel and later in Christian nations. Thus, slaves became the subjects of an even higher power than their masters; therefore, they were under the protection of the same higher power as those who owned them. Many scholars believe this change marked the beginning of the abolition of both the slave trade and slavery itself.[7]

By the middle of the second century B.C., it is believed that the number of slaves in Italy was twelve million, while the number of free citizens numbered only five million.[8] At the time of Christ, the Roman Empire dominated the known world. While Jesus lived and taught, 30 to 40 percent of the population of Italy were slaves. The percent of slaves in Italy at the time of Christ was equal to the number of slaves in the Old South during the time of the War for Southern Independence. This slavery existed not only in Rome and Italy but was a ubiquitous force throughout the empire; it even existed in Palestine, the land of Christ.[9]

The quality of a slave's life in the Roman Empire was more or less dependent upon the good will of his master. Although some laws were passed to protect the life of a Roman slave, he could be sold, mutilated, tortured, or killed by his master. With the slave population being so large, a constant fear existed among the slaveholding class concerning slave uprisings. To prevent such occurrences, Roman law dealt harshly with any slave participating in a revolt or attack upon his master. The most notable slave uprising in Roman history was led by a Thracian slave named Spartacus. After a surprisingly difficult struggle, the Roman army was able to put down the revolt. As a consequence of the uprising, the Roman officials put to death, by crucifixion, more than six thousand slaves who had been captured after Spartacus's defeat. But more than just slaves who revolted against their masters were put to death. Often, innocent slaves were put to death as a warning to other slaves when a slave master had been attacked or killed by his slaves. After the murder of a particular slave master by one of his slaves, the killing of four hundred innocent slaves was ordered by Roman officials. Commenting on this incident, Roman historian Tactitus noted, ". . . you will never coerce such a mixture [slaves] of humanity, except by terror."[10]

Eventually slavery was eliminated in Italy by the slow process of the manumission of slaves as well as by slaves buying their own freedom. Although this event took place at around the time of the rise of the Christian Church, Christianity itself took little direct action to abolish slavery. Rather, it was a Christian emperor, Justinian, who gave slavery its legal foundation in Rome. This system of laws regarding slavery became the basis upon which latter-day European nations established their legal system of slavery. It should be noted that the laws of slavery that were brought to the New World had Roman antecedents.[11]

Although reprehensible to the mind of modern man, slavery carried little or no moral revulsion in the ancient world. For thousands of years, slavery was an integral part of life on earth. By contrast, slavery under Europeans lasted only 383 years in the Western Hemisphere, and only 222 years in the United States. This of course does not take into consideration slavery as practiced by the various Native Americans of North and South America.

In ancient as well as more modern times, slavery was a universal risk of all mankind and not merely a risk confined to one race. Vikings made slaves of various Europeans, Romans made slaves of Germans and Greeks, the English made slaves of the Scottish and the Irish, Moslems made slaves of Christians, Christians made slaves of Moslems, and the list could go on *ad infinitum.*

Most Americans will admit that slavery was a color-blind institution in the far gone days of ancient civilization. But when it comes to more modern times, Americans are reluctant to accept the notion of slavery in any other terms than "white masters and black slaves." Nevertheless, historical records abound with proofs of white slavery both in Europe and in America. Even in the age of political correctness, a few daring souls have come forward and challenged the notion that only Africans were held as slaves in the Americas. Writing in the *New York Times Review of Books,* David B. Davis, a prolific investigator of the slave trade, noted that slave markets from the Black Sea to Egypt maintained a brisk commerce in white slaves throughout the fourteenth and fifteenth centuries. Davis also noted that in the seventeenth century white slavery was not uncommon from Virginia to Barbados.[12]

So great was the enslavement of British subjects that in 1701 it was estimated that of 25,000 slaves in Barbados, 21,700 were white. Many of these "slaves" were indentured servants who had been illegally or at least "extra-legally" taken from their English homeland. Speaking of the indentured servant, Dr. Hilary Beckles, a contemporary English authority, states that "the ownership of which could easily be transferred, like that of any other commodity . . . as with slaves, ownership changed without their participation in the dialogue concerning transfer."[13] Describing the indentured servant as a "White proto-slave," Beckles gives modern readers a more accurate picture of indentured servitude in early America. Early in the history of the English colonies in America, the institution of white slavery provided the bulk of the labor supply. For the most part, prior to 1640 most of the sugar grown in English colonies was produced by forced white labor. With life expectancy reduced for the indentured servant, a five- to seven-year indentureship was often tantamount to slavery for life.

White slavery was not anything new for the English. During the seventeenth and eighteenth centuries in England, as more and more people were removed from their land, a class of poor whites grew at an alarming rate. So great did their numbers become that laws were passed to "control" these poor whites. From these laws, many poor white folks were sold into actual slavery or proto-slavery both in England and the Americas. The most degraded and offensive (to modern sentimentalities) of this class were the children of poor white people. Many of these urchins were "sold" to workhouses, where they worked from twelve to sixteen hours each day. In one 1765 report, it was established that the workhouses in one district had a 90 percent mortality rate for children. It should be noted that these children ranged in age from five to sixteen years. How much abuse and criticism would have been placed upon a Southern plantation that had such a record? The lack of a moral outcry by the abolitionist crowd caused many English labor leaders to question the sincerity of abolitionists' criticisms of the evil institution of slavery. Bemoaning the lack of sympathy for the white slave children of England, Rev. Richard Oastler, a Methodist minister in York, England, stated,

> Thousands of our fellow creatures . . . are this very moment . . . in a state of slavery more horrid than are the victims of that hellish system 'colonial slavery' . . . the very streets which receive the droppings of the 'Anti-Slavery Society' are every morning wet by the tears of innocent victims at the accursed shrine of avarice, who are compelled, not by the cartwhip of the negro slave-driver, but by the dread of the equally appalling thong, or strap, of the overlooker [in the South an overlooker was known as an overseer] to hasten, half-dressed, but not half-fed, to those magazines of British infantile slavery—the worsted mills in the town of Bradford![14]

Thanking Rev. Oastler for his efforts on behalf of the slave children of Bradford, a delegation of labor leaders questioned the "conduct of those pretended philanthropists and canting hypocrites who travel to the West Indies in search of slavery, forgetting there is a more abominable and degrading system of slavery at home."[15] In yet another account of the horrors of white child slavery, there is the account by Charles Shaw, a former child labor slave, who managed to live through the experience:

> Fortunes were piled up on the pitiless toiling of little children, and thousands of them never saw manhood or womanhood. Their young life was used as tillage for the quick growth of wealth . . . these little White slaves were flogged at times as brutally, all things considered, as Legree flogged Uncle Tom. Nearly all England wept about thirteen years later for Uncle Tom, especially the 'classes,' but no fine lady or gentleman wept for the cruelly-used [English] children.[16]

Although white slavery, both in ancient and more modern times, is a provable fact, Africa has the dubious distinction of being the continent from which more slaves have been taken than any other continent. In antiquity, all the major civilizations have taken their share of slaves from Africa. In more modern times Arab slave traders carried on a brisk traffic in black slaves during the days of the Trans-Sahara slave trade. From the ninth century until the advent of the Trans-Atlantic slave trade, around the middle of the fourteenth century, Arab Moslem slave traders were responsible for an estimated ten million slaves taken from Sub-Sahara Africa. Most of these slaves were transported to areas around the Mediterranean Sea, the Red Sea, and the Indian Ocean.[17] Although the Trans-Sahara slave trade did decrease after the commencement of the Trans-Atlantic slave trade, it never ceased. In 1840 the ruler of Egypt, a Moslem, carried on a brisk traffic in slaves from Nubia. A virtual army of more than twenty-seven hundred men armed with rifles, lances, and cannons, struck into the interior of Africa, destroying crops and making slaves out of more than a thousand Africans.

> In this way, the men carrying the sheba [a wooden instrument attached to the neck of one slave then to another], the boys tied together by the wrists, the women and children walking at their liberty, and the old and feeble tottering along leaning on their relations, the whole of the captives are driven into Egypt, there to be exposed for sale in the slave-market. Thus negroes and Nubians are distributed over the East, through Persia, Arabia, India, & Co.[18]

SUMMARY

At this juncture, two points should be clear to all about the institution of slavery. Slavery was neither a European nor a Christian plot; nor was slavery an institution which exclusively oppressed black people as many in the politically correct community maintain. Indeed, as will be demonstrated in upcoming chapters, even in America, slavery crossed racial boundaries. In the nineteenth century, white men were sold into slavery, black men owned black slaves, and Native Americans owned black and red slaves. The myth that slavery was solely a black problem is a position that cannot be supported by historic fact.

MYTH: Slavery is an institution that oppressed only black people.

REALITY: From ancient times to the early part of the nineteenth century, slavery has existed across racial boundaries. The English word "slave," according to the *Oxford World Dictionary,* is derived from the word "Slav," a Caucasian ethnic group. These people were so often taken into slavery by conquering armies of the Ottoman Empire, that from the name "Slav" grew the word "slave."

MYTH: The institution of slavery was a creation of the Christian world.

REALITY: As we have noted, slavery existed from as far back as the earliest record of man's progress. It is foolish to assert that Christianity, which grew from the teaching of Jesus of Nazareth some two thousand years ago, is responsible for the institution of slavery. Most people who espouse this theory merely mean that Christians were responsible for the Trans-Atlantic African slave trade and thus slavery in America. This fact is true, but it overlooks five hundred years of the Trans-Sahara slave trade of the Moslems. This slave trade was responsible for as many African slaves as the Trans-Atlantic trade. If one is to condemn Christianity because of five hundred years of African slave trade, one must also condemn Islam because of five hundred years of the Moslem Trans-Sahara slave trade.

CHAPTER 2

Slavery Comes to the New World

There is no record of either pirates or highwaymen ever having been regarded as persons following an honest calling; whereas, the slave trade, until the early part of the nineteenth century, was a perfectly legitimate business and those engaged therein were considered as respectable as any other traders.[1]

Ernest H. Pentecost in
George Dow
Slave Ships and Slaving

Even while acknowledging slavery as a historical fact in the ancient world, most Americans still think of slavery in the New World as Southern slaves working in fields of cotton. Yet, as we will see, slavery existed in the Western Hemisphere for more than a hundred years before its arrival in Dixie. Even more shocking to modern minds, it was sugar and not cotton that simulated the introduction of African slaves into the New World.

The Trans-Atlantic slave trade had its beginning some fifty years before the discovery of America by Christopher Columbus. Looking for gold for his treasury, Prince Henry the Navigator of Portugal led the way to the exploration of West Africa during the early part of the fifteenth century. As it turned out, the yellow gold he discovered was not nearly as valuable as the black gold he discovered—slaves. Early in the history of the slave trade, slaves were obtained by the simple but crude method of raiding the coast of Africa. It soon became apparent to Europeans that this method would not provide the number of slaves desired. A better system of providing slaves was instituted by the Portuguese, that of peaceful trading with local African slave traders.[2] At first, trading from its ships was adequate, but in 1445 Portugal established a land-based slave trading post, known as a slave factory, fort, or barracoon. This establishment represented the first permanent slave-trading outpost in Africa by a European power. Over the next five hundred years more than fifteen million African slaves[3] flowed from these and other similar factories. During the earliest days of the slave trade, most of the slaves taken from Africa were sold in European markets. Many were used by the Portuguese on their newly established sugar plantations. This one crop, grown at that time along the coast of Africa and in Portugal, was to be the great stimulus for the flow of Africans from their ancestral homeland to Hispaniola, Cuba, and Brazil.[4] George F. Dow, author of *Slave Ships and Slaving,* noted, "Captivated in tribal wars and kidnapped in times of peace, uncounted millions of Negroes were closely stowed in the holds of all kinds of sailing craft and carried to the West Indies and America to be sold as slaves to work the *sugar plantations*" [emphasis added.].[5]

As has been demonstrated, the Trans-Atlantic slave trade had its origins before the exploits of Columbus. Indeed, "Columbus did not take slaves to America but he took the idea."[6] As governor of Hispaniola, Columbus ordered the enslavement of the indigenous peoples. Unfortunately, the local Indian tribes were unable to cope with the requirements of slavery, and their numbers steadily decreased. Starting with a native population of 1,000,000, over one fifteen-year period, the population was reduced to just over 60,000 people.[7] For those who condemn the South for the harshness of Southern slavery, the fate of Native American slaves in the Caribbean Islands should give them pause to reconsider their ill-gotten notion. Nothing in the annals of Southern slavery comes close to the mortality rates seen in Hispaniola.

In an effort to ameliorate the suffering and deaths of the native population,Queen Isabella of Spain authorized the introduction of Negro slaves into Hispaniola. The queen's humanitarian effort is just one of many examples of well-intentioned people attempting to do good and ending up doing harm. As will be demonstrated, the law of unintended consequences (results) often plagued those who were attempting to end suffering and slavery. Queen Isabella and the world would soon learn that good intentions do not always produce good results. As African slaves were introduced into the New World, the Native American population became less valuable and soon virtually disappeared. As sad as that result was, even worse, the African slave trade was given a boost that would not subside for the next 250 years—good intentions, bad results.

The individual who is credited for the introduction of African slaves into America was a Catholic missionary by the name of Bartolomé de Las Casas. Although there were African slaves in the New World before Las Casas, it was he who convinced Queen Isabella that Negroes were more suited for the work at hand in Hispaniola than the indigenous population. It is of interest to note that at this time Cardinal Ximenes opposed the plan by Las Casas and Queen Isabella. Cardinal Ximenes felt that the Negroes would find Hispaniola too favorable and reproduce faster than the Spanish and become a threat to Spanish rule on the island. History would prove Cardinal Ximenes correct.

SLAVERY IN THE SOUTHERN UNITED STATES

From 1503, the date of the introduction of the first African slaves into the New World, it would be another 117 years before African slaves were introduced into Virginia and subsequently New England. In 1620, thirteen years after the settlement of Jamestown, Virginia, the first African slaves were sold in what was to become the United States of America. It should be noted that the first African slaves were sold in Virginia more than 117 years *after* African slavery had been established in the New World. Virginians (i.e., Southerners) did not invent African slavery. Yet, because this form of slavery was introduced first in Virginia, Southerners are often blamed for all the evils of American slavery. Nothing could be more incorrect than the idea that Southerners are responsible for slavery in America. Nevertheless, due to the unique form of agriculture practiced in the South (that is, labor-intensive plantation agriculture), by 1833 the South was the last English-speaking section of the world in which slavery had not been abolished or was not in the process of being abolished. It should not be forgotten that even after the end of slavery in the South, slavery existed in Cuba under Spanish rule for another ten years and in Brazil under Portuguese rule for another twenty-two years. Also it should be remembered that the United States was on the most cordial of relations with both countries during this time. Even in the face of these facts, Northern propagandists, both before and after the War, continued "to paint the South to all the rest of the world, in the blackest colours of misrepresentations, so as to have us [Southerners] regarded as a semi-barbarous race of domestic tyrants, whose chief occupations were chaining or scourging negroes, and stabbing each other with bowie-knives."[8] It has been more than 130 years since noted theologian and defender of the South Rev. Robert L. Dabney made the preceding comment; yet, the vicious anti-South propaganda continues unabated even today.

As will be demonstrated, early in the history of the United States, the South led the nation in efforts to limit the African slave trade and promote the end of slavery. Southern historian Francis B. Simkins states that, "In the period of the American Revolution the interest of the South in slavery declined."[9] The passing of the Northwest Ordinance in 1787 offers positive proof of this decreased interest in slavery by the South. Virginia, the state that was most responsible for the acquisition of the Northwest Territory during the War for American Independence, ceded to the Federal government all that territory that would later form more than five new states. With the passage of the Northwest Ordinance by Congress, slavery was disallowed in all of that territory. Virginia and all other Southern states in existence at the time voted for the bill that limited slavery in the Northwest Territory. If, as many politically correct folks maintain, the South is the one entity in America that is responsible for slavery, why did Virginia's and all the other Southern states' representatives in Congress vote for the Northwest Ordinance's limitation on slavery?

Still another example of the South's willingness to limit the growth of slavery in the United States, every Southern state except South Carolina had made further importation of African slaves illegal prior to such measures being passed by Congress. South Carolina repealed its law against the importation of African slaves because of its inability to police its many rivers and lengthy shoreline against Yankee slave traders. In 1808, the year appointed by the Constitution for an act to prevent further importation of African slaves into the United States, the anti-slave trade bill passed with representatives from only two Southern states (Virginia and South Carolina) and two Northern states (Vermont and New Hampshire) voting against the bill.

There are a few little-known facts about early American slavery that demonstrate the willingness of the South to promote the abolition of slavery. One overlooked fact is that in the two decades after the adoption of the United States Constitution (1788), manumission (the voluntary freeing of slaves by a slaveholder) doubled each decade in the South. An example of this spirit of freedom was demonstrated when Robert Carter freed more than five hundred slaves in 1791. George Washington manumitted his slaves on his death, which was not an uncommon practice. The willingness of masters to free their slaves upon their death occurred frequently during the early part of the antebellum South. John Randolph of Roanoke, the father of Southern Nationalism, freed four hundred slaves at his death in 1833.[10]

The first attempt to bring about the abolition of slavery was instituted in 1817 with the founding of the American Colonization Society. This organization was formed by slaveholders in Virginia, Kentucky, and Maryland. During the nineteenth century in the United States, both in the North and in the South, the theory of Negro inferiority was widely accepted. Most white people doubted the ability of free black people to cope with the demands of an industrial-age society. Modern Americans are acquainted with Jefferson's words about freedom for American slaves, "Nothing is more clearly written in the book of fate than that these people will be free." These stirring words are engraved on Jefferson's memorial in Washington. But the stonecutters put a period at the end of that remark, whereas Jefferson had placed a semicolon and went on to state, "And it is equally certain that the two races will never live in a state of equal freedom under the same government, so insurmountable are the barriers which nature, habit, and opinions have established between them."[11] Even the most "enlightened" philosopher of the American Revolution held the view of Negro inferiority that was common throughout all European societies at that time. Nevertheless, up until the year of his death, Jefferson also held the view that slavery should be abandoned. Eleven months prior to his death, Jefferson stated, "The abolition of the evil [slavery] is not impossible; it ought never to be despaired of."[12] Jefferson's view of the black slaves and slavery in general is reflected in his *Notes on the State of Virginia,* 'Proposed Revision of Constitution of Virginia.' Jefferson states:

> To emancipate all slaves born after the passing the act. The bill reported by the revisers does not itself contain this proposition; but an amendment containing it was prepared, to be offered to the legislature whenever the bill should be taken up, and further directing, that they should continue with their parents to a certain age, then to be brought up, at the public expense, to tillage, arts, or sciences, according to their

geniuses, till the females should be eighteen, and the males twenty-one years of age, when they should be colonized to such place as the circumstances of the time should render most proper, sending them out with arms, implements of household and of the handicrafts arts, seeds, pairs of the useful domestic animals, &c., to declare them a free and independent people, and extend to them our alliance and protection, till they have acquired strength; and to send vessels at the same time to other parts of the world for an equal number of white inhabitants; to induce them to migrate hither proper encouragements were to be proposed. It will probably be asked, Why not retain and incorporate the blacks into the State, and thus save the expense of supplying by importation of white settlers, the vacancies they will leave?

Deep-rooted prejudices entertained by the whites; ten thousand recollections, by the blacks, of the injuries they have sustained; new provocations; the real distinctions which nature has made; and many other circumstances, will divide us into parties; and produce convulsions, which will probably never end but in the extermination of the one or the other race. To these objections, which are political, may be added others, which are physical and moral.

A black, after hard labor through the day, will be induced by the slightest amusements to sit up till midnight, or later, though knowing he must be out with the first dawn of the morning. They are at least as brave, and more adventuresome. But this may perhaps proceed from a want of forethought, which prevents their seeing a danger till it be present. When present, they do not go through it with more coolness or steadiness than the whites. . . . Love seems with [them] to be sentiment and sensation. Their griefs are transient. Those numberless afflictions, which render it doubtful whether Heaven has given life to us in mercy or in wrath, are less felt, and sooner forgotten with them. In general, their existence appears to participate more of sensation than reflection. To this must be ascribed their disposition to sleep when abstracted from their diversions, and unemployed in labor. An animal whose body is at rest, and who does reflect must be disposed to sleep of course. Comparing them by their faculties of memory, reason, and imagination, it appears to me that in memory they are equal to the whites; in reason much inferior, as I think one could scarcely be found capable of tracing and comprehending the investigations of Euclid; and that in imagination they are dull,

> tasteless, and anomalous. . . . Never yet could I find that a black had uttered a thought above the level of plain narration; never saw even an elementary trait of painting or sculpture. In music they are more generally gifted than the whites with accurate ears for tune and time, and they have been found capable of imagining a small catch.[13]

These comments, by one of America's most celebrated "enlightened" leaders, demonstrates the common nineteenth-century view of the African in America. Jefferson and the vast majority of Americans, North or South, did not believe that emancipation of the slaves could be accomplished without removing the African after freedom. This view was held by United States presidents from George Washington to Abraham Lincoln.

Nor was this view of African inferiority in European society held only by Americans. The French writer Alexis de Tocqueville noted:

> You may set the negro free, but you cannot make him otherwise than an alien to the European. Nor is this all; we scarcely acknowledge the common features of mankind in this child of debasement whom slavery has brought amongst us. His physiognomy is to our eyes hideous, his understanding weak, his taste low; and we are almost inclined to look upon him as a being intermediate between man and the brutes. The moderns, then, after they have abolished slavery, have three prejudices to contend against, which are less easy to attack, and far less easy to conquer, than the mere fact of servitude: the prejudice of the master, the prejudice of the race, and the prejudice of color.[14]

With society at large holding the view of black racial inferiority, it was difficult to promote the abolition of slavery. If the black population were freed, they would become free citizens in a European society. This was unacceptable to Northerners and Southerners of the eighteenth and nineteenth centuries. Thus, in an effort to overcome fears of creating a free black underclass in the United States, the American Colonization Society urged the freeing of slaves and their subsequent removal to their ancestral homeland, Africa. In 1822 this society was instrumental in establishing the African nation of Liberia.[15] To this day, the capital of Liberia has been Monrovia. That city was named in honor of a Southern slaveholder, President James Monroe, who was also a strong supporter of the effort to end slavery in the United States.

In America today, most people view the abolition movement as a Northern idea and cause; thus, the South is viewed as the deadly foe of abolitionism. In the defense of truth, it will be demonstrated that the movement for the abolition of slavery was not just a Northern idea. Indeed, some of the first abolition societies were formed in the South with the assistance of Southern slaveholders. Both slaveholders and non-slaveholders in the South were active in the early *Southern* abolition movement. Having been educated and indoctrinated by America's liberal establishment, most Americans find these facts shocking. But even more shocking to modern minds is the fact that by 1827 fully four-fifths of all the abolition organizations and four-fifths of the members of those organizations were from the South.[16] The fact that there was little or no difference between the North and South over the issue of slavery has been noted by Southern historian Francis B. Simkins: "Before 1820 there was little difference between the North and the South in the volume and vigor of antislavery expression."[17] Governor John Randolph of Virginia even condemned earlier Virginians for "copying a civil institution [slavery] from savage Africa."[18]

Early in the history of the United States, it was not uncommon for Northerners to work with Southerners to promote the end of slavery. For example, William Rawle of Pennsylvania was, until his death, president of the Maryland Society for Promoting the Abolition of Slavery.[19] Maryland at that time was truly a Southern state, having more than a hundred thousand slaves within its borders.[20] Even though Rawle was a Northerner, Southerners worked closely with him in promoting a common goal (that is, the abolition of slavery). It should be obvious to any thinking person that as long as Northerners and Southerners worked together, with mutual respect and understanding, there was positive movement for the abolition of slavery. It was not Northern abolitionists such as Rawle who caused such a fright and negative reaction to abolitionism in the South. That would come later in the form of the Radical Abolitionists.

The desire for the removal of the system of slavery in Virginia was so strong that by 1832 its legislature was seriously debating the issue of the abolition of slavery.[21] This history of Southern abolitionism goes all the way back to the colonial period. In the eighteenth century the elected government of Virginia passed laws to curb the influx of slaves. The effort of these Virginians was thwarted by the British rulers. Reverend P. Fontaine of Virginia noted:

> Our Assembly, foreseeing the ill consequences of importing such numbers among us, hath often attempted to lay a duty upon them which would amount to a prohibition, such as ten or twenty pounds a head; but no governor dare pass such a law, having instructions to the contrary from the Board of Trade at home. By this means they are forced upon us, whether we will or not. This plainly shows the African Company hath the advantage of the colonies, and may do as it pleases with the ministry.[22]

It should be noted that the governor who would not sign a bill to limit the importation of more African slaves was a royally appointed agent. In other words, he was neither elected nor appointed by the people of Virginia; he was performing his duties as directed by the king, not by Virginians. The following extract from a petition to the king of England by the House of Burgesses of Virginia will demonstrate how the early inhabitants of Virginia felt about the importation of more slaves.

> The importation of slaves into the colonies from the coast of Africa hath long been considered as a trade of great inhumanity, and under its *present encouragement,* we have too much reason to fear *will endanger the very existence* of your majesty's American dominions.
>
> We are sensible that some of your majesty's subjects of *Great Britain* may reap emoluments from this sort of traffic, but when we consider that it greatly retards the settlement of the colonies with *more useful* inhabitants, and may, in time, have the most destructive influence, we presume to hope that the *interest of a few* will be disregarded when placed in competition with the security and happiness of such numbers of your majesty's dutiful and loyal subjects.
>
> Deeply impressed with these sentiments, we most humbly beseech your majesty to *remove all those restraints* on your majesty's governors of this colony, *which inhibit their assenting to such laws as might check so very pernicious a commerce.*[23]

Unfortunately, this petition had no effect in curbing the influx of African slaves into the colony of Virginia. This is one reason that Thomas Jefferson inserted into the text of the Declaration of

Independence the complaint that the king refused the colonies the right to prevent the introduction of slaves by "the inhuman use of the royal negative."

In a span of seventy-three years, the House of Burgesses of Virginia passed no less than twenty-three resolutions, acts, and/or bills that tended to limit or prohibit the continued importation of African slaves into Virginia.[24] Likewise, in 1760 South Carolina attempted to put a limit on the radical increase in the importation of slaves into that colony, only to be rebuffed by the king. The colony of Georgia was the first American colony to adopt a constitution prohibiting the importation of slaves. In 1798 the state of Georgia prohibited the further importation of slaves into that state, a full ten years before the Federal Congress did so.[25] At the time of Jefferson's writing of the Declaration of Independence, one charge that he desired to level against the king was that the king pursued a policy on the importation of African slaves that went against the wishes of the people of the colonies. The part of the declaration that was removed by the votes of New England states: "By prompting our negroes to rise in arms among us; those very negroes whom, by an inhuman use of his negative, he had refused us permission to exclude by law."[26] Unfortunately, the major charge against King George was stricken from the declaration. Perhaps, in striking the clause from the Declaration of Independence, the financial greed of Yankee slave traders was being considered. It might be pointed out here that in 1776, the British government was attempting to do the very same thing that Abraham Lincoln's government attempted to do in 1862. Both King George and Abraham Lincoln were attempting to instigate a slave rebellion. They were attempting to cause the slave population to rise up and butcher the families of the "Rebel" forces. These were the very same slaves that the king's men and Lincoln's men had sold to the people of the South.

The fear of a slave uprising had always been a reality in any slave society; the North and the South were no different. The brutal massacre of the white population in Haiti and Santo Domingo during those successful slave uprisings was a constant source of fear for many Southerners. White non-slaveholders as well as white slaveholders felt victimized by the demands of Radical Abolitionists insisting on immediate abolition of slavery. This demand was often linked with the threat of "servile insurrection," or slave uprising.

If Southerners and Northerners were attempting to end slavery early in the history of the United States, what happened to change this feeling of good will? Two factors can be pointed to as major reversals in the attempt to end slavery in the South. The first factor is a Yankee by the name of Eli Whitney, who invented the cotton gin in 1793. Before the invention of Whitney's cotton gin, cotton fiber was removed from cotton seed by hand. This was a very difficult and time-consuming process. It took a slave all day to produce one pound of cotton fiber. It required five hundred slave-days of labor to produce the fiber for one five-hundred-pound bale of cotton. While living on a Georgia plantation, Whitney invented a machine that cut that workload to a mere fraction of what it once was, and thus revolutionized the cotton industry. When operated by hand, the machine could do the work of ten slaves. When operated by horsepower, it could do the work of fifty slaves. This development made cotton production immensely profitable. As often happens, despite the best of intentions, much harm can be done. The unintentional result of Whitney's invention was that the slaves now had a new and very lucrative job description: the production of cotton. And as would become obvious, cotton was best grown in the South.

With fortunes to be made both by Southern planters and Northern shippers and industrialists, moral qualms about the enslavement of an "inferior" class of people quickly abated. Not only did the South gain by this process, but all of the United States were benefiting from Southern agriculture. By 1850 two-thirds of America's exports, many of them carried in Northern ships, came from the fields of the South.[27] During this time, Southern slaveholders questioned the honesty of Northerners who condemned the South for making profits from slave-grown produce, while Yankees in textile mills, shipping, and banks were making profits from the very same slave-grown produce.

In 1791, before the invention of the cotton gin, America's total cotton production was a mere four hundred bales. By 1810, the production was up to 177,824 bales; in 1830, production was at 732,218 bales; and by 1860, it was at 3,841,416 bales or two-thirds of the world's cotton production. From four hundred bales to almost four million bales in less that seventy years, thanks largely to a Yankee with good intentions.[28]

Even with fortunes to be made and maintained by cotton production, the movement to abolish slavery in the South was a viable movement until the second decade of the nineteenth century. The death knell to the Southern abolition movement was heard across the South when the Radical Abolitionists of the North demanded immediate abolition of slavery with no compensation to slaveholders. Here is seen a movement by the people of one section of the United States who were dedicated to destroying a system of labor in another section of the country that had been recognized as legitimate by the Founding Fathers, both North and South. No longer was the movement to abolish slavery a mutual endeavor by all Americans; rather, it had now become the focus of sectional dispute. Still worse, as the issue of slavery became politicized, feelings on both sides of the issue began to harden. At that point rational discussion and positive movement for the elimination of slavery in America died. Southern historian John S. Tilley notes, "The record has disclosed that a reaction set in concurrently with the advent of the group known as abolitionists. . . . [I]n the thinking of the abolitionist, the slave-owner was an inhumane monster."[29]

Even as late as 1828, in faraway Mississippi, a frontier region of the United States at that time, the cry for the end of slavery was to be heard. Gerard C. Brandon, Mississippi's governor in 1828, urged the banning of further importation of slaves into the state. In a speech on the subject of elimination of the slave trade, Governor Brandon struck at the heart of slavery itself. Brandon stated:

> Slavery is an evil at best, and has invariably operated oppressively on the poorer class in every community into which it has been introduced, and excludes from the State, in proportion to the number of slaves, a free white population, through the means of which alone can we expect to take rank with our sister States. With these reflections I submit to the wisdom of the general assembly to say whether the period has not arrived when Mississippi, in her own defense should, as far as practicable, prevent the further introduction of slaves for sale.[30]

With the adoption of the 1832 constitution of Mississippi, a limit was placed upon the introduction of slaves into the state. Unfortunately, with the coming of the cotton boom in Mississippi, and the attacks upon the South by Radical Abolitionists, the abolition movement in that state slowly died. In discussing the change that overtook Mississippi as it related to the institution of slavery, one historian observed that "this changed attitude resulted from the ever more insistent attacks of the Abolitionists, who forced Mississippians to defend themselves in any way they could."[31] What was said about Mississippi could be truthfully said about any of the Southern states during this time in history.

Slowly at first, a new attitude about slavery had begun to take hold in the North. The new attitude replaced the older and more benevolent view of slavery. It was the latter attitude that existed in the North as long as slavery was viable there. From co-labors with other abolitionists, the Southern slaveowner was now seen as the embodiment of all forms of sin and evil in America. Remember, some of the first abolitionists in the South were slaveowners. They led the way in freeing slaves at their own expense and in fostering the early Southern abolition movement. As has been noted, both the North and the South held similar views regarding the elimination of slavery in America during the first forty-five years of this nation's existence. Nevertheless, by 1830, an obvious change had taken place in the views of both the North and the South on the issue of slavery. The need for black labor decreased in the North while, with the invention of the cotton gin, the usefulness of black labor increased in the South. At the same time the black population was increasing in the South, stories of gruesome atrocities perpetrated by slaves during the slave uprising in Santo Domingo reached the United States. Thus, the possibility of a bloody "servile insurrection" became a daily reality to Southerners, both slaveholders and non-slaveholders. Is it any wonder that Southerners became just a little irritated and nervous by the actions of Northern Radical Abolitionists?

As the radicals increasingly indulged in slanderous propaganda against Southern slaveholders, soon everything Southern, not just slavery or slaveholders, was viewed as evil. Noting the tendency of the Radical Abolitionists to falsely accuse Southern slaveholders of any number of evils, historian Francis B. Simkins states:

> Having lost faith in a heaven beyond the sky, they [Radical Abolitionists] hoped to make heaven—or at least a New England—of that section of the country cursed with slavery. . . . They indulged in slanderous propaganda against slaveholders, calling them robbers, manstealers, and thieves who worked the slaves to death in seven years, beat them with many lashes, cropped their ears for purposes of identification, threw them to bloodhounds to be chewed, put red pepper, turpentine, and

> vinegar in their wounds, and failed to give them enough clothes to protect them from the weather.[32]

Early in the history of America's abolitionist movement, the radicals were few in number and influence. Nevertheless, they had an effect upon the South that was unrelated to their size or influence in the North. In the South the ranting of radicals such as William Lloyd Garrison "evoked such fear and anger that a peaceful attainment of his aims was made impossible."[33] Here is seen another example of good intentions (the elimination of slavery) having an unintended result—the impossibility of the peaceful attainment of ending slavery.

Few if any Southerners believed that the slave-master relationship was free of abuse. With their typical biblical world-view, most Southerners understood the innate evil that resides within all men. Holding such a world-view, they believed that the system of slavery, just as any other system of labor or human endeavor, was likely to be abused. Southerners viewing the system of Southern slavery believed this abuse was the exception to the rule and not the rule. Yet, the strident and abusive rhetoric of the Radical Abolitionists, declaring that the sins occurring within the system of Southern slavery were the rule and not the exception, poisoned the last well of good feelings between the North and the South. Worse yet, every Southerner became the chosen object of scorn and ridicule because of the supposed "sin" of slavery. Thus, whether it was the atrocities committed by arch-abolitionist John Brown in Kansas or the incendiary actions of the invading Union Army during the War for Southern Independence, the viewpoint was the same: All Southerners were the enemy. Little or no protection was afforded any members of the non-slaveholding class, which comprised 80 to 90 percent of the Southern population. Thus is seen the outcome of radicalism in the North as it sought to end slavery in the South.

The radicals' anti-South view has its modern equivalent in the politically correct notion that anyone who defends the honor of his Confederate ancestors is "defending slavery." Even though 80 percent or more of the Confederate soldiers were non-slaveholders, politically correct society stigmatizes them as evil defenders of slavery and therefore not worthy of honor or respect. Any descendent of such a Confederate soldier who insists on honoring his ancestor is quickly labeled a buffoon or, worse yet, a racist by the modern-day

Radical Abolitionist. Even Confederate heroes who held anti-slavery views are castigated or consigned to the Orwellian memory-hole. At this point, one can see how the "hate the South" movement of the Radical Abolitionists has continued into the twenty-first century.

With the passage of time, the antics of the Radical Abolitionists continued to increase. What started out as a few fanatics rapidly grew in numbers and influence. Soon, Northern industrialists saw the issue of slavery as the Achilles heel of the Southern free-trade block. By scandalizing everything Southern, Northern congressmen and senators could be intimidated to vote *against* the interests of Southern agriculture and *for* the interests of Northern industry (i.e., protective tariffs). Northern industrial and commercial interests found a natural ally in the new abolitionist movement.

As their numbers increased, the Radical Abolitionists redoubled their efforts to denounce the South, not just slavery. By 1830, Radical Abolitionists were flooding the Southern mails with magazines and tracts denouncing slaveholders. Radical Abolitionist Lydia Child asserted that slavery in the South was the outgrowth of licentiousness inherent in Southern character.[34] Wendell Phillips, a leading radical, stated that due to the nature of slavery the South was "one great brothel."[35] Garrison even charged that Southern ministers of the gospel were protecting slavery because slavery made it easier for them to secure concubines. According to Garrison, these clergyman of the South were engaged in the raping of black parishioners.[36] The actions of the early abolitionists were so offensive that President Andrew Jackson called such activity "a wicked plan of exciting the negroes to insurrection and to massacre."[37]

Southern historian John S. Tilley correctly analyzed the effects of the Radical Abolitionists

> The record has disclosed that a reaction set in concurrently with the advent of the group known as abolitionists. These agitators centered their attention largely upon the Southern states in which, for climatic and economic reasons plus a shrewd transfer of slave holdings, the institution had let down its anchor. To the Southerner, who knew well the ugly story of incredible exploitation of child-workers in Northern mills, it was more than passing strange that crusading zeal emanating from that section should adopt as a goal the uprooting of the economic system of the South.[38]

More and more, men of the North read, believed, and passed on the incendiary words of the Radical Abolitionists. The radicals' depiction of the South as an ethical and a moral cesspool in America did not have the desired effect of ending slavery. As a result of a torrent of insults, lies, and other abuses, the near universal desire for gradual abolition of slavery in the South was dealt a death blow.

The South had given America such men as George Washington (a slaveholder), Thomas Jefferson (a slaveholder), and Patrick Henry (a slaveholder), just to name a few. This same South had also provided more men per capita for the defense of the nation than any other section in both the War of 1812 and the Mexican War.[39] Now, after giving so much to the nation, the South found itself being portrayed as a place of ignorant, brutal, and wicked people, one whose equal rights within the union were increasingly under attack. Within the span of fifty years the South, according to the Northern view, went from being the foremost defender of liberty ("give me liberty or give me death") to being a cruel tyrant. Within the same time frame, it went from being a co-laborer with the North for the abolition of slavery to being the defender of its rights, one of which was its peculiar system of labor. In reality, the South had changed, but not nearly as much as the North had changed.

It is difficult to discern the motives of men. But one thing is for sure, if abolition of slavery had been the desire of the Radical Abolitionists, they would have put forth a plan for gradual emancipation with compensation for slaveholders and proper training for all perspective freemen. Great Britain had ended slavery in its colonies using just such a plan. But the Radical Abolitionists ridiculed and disregarded the British plan. Moreover, they "scorned the British example . . . the radicals refused to consider [compensation to slaveholders] . . . refused to accept the legalities of laws passed when the nation was formed. They argued that slavery was a sin."[40] The definition of slavery as a "sin" was a godsend for Yankee abolitionists. If slavery was a sin, then its end had to be immediate, not gradual, and no compensation could be countenanced for the sinful slaveholders. And conveniently, the tax money that would have gone South to compensate slaveholders could then be spent on Northern internal improvements. Also, Northerners who had sold slaves to the South for almost two hundred years, and having thus liquidated their slave assets before this dreadful "sin" had become "self-evident," had nothing to lose by this process.

Thus the radicals succeeded in changing the definition of slavery and the focus of the abolition of slavery. From a debate on how to control and eliminate a poor political policy, the debate had become a question of sin and therefore morality. The definition of slavery having been changed, the question then moved to a different level. No longer were Americans discussing changes in social or political policy; they were discussing the nature of the individuals who were responsible for the sinfulness of a nation. As long as social and political policy was under discussion, compromise and progress (incremental as it may have been) was possible. But no one can compromise on accepted morality or he will become an immoral person. With the possibility of compromise withdrawn, the only solution was total war on the offending party (the South). Thus is seen the steady progress from mutual respect and compromise between the North and the South to an attitude of open hostility.

In reaction to the activity of the Radical Abolitionists, the Fire-Eater movement surged to the forefront in Mississippi and other Deep South states. The Fire-Eaters were a group of Southerners who believed that the "safety and happiness"[41] of the South demanded the creation of a new form of government. To achieve this end, they pushed for secession of the Southern states from the Union. In 1853, the Fire-Eaters of Mississippi published a series of articles under the title "Chronicles of the Fire-Eaters of the Tribe of Mississippi." Utilizing biblical phraseology, these articles, reportedly written by one "Seraiah the Scribe," used humor to demonstrate how the South was in danger from attacks by the North. In part, the Chronicles stated:

> Seraiah the Scribe unto the Fire-Eaters, and Filibusters, and the State Righters, and the Submissionists, and the Unterrified, and the Hard-fisted, the United and Harmonious Democracy of the tribe of Mississippi, sendeth greetings.
>
> He that hath ears to hear let him hear; he that hath eyes to see let him see; he that hath knowledge let him understand; for the end of these things, even the "finality" thereof, is not yet come.
>
> And it came to pass in the fifth month, on the seventh day of the month, in the second year, that Joseph, whose surname was Copperas Breeches, ruled over the land of Mississippi.
>
> That the wise men of the city of Jackson and the county round about assembled together in the Great Hall of the city, and said with one accord, what do we here, and why sit we

here idle when dangers are pressing us from the North, and from the East and from the West, on account of the children of Ham, whom we hold in servitude in our midst.

Go to, now let us act as becometh wise men, and assemble together the whole people, . . . lest we be blotted out from the face of the earth.

And when they had assembled together, Daniel the son of Adam arose in the midst of the congregation and said unto them, lo, now as ye are assembled is it not wise and proper that our Governor, even Joseph, whose surname is Copperas Breeches, should preside over you; for he is a man that is wise in counsel, and he will show us his opinion; and the whole congregation said, Amen.

And Joseph arose and said unto them, men and brethren, I pray you hearken unto my speech, and give ear unto that which I now say, that ye may live long in the land which ye now possess, and that it may be well with thee and thy children after thee forever.

For behold the day cometh and is even now at hand that ye must rise in your might and your strength and show unto the tribes of the North, even the Yankees and the Free Soilers, that ye are a great and mighty people, and that none can withstand you, yea not even the tribes of the Yankees, the people of all nations, nor the rest of mankind.

Now therefore . . . let there be no division, but be ye reconciled one to another, be united as brethren, be strong, be courageous and be valiant.

For know ye not that evil betideth you, that the tribes of the Yankees in the North have said ye shall not go over to the land of California if ye take any of the children of Ham with you as bond men or bond women. [Here, the speaker is making reference to lands won by the United States from Mexico during the late war. In that war, Southerners represented the largest portion of men who fought. Then, after Southern blood had won the territory, the North told Southerners that they could not take their property into the commonly held territory of the Union.]

Is not this the land for which you have fought, bled and died; yea, for which the bones of your sons and your brethren now lie on the plains of Mexico and none are there to bury them? And the whole congregation said, Amen.

Behold California is as the land of Ophir, its mountains and its streams aboundeth in gold, its traffic is with the isles of the ocean and in silks of China and riches of the Indies.

Who are they that defy the might of Southern chivalry? Are they not the white-livered, cold-blooded, and brazen-faced Yankees, that deal and traffic in *notions,* and all sorts of wares and brazen clocks, and blue vessels and wooden nutmegs? They think of naught but gain, they are full of treachery and deceit, their words are smooth like oil, but under their tongues is poison of asps, and their cry is as the horseleech, "give, give." [One complaint Southerners had against the North was its use of the Federal government's taxing powers to extract revenue from the South and spend it for internal improvements in the North.]

And the Yankees have not regarded the covenants of their fathers, which were made in the days of old, when this land was delivered from the oppression of our British rulers, when the Free Soilers held the children of Ham in bondage, as we now do. [This is a cry against Yankee hypocrisy that is still heard today by the defenders of the South.]

And they have refused to deliver them [that is, return fugitive slaves as directed by Article IV, Section 2, of the United States Constitution] again unto us as they had promised, but they have held them in their own land to be hewers of wood and drawers of water.

Behold these things have been done in their solemn assemblies. Their leaders have led them astray.

Now, therefore, that which seemeth right in mine eyes is that ye should call upon all the people, in every town and village, upon the highways and by ways, and send forth your wise men and your eloquent orators, that they may raise a commotion, and sound an alarm throughout the length and breadth of the land, even from Bull mountain, in the land of Itawamba, to the sea shore, and from the borders of Alabama to the waters of the Mississippi.

And let them say, behold the Yankees have robbed you of all the gold in California; they have stolen your servants, they have wasted your substance, they have utterly condemned the laws and the covenants which have heretofore been made, and all which ye have faithfully observed.

And your labor and that of your servants profiteth you not; for the Yankees . . . sell unto corn, and wine, and Nock & Rawson, and swine's flesh, and all your fabrics of wool, and your land is emptied year after year.

And buy ye no more of the Yankees and Gothamites, the blue cloths and fabrics of English dye, or purple, or scarlet, or fine linen, or needle work, garments of all kinds, and color all

> your breeches with copperas, as this day you see that your servant Joseph has done.
>
> And when Joseph had made an end of speaking, the whole congregation shouted with a great shout, and clapped their hands and said, God save our Governor, even Joseph whose surname is Copperas Breeches.[42]

Governor Joseph W. Matthews, "Old Copperas Breeches," was elected as a candidate of the people. As a Democrat, he reflected the political philosophy of the common free white male population of Mississippi. It should be noted here that the common people of Mississippi were not the folks who owned large plantations and, therefore, slaves. The rich plantation owners were more likely represented by the Whig party. The people of the South were, by the time of the writing of this Fire-Eaters article, so enraged by the antics of the Radical Abolitionists that the Democrats (i.e., the common people of the South) were now defending the right of slavery under the Constitution. Rather than increasing the spirit of abolitionism in the South, the Radical Abolitionists had polarized the Southern people, even those who owned few or no slaves, to stand with the large plantation owners (Whigs) and against Radical Abolitionism. But the history of slavery in America neither begins nor ends in the South. We now must look at the history of slavery in the North.

SLAVERY IN THE NORTHERN UNITED STATES

Slave auctions, slave codes, slave families being broken apart, slave beatings, and slave uprisings in the minds of modern Americans are unquestionably associated with the Old South. The fact that all the above-mentioned blights upon American history are part of Northern history is poorly appreciated in modern America. Thus, whenever the aforementioned evils are discussed, it is the South that is placed in a negative light.

As will be demonstrated, in the early days of the Northern colonies slavery was as important to the North as it was to become to the South. On the third of August, 1713, Josiah Franklin, the stepbrother of Benjamin Franklin, ran the following advertisement in the *Boston News Letter*:

> Three negro men and two women to be Sold and to be seen at the House of Mr. Josiah Franklin.[43]

Franklin, a well-established merchant of Boston, sold many articles at his place of business, including slaves. His place of business was also used by many other slave traders as a convenient place to sell their slaves. Although not directly involved in the slave trade, Benjamin Franklin did publish ads in his newspaper advertising the sale of slaves. This was done by Benjamin Franklin at the same time as other newspapers in the area were, in principle, refusing to publish such ads.[44]

Slavery, north of the Mason-Dixon line (i.e., in the North) existed from 1626 until the eve of the War for Southern Independence. For all practical purposes, the history of slavery in the North lasted approximately 225 years.[45]

The use of Native American and Negro slaves was not uncommon throughout the British American colonial empire. But the British were not alone in this practice. In 1626, the Dutch found it expedient to bring Negro slaves to their colony of New Netherlands (New York). For what purpose did the Dutch inject the system of African slavery into their colony? The answer is rather simple: the need for a reliable labor force. It was not racism that stimulated slavery; rather, it was an economic imperative that was the driving force in the establishment of slavery in the North. In this respect, the North and the South have a common history. As historian Eugene D. Genovese points out, "[S]lavery as a system of class rule predated racism and racial subordination in world history and once existed without them."[46] Regardless of which colony one looks at—North or South, North America or South America—it was slavery, Negro slavery for the most part, that provided the means of obtaining a degree of prosperity that assured the colony's success.[47]

At this point, it must again be pointed out that the mechanism driving slavery in the Americas was the need for a stable and reliable labor force. Fields had to be cleared, homes built, food grown, forts constructed, and roads established. All the work of clearing, building, and growing was done by hand. This fact alone demonstrates why slavery was needed in the North as well as in the South in the early colonial period. Today, one man with a chain saw and a small tractor can do the work of ten or more men of the 1600s. If slavery is a system to provide labor sufficient to get the job done, then mechanization and the internal combustion engine would have ended slavery. Given the proper amount of time, progress, not Radical Abolitionists and war, would have freed America from the institution of slavery and spared hundreds of thousands of young American lives in the process.

One of the many hardships suffered by the early colonies was the chronic shortage of free white labor. This shortage was acute as well as chronic, so much so that a system of "unfree" labor (i.e., indentured servants) was established early in colonial history. Unfortunately for all parties concerned, the system of unfree white labor did not provide the number of workers needed to make the colony self-sustaining. After all, not every European was eager to risk a perilous Atlantic crossing only to land in the American wilderness as the property of another man. Another problem often surfaced with indentured servants. More often than not, when their indentureship expired, they left the farms of their masters and followed the lucrative fur trade or went into a trade for their own benefit. This tendency reduced the available free labor force. Without an adequate and stable labor force, the colony would fail. Therefore, African slavery was the only logical alternative.[48]

With an increase in African slavery in addition to the "unfree" white indentured servants, land and infrastructure development increased. In essence, the unfree laborers were conquering the wilderness of America and making civilization possible. What was true in the colony of New York was true throughout the Northern and Southern colonies.[49]

New England, home of some of the most radical, blue-blooded abolitionists, has a remarkable slavery history. Historian Lorenzo Greene places the beginning of New England's affair with slavery between 1624 and 1630.[50] Other historians, such as George H. Moore, place the inception of New England slavery at 1637.[51] During that time, the colony of Massachusetts engaged in war with the Pequod Indians. As in Africa and Europe, success on the field of battle yielded prisoners who were sold into slavery. Thus we see the beginnings of slavery in New England with the enslavement of the Native American population of Massachusetts. The beginning of African slavery in Massachusetts can be pinpointed to the arrival of New England's first slave ship, *Desire,* back in its home port of Salem, Massachusetts. Returning from the Bahamas, the *Desire* brought back to Massachusetts several African slaves who were quickly bought by the local population.

The *Desire* was one of the first ships built in New England. It worked the trade route between New England and the West Indies. In the West Indies, the New England captain exchanged New England goods—fish, trade goods, and Indian slaves—for cotton, tobacco, salt, and Negro slaves.[52] Governor Winthrop of Massachusetts recorded the type and amount of goods brought from the West Indies to Massachusetts in his journal. Among the items which he identified as landing from the *Desire* were African slaves. It should be noted that not one word of protest was made by the governor about this traffic in humans.

As has been noted, one of the items the folks of Massachusetts were sending to the West Indies was Indian slaves. In *Notes on the History of Slavery in Massachusetts,* George H. Moore states that in 1637 the Pequod Indians were being pushed off their ancestral homeland by the colonists of Massachusetts. Responding to the encroaching white settlers, the Pequods went to war with the colonists. The war ended with the near decimation of the Pequod Nation. Those who escaped slaughter were captured and sold into slavery. The women and children were enslaved in New England; the men and older boys were shipped to the West Indies and sold into slavery. Of the three stages (passages) of the slave trade, we can observe in the history of New England the active enslavement of Indians (first passage), the movement of slaves from their homeland to the slave market (middle passage), and, completing the history of the nefarious trade in humans, the final purchase and employment of slaves (third passage).

It may be of interest to note the description given by Moore of how the Indians, who were taken prisoner by the Massachusetts military, were treated:

> [I]t is certain that in the Pequod War they took many prisoners. Some of these, who had been "disposed of to particular persons in the country" *(Winthrop, I),* 232 ran away, and being brought in again were "branded on the shoulder," *ib.* In July, 1637, Winthrop says, "We had now slain and taken, in all, about seven hundred. We sent fifteen of the boys and two women to Bermuda, by Mr. Peirce. . . . Governor Winthrop, writing to Governor Bradford of Plymouth, 28th July, 1637, an account of their success against the Pequods—"Ye Lords greate mercies towards us, in our prevailing against his & our enemies"—says: The prisoners were divided, some to those of ye river [the Connecticut colony] and the rest to us. Of these we

> send the male children to Bermuda, by Mr. William Peirce, & ye women & maid children are disposed aboute in ye tounes. Ther have now been slaine and taken, in all, aboute 700.[53]

New England did not stand alone in the commerce of African slave trading. All the major European powers vied for their portion of the lucrative trade in slaves. The demand for slaves by Europeans stretched from Canada in the North to Chile in the South. The requests for slaves was so extensive and unrelenting that from 1640 until 1820 more than four times as many Africans as Europeans were brought to the Western Hemisphere.[54] It should be remembered that of this total African immigration, only 6 percent were brought to the United States. A full 94 percent of all Africans brought to the New World from Africa were sent to Cuba, Brazil, and the islands of the Caribbean. Is it not just a little unusual that in only two countries was slavery ended by a bloody war? Those countries that ended slavery by war were Haiti and the United States. The British West Indies, Cuba, Brazil, and the other Latin American nations did what the United States and Haiti could not do—end slavery peacefully.

As appalling as the revelations about New England slavery have been thus far, the history of New England vis-à-vis the institution of slavery offers more shocking surprises. Although Virginia is often cited as the first American colony in which slavery existed, few people know that it was Massachusetts and not a Southern colony that passed the first law to recognize and protect the master's right in the property of his slave; this was done in 1641.[55]

It may be beneficial to look at a few notable firsts in the history of slavery in America. For example, the first attempt at slave breeding took place in Massachusetts. George H. Moore gives this account of the attempt:

> An early traveller in New England has preserved for us the record of one of the earliest, if not, indeed, the very first attempt at breeding of slaves in America. The following passage from Josselyn's *Account of Two Voyages to New England*, published at London in 1664, will explain itself:
>
> The Second of October [1639], about 9 of the clock in the morning Mr. Mavericks Negro woman came to my chamber window, and in her own Countrey language and tune sang very loud and shrill, going out to her, she used a great deal of respect towards me, and willingly would have expressed her grief in English; but I apprehended it by her countenance and

> deportment, whereupon I repaired to my host, to learn of him the cause, and resolved to intreat him in her behalf, for that I understood before, that she had been a Queen in her own Country, and observed a very humble and dutiful garb used towards her by another Negro who was her maid. Mr. Maverick was desirous to have a breed of Negroes, and therefore seeing she would not yield by persuasions to company with a Negro young man he had in his house; he commanded him will'd she nill'd she to go to bed to her, which was no sooner done but she kickt him out again, this she took in high disdain beyond her slavery, and this was the cause of her grief.[56]

This first recorded attempt at slave breeding in America was as unsuccessful in the North as any like attempt in the South. In their classic work on slavery in the Old South, Robert W. Fogel and Stanley L. Engerman call the idea of slave breeding in the Old South a "myth." The very idea that the normal sexual habits of a people could be harnessed by a "master" class in order to "breed" humans is not only repugnant but ridiculous. These Nobel Prize-winning economists assert that the myth of slave breeding is supported only by the most meager of evidence. They then proceed to present evidence to show that the myth is a total fallacy.[57] Southerners are not unaccustomed to being ridiculed because of the supposed slave-breeding habits of their ancestors. As previously pointed out, New England holds the record for the first attempt at this activity, and noted scientists have challenged the notion of slave breeding in the Old South.

Nothing provokes more rage against the South in general, and Southern slaveholders in particular, than the thought of the use of a whip on slaves. From *Uncle Tom's Cabin* to the latest Hollywood Civil War miniseries, the theme of Southerners whipping slaves guarantees the proper response from the audience. But why just the South? In Massachusetts and throughout the North, the whip was liberally employed. As early as 1705, the legislative body of Massachusetts was passing laws that instituted whipping as a means of punishment for both free and slave. Moore gives the following account of such an early law:

> The Law of 1705, Chapter 6, "for the better preventing of a Spurious and Mixt Issue, &c.;" punishes Negroes and Molattoes for improper intercourse with whites, by selling them out of the Province. It also punishes any Negro or

> Molatto for striking a Christian, by whipping at the discretion of the Justices before whom he may be convicted. It also prohibits marriage of Christians with Negroes or Molattoes—and imposes a penalty of Fifty Pounds upon the persons joining them in marriage.[58]

Although this is the first account of the legislature of Massachusetts passing a law for the whipping of Negroes, it should be pointed out that the practice of whipping was not confined to black people. Moore records that as early as 1658, the inhabitants of Massachusetts were imposing whipping and slavery as a punishment for white people. Having been caught attending a meeting of Quakers, the family of Lawrence Southwich was ordered to pay a fine. Refusing to pay the fine or work as payment of their fine, the general court took action. Moore relates:

> This they did, after due deliberation, by resolution empowering the County Treasurers to sell the said persons to any of the English nation at Virginia or Barbadoes [white slavery]—in accordance with the law for the sale of poor and delinquent debtors. . . . Provided Southwick [daughter of Lawrence Southwich] was subsequently in the same year, in the company of several other Quaker ladies, "whipt with tenn stripes," and afterwards "committed to prison to be proceeded with as the law directs."
>
> The indignant Quaker historian, in recounting these things, says, "After such a manner ye have done to the *Servants* of the Lord, and for *speaking* to one another, . . . and for *meeting* together, ransacking *their Estates,* breaking open *their Land*; and when ye have left *them nothing,* fell *them* for this which *ye* call *Debt.* Search the Records of former Ages, go through the Histories of Generations that are past; read the Monuments of the Antients, and see if *ever* there were *such* a thing as this since the Earth was laid, and the Foundations thereof in the *Water,* and *out of the Water* . . . O *ye* Rulers of Boston, ye Inhabitants of the *Massachusetts*! What shall I say unto *you*? Indeed, I am at a stand, I have no Nation with *you* to compare, I have no people with *you* to parallel, I am at a loss with *you* in this point.[59]

Many apologists for New England will argue that although the system of slavery and whippings was common during the early period of the area, it surely had changed by the time of the War for American Independence. Nevertheless, one year after the signing of the Declaration of Independence, in 1777, the following bill of sale was issued for a slave from Middletown, Connecticut:

> Know all men by these Presents that I Joseph Stocking of Middletown in the County of Hartford and State of Connecticut for the Consideration of Thirty Pounds lawful Money received to my full satisfaction of George Wyllys Esquire of Hartford in the County aforesaid do give grant Bargain sell & convey and deliver to the said George Wyllys Esqr his Heirs and Assigns a certain Negro woman slave name Silvia of the Age of twenty three years. To have & to hold the said Negro slave to him the said George Wyllys Esq. his Heirs & Assigns for and during the Term of her Natural Life to his & their Use benefit & behoof.[60]

Even after the end of the American War for Independence and twenty years after Massachusetts's judicial form of emancipation was in place, Massachusetts nevertheless maintained a hostile attitude toward free people of color in the state. The following notice was published in the *Massachusetts Mercury,* in Boston, on September 16, 1800:

> Notice To Blacks
>
> The Officers of Police having made return to the Subscriber of the names of the following persons, who are Africans or Negroes, not subjects of the Emperor of *Morocco* nor citizens of the *United States,* the same are hereby warned and directed to depart out of this Commonwealth before the 10th day of October next, as they would avoid the pains and penalties of the law in that case provided, which was passed by the Legislature, March 26, 1788. [61]

Following the notice were the names of several Africans or Negroes who were commanded to leave the state of Massachusetts or suffer the "pains and penalties of the law." After a list of names, the ad continued:

> List of INDIANS and MULATTOES
>
> The following persons from several of the *United States,* being people of color, commonly called Mulattoes, are presumed to come within the intention of the same law; and are accordingly warned and directed to depart out of the Commonwealth before the 10th day of October next.[62]

Moore explains the rationale for this and similar notices that ran throughout the North at that time:

> This notice must have been generally published in Boston, and was copied in other cities without the list of names. We have met with it in Commercial Advertiser of the 20th September, 1800, and the Daily Advertiser, 22rd September, 1800, both in New York. Also in the Gazette of the United States and Daily Advertiser of 23rd September, 1800, in Philadelphia. . . .
>
> In the year 1800, the whole country was excited by the discovery of an alleged plot for a general insurrection of negroes at the South. . . .
>
> But the alarm was not confined to Virginia. Even in Boston, fears were expressed and measures of prevention adopted. . . . The Gazette of the United States and Daily Advertiser . . . Philadelphia, September 23, 1800, copies the "Notice" with these remarks:
>
> "The following notice has been published in the Boston papers: It seems probable, from the nature of the notice, that suspicions of the design of the negroes are entertained, and we regret to say there is too much cause."
>
> Such was the act, and such was one of its applications. Additional acts were passed in 1798 and 1802, but this portion was neither modified nor repealed.[63]

As the history of New England proves, the whip was liberally applied by the people of Massachusetts both during and after slavery, and it was applied to white people as well as black people.

In the early part of the nineteenth century, many Northern states, including Massachusetts, refused to honor the fugitive slave section of the United States Constitution. It was not unusual to hear Northerners refer to this section of the Constitution as a "Southern" section. Both in the past and in the present, people assume that this section of the Constitution was the brainchild of evil Southern slaveholders. Yet, the history of the Fugitive Slave Law will, again, demonstrate the hypocrisy and ignorance of many people in this regard.

The fugitive slave section of the United States Constitution is patterned after the *first* Fugitive Slave Law, which was established in America by the United Colonies of New England. As Moore points out:

> The Articles of Confederation of the United Colonies of New England, 19th May, 1643, which commences with the famous recital of their object in coming in to those parts of America, viz., "to advaunce the Kingdome of our Lord Jesus

Christ, and to enjoy the liberties of the Gospell in puritie with peace," practically recognized the lawful existence of slavery.

The fourth Article, which provides for the due adjustment of the expense or "charge of all just warrs whether offensive or defensive," concludes as follows:

"And that according to their different charge of eich Jurisdiccon and plantacon, the whole advantage of the warr (if it please God to bless their Endeavors) whether it be in lands, goods, or PERSONS, shall be proportionably devided among the said Confederates." The same feature remained in the Constitution of the Confederacy to the end of its existence.

The original of the Fugitive Slave Law provision in the Federal Constitution is to be traced to this Confederacy, in which Massachusetts was the ruling colony. The Commissioners of the United Colonies found occasion to complain to the Dutch Governor of New Netherlands, in 1646, of the fact that the Dutch agent at Hartford had harbored a fugitive Indian woman-slave, of whom they say in their letter: "Such a servant is parte of her master's estate, and a more considerable parte than a beast." A provision for the rendition of fugitives, etc., was afterwards made by treaty between the Dutch and the English.[64]

The unwillingness of the North to abide by the constitutional mandate set forth in the fugitive slave section of the Constitution will be discussed in the following chapter. But it should be clear by now, as long as the North needed slavery, it demanded obedience to the Fugitive Slave Law of its making.

A fictional Southern slaveholder who routinely beats and then murders his slave is a common theme in Hollywood dramas. Human nature being what it is, no one should doubt that this type of activity was possible. Yet, in the history of Northern slavery, one can find a not-so-fictional account of a master murdering his slave. In 1639, a slave master from Hartford, Connecticut, is said to have killed his slave.[65] We can only speculate just how long we must wait before Hollywood responds with a story line "poor innocent slave murdered by his evil Yankee slave master." Obvious, that story line does not comport with the modern stereotypical view of slavery in America. More to the point, it does not caress the anti-South cultural bigotry held by so many modern politically correct individuals.

Several forms of "unfree" labor existed during the early days of the Northern colonies. As has been shown, slavery extended to more than just Africans. Native Americans, Africans, and the occasional white were all yoked for life to their master's will. In 1641, the General Court of Massachusetts condemned a white indentured servant to slavery for assaulting his master. Even white children were the objects of the "tender" mercy of the Massachusetts court when, in 1658, two white children were sold into slavery by order of the court.[66] Although not routinely linked today, slavery was a major factor in the early life of the Puritan Fathers. Noting the extensive use of Negro slaves in Boston, Frenchman Antoine Court wrote, "[T]here is not a house in Boston, however small may be its means, that has not one or two [African slaves]."[67] Lorenzo Greene, chronicler of slavery in New England, notes that a registry of New England's aristocracy and Puritan slaveholders would be almost identical.

A common complaint by Southerners before and after the War is that just because 6 percent of Southerners owned slaves, that should not indict the other 94 percent of non-slaveholding Southerners. Southerners also point to leaders such as Robert E. Lee and St. George Tucker, who were firm opponents of slavery. In his defense of the people of New England, Greene states that "most New England families had no connection with slavery."[68] He goes on to point out notable leaders of New England such as John Adams who were vocal opponents of slavery. The question that begs to be asked is: "Why should we overlook New England's complicity in the system of slavery while condemning the South?"

As has already been shown, New York and Massachusetts were early players in the system of slave labor, but they were not the only Northern colonies utilizing slave labor. In 1652 Rhode Island, following the lead of Massachusetts, enacted laws to protect a master's right in his slave property.[69] By this date, all of New England had passed laws defining and defending the institution of slavery.

A survey of the history of slavery in the North would not be complete without a look at the "cradle of liberty"—Philadelphia, Pennsylvania. On the eve of the American War for Independence, Philadelphia was the largest city in British North America. For various reasons, historians have underreported the number of slaves and the impact of slavery in Pennsylvania in general and in Philadelphia in particular. Yet, with a little investigation one will discover the same pattern of slave employment in this Northern colony as is seen in the Southern colonies of North America.

The prime factor in the employment of slaves in Pennsylvania was the need for a reliable labor force (does this sound familiar?). Although the genesis of African slavery in Pennsylvania is difficult to ascertain, three years after the Quaker founders established Philadelphia, a shipload of 150 Africans arrived in port. Now, did the pious "Friends" rush down to the port and demand liberation for their fellow man? Yes, the Quakers rushed to the port—rushed to buy a few good African slaves.[70] So great was the demand for slaves that Nicholas More wrote to William Penn stating that most of the silver and gold that had been brought to the colony had been exchanged for the purchase of slaves.[71] Again it must be pointed out that slavery existed in Pennsylvania for one reason—labor. In the wilderness that was America, sufficient and reliable labor was needed to carve out a civilization and ultimately make prosperity possible. As long as the need for slavery existed, scruples against slavery, even when held by Quakers, could not stop the institution. Slavery was the "necessary" evil in the North just as it was to become in the South.

The stream of slaves into Philadelphia ebbed and flowed in response to the availability of white laborers. Thus, we see two high points in the flow of slaves into Philadelphia. Around 1730, the stream of slaves into Philadelphia peaked and then slowly declined as the numbers of Scotch-Irish and German unfree laborers (i.e., indentured servants) increased.[72] From the first peak in the importation of slaves into the colony, the number of slaves brought to the colony slowly decreased but never ceased. The second high point for the importation of slaves into the colony occurred in the year 1756.

As a consequence of the Seven Years War (the French and Indian War), many indentured servants were conscripted into the British Army, and unfree white laborers became a scarce commodity. The resulting decrease in the available white laborers stimulated a renewed interest in African labor and thus a second peak in the importation of slaves.[73] The necessity of obtaining African slaves in 1756 was noted in a letter by Thomas Penn to William Peters. Peters stated that the decrease in the number of available indentured servants was forcing the people of the colony to "the necessity of providing themselves with negro slaves, as the property in them and their service seems at present more secure."[74]

The second peak in importation of slaves took place at the very same time that the colonial abolition movement was well established. The efforts of the colonial abolitionists were an abject failure. Their failure had more to do with the severe decrease in an alternative labor supply than a lack of good arguments for the ending of slavery. To emphasize the point already made, *as long as slavery was an economic necessity, appeals to conscience were of little benefit in ending it.*[75] What was true for the North before the War for American Independence was also true for the South before the War for Southern Independence.

The pressing need to secure labor was so strong that even pious men of the Quaker faith refused to follow the principles laid down by their religious leaders to refrain them from buying slaves. Even the boldest efforts by fellow Quakers and their leaders did not prevent members of that faith from utilizing slave labor. Only with the cessation of the Seven Years War and an increase in the supply of white laborers did the Quakers free themselves from the use of slave labor. The institution of slavery was so intrenched in and around Philadelphia that by 1751 more than six thousand slaves, or about one-half of the total number of slaves in Pennsylvania, were residents of the area.[76] The Philadelphia tax assessor's report of 1767 (just nine years before the signing of the Declaration of Independence) demonstrates that almost 16 percent of the taxpayers of Philadelphia were slaveholders.[77] By the year of the signing of the Declaration of Independence, there were between six hundred and seven hundred African slaves in the city.

The story of the founding of the Confederate States of America is often accompanied by sketches of slaves toiling away in fields of cotton. The subliminal message is "Confederacy equals slavery." Yet, as has been shown, the very city where the Declaration of Independence was signed was one of the largest "slave" cities in the North. Moreover, every delegate who signed the Declaration of Independence was from a state that had a long and successful history of slavery. Nevertheless, no one calls the independence movement of America a "slaveholders'" rebellion.

This brief review of the history of slavery in the North demonstrates four facts:

1. Slavery was an important part in the early development of the Northern colonies. Both the existence of actual slaves working for Northern masters and the commercial ventures into the African slave trade made Northern prosperity more attainable.
2. The evils normally associated with Southern slavery were just as

prevalent within Northern slave society, such as: attempts at slave breeding, slave whippings, seeking fugitive slaves, or slave branding.

3. Slavery existed for one major reason—labor. Early in the history of the Northern colonies, African slavery was instituted as an alternative to the lack of an adequate white labor force.
4. As long as slavery was an economic necessity, its abolition was impossible—even among Quakers.

In the history of slavery in America, one factor has been noted by many defenders of the South.[78] In those areas of the nation where slavery was not as prevalent, the commerce in the African slave trade was very prominent. Also, in those areas of the nation where slavery was prevalent, the African slave trade was not very prominent. While it is easier to see the results of slavery in the South, the results of the North's participation in the institution of slavery and the slave trade should be of equal concern to all open-minded individuals.

The scope of the practice of African slavery in the North can be gauged by the number of slaves in each Northern state in 1790. It should be noted that by this time the supply of free white laborers was more than adequate to meet the needs of the Northern states. As a result, a system of gradual emancipation was either in place or would soon be established. Nevertheless, a few slaves would be held in bondage in the North until the eve of the War for Southern Independence.

Northern Slaves

Date	**State**	**Number**
1790	Connecticut	2,757
1790	New Hampshire	8—46
1790	New Jersey	12,422
1790	New York	22,306
1790	Pennsylvania	3,761
1776*	Massachusetts	5,249
1790	Rhode Island	948

*With the adoption of its 1780 constitution, the Massachusetts Supreme Court ruled that slavery could not exist within the state. This judicial emancipation eliminated *de jure* slavery in the state; nevertheless, it remained as a *de facto* institution for several years, while many slaveholders sold their slave property.

As a final look at the institution of slavery in the North, let us return to New England. In the year 1700, one of the earliest anti-slavery tracts appeared in Massachusetts. Judge Samuel Sewell wrote and circulated a tract titled "The Selling of Joseph, a Memorial." This work, according to historian George H. Moore, was received with "amazement and wonder, not unmingled with sorrow and contempt."[79]

The tract used biblical imagery and language to assert that slavery could not be condoned by Christians. This tract has been alluded to by those who would declare slavery as a sin. Yet, Judge Sewell's words were not well received when first published. Many a student of American history has been virtually brought to tears as a result of the story of slavery as told by Judge Sewell.[80] Nevertheless, very few history teachers have taken the time to tell the story of Judge John Saffin's reply to "The Selling of Joseph, a Memorial." In 1701 Judge Saffin, a slaveholder of Massachusetts and a member of the same court as Judge Sewell, wrote the following reply which was titled, "A Brief and Candid Answer to a late Printed Sheet, Entitled, The Selling of Joseph." Once again it must be pointed out that this Northern defense of the biblical view of slavery is not being reprinted as a defense of slavery. The point being made is that these views were held by Americans both in the North as well as in the South and that as long as slavery or the slave trade was deemed necessary for the advancement of the society, opposition—biblical or otherwise—was ineffectual. While defending the view that slavery was sanctioned by the Bible, Judge Saffin made several points that would reassert themselves throughout the first two hundred years of American history: (1) Because of the prejudice of color, white laborers were preferred to black laborers. The same reasoning on this subject was expressed by John Adams of Massachusetts sixty years later. (2) It is not moral to demand someone to free his slave at the cost of losing the price of that slave (something the people of Massachusetts conveniently forgot after they sold their slaves to Southerners). (3) Once freed, the "Negroes must be sent out of the Country."[81] Here we see a Northerner making the argument of how difficult it would be to have a free black underclass within a white society. This is the same problem that had to be faced any time abolition of slavery was considered in nineteenth-century America—North or South. After we have reviewed the statements of Judge Saffin of Massachusetts, Dr. N. L. Rice of Ohio, Bishop John H. Hopkins of Vermont, and Dr. R. L. Dabney of Virginia, it will become apparent that each man made the same point—that slavery was not sinful and that it was difficult to abolish.

While Judge Sewell's tract denouncing slavery as a sinful act is often cited and published, Judge Saffin's reply is seldom seen. Therefore, in the interest of fairness, Judge Saffin's reply will be reprinted, in full, below. Unlike our detractors, we will provide you with both sides of this argument. Judge Sewell's tract can be found in the appendix of this book.

Judge Saffin's Reply to Judge Sewell, 1701

THAT Honourable and Learned Gentleman, the Author of a Sheet, Entituled, *The Selling of Joseph, A Memorial,* seems from thence to draw this conclusion, that because the Sons of *Jacob* did very ill in selling their Brother *Joseph* to the *Ishmaelites,* who were Heathens, therefore it is utterly unlawful to Buy and Sell Negroes, though among Christians; which Conclusion I presume is not well drawn from the Premises, nor is the case parallel; for it was unlawful for the *Israelites* to sell their Brethren upon any account, or pretence whatsoever during life. But it was not unlawful for the Seed of *Abraham* to have Bond men, and Bond women either born in their House, or bought with their Money, as it is written of *Abraham, Gen.* 14:14 & 21:10 & *Exod.* 21:16 & *Levit.* 25:44, 45, 46 *v.* After the giving of the Law: And in *Josh.* 9: 23. That famous Example of the *Gibeonites* is a sufficient proof were there no other.

To speak a little to the Gentleman's first Assertion: *That none ought to part with their Liberty themselves, or deprive others of it but upon mature consideration*; a prudent exception, in which he grants, that upon some consideration a man may be deprived of his Liberty. And then presently in his next Position or Assertion he denies it, *viz.: It is most certain, that all men as they are the Sons of* Adam *are Coheirs, and have equal right to Liberty, and all other Comforts of Life,* which he would prove out of *Psal.* 115: 16. *The Earth hath he given to the Children of Men.* True, but what is all this to the purpose, to prove that all outward comforts of this life; which Position seems to invert the Order that God hath set in the World, who hath Ordained different degrees and orders of men, some to be Monarchs, Kings, Princes and Governors, Masters and Commanders, others to be Subjects, and to be Commanded; Servants of sundry forts and degrees, bound to obey; yea, some to be born Slaves, and to remain during their lives, as hath been proved. Otherwise there would be a meer parity among men, contrary to that of the Apostle, *I Cor. 12 from the 13 to the 26 verse,* where he sets forth (by way of comparison) the different sorts and offices of the Members of the Body, indigitating that they are all of use, but not equal, and of like dignity. So God hath set different Orders and Degrees of Men in the World, both in Church and Common weal. Now, if this Position of parity should be true, it would then follow that the ordinary Course of Divine Providence of God in the World should be wrong, and unjust, (which we must not dare to think, much less to affirm) and all the sacred Rules, Precepts and Commands of the Almighty which he hath given the Sons of Men to observe and keep in their respective Places, Orders and Degrees, would be to no purpose; which unaccountably derogate from the Divine Wisdom of the most High, who hath made nothing in vain, but hath Holy Ends in all his Dispensations to the Children of men.

In the next place, this worthy Gentleman makes a large Discourse concerning the Utility and Conveniency to keep the one, and inconveniency of the other; respecting white and black Servants, which conduceth most to the welfare and benefit of this Province: which he concludes to be white men, who are in many respects to be preferred before Blacks; who doubts that? Doth it therefore follow, that it is altogether unlawful for Christians to buy and keep Negro Servants (for this is the Thesis) but that those that have them ought in Conscience to set them free, and so lose all the money they cost (for we must not live in any known sin) this seems to be his opinion; but it is a Question whether it ever was the Gentleman's practice? But if he could perswade the General Assembly to make an Act, That all that have Negroes, and do set them free, shall be Reimbursed out of the Publick Treasury, and that there shall be no more Negroes brought into the Country; 'tis probable there would be more of his opinion; yet he would find it a hard task to bring the Country to consent thereto; for then the Negroes must be all sent out of the Country, or else the remedy would be worse than the Disease; and it is to be feared that those Negroes that are free, if there be not some strict course taken with them by Authority, they will be a plague to this Country.

Again, If it should be unlawful to deprive them that are lawful Captives, or Bondmen of their Liberty for Life being Heathens; it seems to be more unlawful to deprive our Brethren, of our own or other Christian Nations of the Liberty, (though but for a time) by binding them to Serve some Seven, Ten, Fifteen, and some Twenty Years, which oft times proves for their whole Life, as many have been; which in effect is the same in Nature, though different in the time, yet this was allow'd among the *Jews* by the Law of God; and is the constant practice of our own and other Christian Nations in the World: the which our Author by his Dogmatical Assertions doth condemn as Irreligious; which is Diametrically contrary to the Rules and Precepts which God hath given the diversity of men to observe in their respective Stations, Calling, and Conditions of Life, as hath been observed.

And to illustrate his Assertion our Author brings in by way of Comparison the Law of God against man Stealing, on pain of Death: Intimating thereby, that Buying and Selling of Negro's is a breach of that Law, and so deserves Death: A severe Sentence: But herein he begs the Question with a *Caveat Emptor.* For, in that very Chapter there is a Dispensation to the People of *Israel,* to have Bond men, Women, and Children, even of their own Nation in some case; and Rules given therein to be observed concerning them; Verse the *4th.* And in the before cited place, *Levit.* 25:44, 45, 46. Though the *Israelites* were forbidden (ordinarily) to make Bond men and Women of their own Nation, but of Strangers, they might: the words run thus, verse 44. *Both thy Bond men, and thy Bond maids which thou shalt have shall be of the Heathen, that are round about you: of them shall you Buy Bond men and Bond maids, & c.* See also, *I Cor.* 12:13. Whether we be Bond or Free, which shows that in the times of the New Testament, there were Bond men also, & c.

In fine, The sum of this long Haurange, is no other, than to compare the Buying and Selling of Negro's unto the Stealing of Men, and the Selling of Joseph by his Brethren, which bears no proportion therewith, nor is there any congruiety therein, as appears by the foregoing Texts.

Our Author doth further proceed to answer some Objections of his own framing, which he supposes some might raise.

Object. 1. *That these Blackamores are of the Posterity of* Cham, *and therefore under the Curse of Slavery. Gen.* 9: 25, 26, 27. The which the Gentlemen seems to deny, saying, *they ware the Seed of Canaan that were Cursed, &c.*

Answ. Whether they were so or not, we shall not dispute: this may suffice, that not only the seed of *Cham* or *Canaan,* but any lawful Captives of other Heathen Nations may be made Bond men as hath been proved.

Obj. 2. *That the Negroes are brought out of Pagan Countreys into places where the Gospel is Preached.* To which he Replies, *that we must not doe Evil that Good may come of it.*

Ans. To which we answer, That it is no Evil thing to bring them out of their own Heathenish Country, where they may have the Knowledge of the True God, be Converted and Eternally saved.

Obj. 3. *The* Africans *have Wars one with another*; our Ships bring lawful Captives taken in those Wars.

To which our Author answers Conjecturally, and Doubtfully, *for ought we know,* that which may or may not be; which is insignificant, and proves nothing. He also compares the Negroes Wars, one Nation with another, with the Wars between *Joseph* and his Brethren. But where doth he read of such War? We read indeed of a Domestick Quarrel they had with him, they envyed and hated *Joseph*; but by what is Recorded, he was meerly passive; and meek as a Lamb. This Gentleman farther adds, *That there is not any War but is unjust on one side, &c.* Be it so, what doth that signify: We read of lawful Captives taken in the Wars, and lawful to be Bought and Sold without contracting the guilt of the *Agressors*; for which we have the example of *Abraham* before quoted; but if we must say while both parties Warring are in the right, there would be no lawful Captives at all to be Bought; which seems to be rediculous to imagine, and contrary to the tenour of Scripture, and all Humane Histories on the Subject.

Obj. 4. *Abraham had Servants bought with his Money, and born in his House. Gen.* 14:14. To which our worthy Author answers, *until the Circumstances of Abraham's purchase be recorded, no Argument can be drawn from it.*

Ans. To which we Reply, this is also Dogmatical, and proves nothing. He farther adds, *In the mean time Charity Obliges us to conclude, that he knew it was lawful and good.* Here the gentleman yields the case; for if we are in Charity bound to believe *Abrahams* practice, in buying and keeping *Slaves* in his house to be lawful and good: then it follows, that our Imitation of him in this his Moral Action, is as warrantable as that of his Faith; *who is the Father of all them that believe. Rom.* 4:16.

In the close of all, Our Author Quotes two more places of Scripture, *viz.; Levit.* 25:46, and *Jer.* 34, from the 8 to the 22 *v.* To prove that the people of Israel were strictly forbidden the Buying and Selling one another for *Slaves*: who questions that? And what is that to the case in hand? What a strange piece of Logick is this? Tis unlawful for Christians to Buy and Sell one another for slaves. *Ergo,* It is unlawful to Buy and Sell Negroes that are lawful Captiv'd Heathens.

And after a Serious Exhortation to us all to Love one another according to the Command of Christ. *Math.* 5: 43, 44. This worthy Gentleman concludes with this Assertion, *That these Ethiopeans as Black as they are, seeing they are the Sons and Daughters of the first* Adam; *the Brethren and Sisters of the Second* Adam, *and the Offspring of God; we ought to treat them with a respect agreeable.*

Ans. We grant it for a certain and undeniable verity, That all Mankind are the Sons and Daughters of *Adam,* and the Creatures of God; But it doth not therefore follow that we are bound to love and respect all men alike; this under favour we must take leave to deny; we ought in charity, if we see our Neighbour in want, to relieve them in a regular way, but we are not bound to give them so much of our Estates, as to make them equal with our selves, because they are our Brethren, the Sons of *Adam,* no, not our own natural Kinsmen: We are Exhorted *to do good unto all, but especially to them who are of the Household of Faith, Gal.* 6:10. And we are to love, honour and respect all men according to the gift of God that is in them: I may love my Servant well, but my Son better; Charity begins at home, it would be a violation of common prudence, and a breach of good manners, to treat a Prince like a peasant. And this worthy Gentleman would deem himself much neglected, if we should show him no more Defference than to an ordinary Porter: And therefore these florid expressions, the Sons and Daughters of the First *Adam,* the Brethren and Sisters of the Second *Adam,* and the Offspring of God, seem to be misapplied to import and insinuate, that we ought to tender Pagan Negroes with all love, kindness, and equal respect as to the best of men.

By all which it doth evidently appear both by Scripture and Reason, the practice of the People of God in all Ages, both before and after the giving of the Law, and in the times of the Gospel, that there were Bond men, Women and Children commonly kept by holy and good men, and improved in Service; and therefore by the Command of God, *Lev.* 25:44, and their venerable Example, we may keep Bond men, and use them in

> Service still; yet with all candour, moderation and Christian prudence, according to their state and condition consonant to the Word of God.
>
> The Negroes Character
>
> *Cowardly and cruel are those* Blacks *Innate,*
> *Prone to Revenge, Imp of inveterate hate.*
> *He that exasperates them, soon espies*
> *Mischief and Murder in their very eyes.*
> *Libidinous, Deceitful, False and Rude,*
> *The spume Issue of Ingratitude.*
> *The Premises consider'd, all may tell,*
> *How near good* Joseph *they are parallel.*[82]

Nothing written by any Southern racist could equal the preceding racist diatribe by a leading member of Massachusetts society. This is an example of the strong feelings of racial superiority held by Europeans of that time. Even when slavery was eliminated in the North, the racist ideology remained intact. Thus, in 1858, when Abraham Lincoln stated that he was in favor of maintaining the white race in the position of the superior race in America,[83] no one was surprised.

THE VICTIMIZATION SCANDAL

Toward the latter quarter of the twentieth century, American society became painfully aware of the term "political correctness." Not since the age of the Alien and Sedition Acts, a time when publishers or even congressmen could be jailed for speaking ill of the government, have Americans experienced such a stifling of free expression and free inquiry. Political correctness has its antecedents in the Marxist movements around the world. Mao Tse-tung was an early practitioner of Red Chinese political correctness. In the mid-sixties, Mao released hordes of young radicals (Red Guards) who terrorized citizens of China whom they deemed to be less than totally loyal to the communist revolution. To be charged by the Red Guards was tantamount to being tried and convicted. The hallmark of the Red Guard movement was, as is true with all "p.c." movements, that no evidence was needed to convict a citizen; the charge alone was sufficient to convict. Pol Pot's Khmer Rouge filled the killing fields of Cambodia with people who were charged with being too "bourgeois" in their lifestyles. Again, only the charge needed to be made; no evidence was necessary nor was it allowed in defense of the accused.

Group victimization is the foundational principle upon which the political-correctness movement stands. A victim group must first identify its "victimizer" group from which innumerable amounts of apologies and retribution will be extracted. Since the victim group is usually a minority group within society, several victim groups will unite under the banner of political correctness and advance using their collective political strength. Thus, we see the Red Guards minority in China uniting with a powerful central government to pursue their agenda; the minority Khmer Rouge of Cambodia using force to pursue their agenda; and, in the United States, various minorities uniting, with the assistance of the central government, to achieve the goals of political correctness.

Political correctness does not present itself to the public with the notion that it desires to do evil. Far from announcing evil intent, the movement is presented as the vanguard of those seeking only the betterment of people. This was the case in China, Cambodia, and even Nazi Germany. Shortly after his election as chancellor of Germany, Adolph Hitler signed into law a euthanasia act that allowed "competent" physicians to end the life of the incurably sick. This law was presented to the public as an act for the *benefit* of the incurably sick. Soon anyone who disagreed with the established (politically correct) view was subject to adversity. The world does not have to be reminded of the end results of this "beneficial" law.

In the United States, politically correct African-American leaders compose the most vociferous "victim" group. The self-anointed leadership continues to demand all forms of payment for what they term "the legacy of slavery." White Americans in general and Southern white Americans in particular are the objects (i.e., the victimizer group) of the mantra of "the legacy of slavery." Today, when it is noted that more African-American males are in prison than in college,[84] that 68 percent of African-American children are born out of wedlock,[85] or that the leading cause of death among young African-American males is murder at the hands of other African-American males,[86] the response among these advocates is "the legacy of slavery." So strong is their political and social clout that few if any will dare to challenge these assertions.

For example, when attacking Southern ideas, history, or culture, facts are never allowed to stand in the way of political correctness. The charge that the Confederate flag is a symbol of racism is all that is needed to have it removed from public display. Note that an intelligent discussion of the issue of slavery and the Confederate flag has been stifled by the charge of racism. Adding insult to injury, the advocates of political correctness will charge anyone who disagrees with their interpretation of an issue as, *ipso facto,* part of the problem. Thus, freedom of thought, speech, and action is stifled.

The most obvious fallacy of "the legacy of slavery" myth is that slavery was a white-versus-black institution. As will be demonstrated in chapter 4, the complexion of slave ownership was never totally white. Throughout the history of American slavery, thousands of African-Americans were slaveholders. Furthermore, several historians have reported that the institution of slavery itself has its origins in a lawsuit filed by an early African-American slaveholder.[87] According to this account, Anthony Johnson, one of the original Africans landed in Virginia in 1619, was sold as an indentured servant. After completing his indentureship, Johnson became a rather successful farmer and bought several indentured servants for his own use. Upon a demand by one of his servants, the servant, named John Castor, was freed from his indentureship. When Castor bound himself to another man, a Mr. Parker, Johnson filed suit against Parker (*Johnson v. Parker,* Northampton County, Virginia). The suit resulted in Castor being returned to Johnson as his servant for life. From this landmark decision in 1653, slavery in the South sprang. It should be noted that the main characters in this event were all Africans. Even if it can be proven that the father of Southern slavery was an African-American, supporters of victimization will still try to fix the guilt of slavery on white racists. When faced with the fact that Africans in Africa sold their fellow citizens to Europeans or with the fact of African-American involvement in the institution of slavery in America, this crowd never allows these facts to get in the way of their crusade. As with the communist purveyors, anyone who wishes to discuss facts will be charged with aiding and abetting the so-called criminal activity.

As shocking as the above-mentioned facts are, many will still maintain that a sober look at African-American society today is proof that there is a "legacy of slavery" that is causing many problems. For example, a recurring debate focuses on the allegation that the high rate of illegitimacy among African-American women is a result of the breakup of slave families. Yet the record reveals that the illegitimacy rate for African-Americans increases the *further removed* African-American women are from slavery. From 1890 through 1950, African-American women were just as likely to be married with children as were white women.[88] Even during slavery, slave family unity was much higher than it is in modern African-American families.[89] One would think that the most provable cause for the failure of the African-American families would be found in the present and not two or three centuries in the past.

Even if white America should concede that the legacy of slavery is deleterious to modern African-Americans, why should present-day citizens of the United States shoulder the bulk of the cost? After all, slavery existed in North America from 1641 (the date that Massachusetts legalized slavery) until the adoption of the Thirteenth Amendment in 1865—a period of more than 244 years. If the date of the birth of the United States is set at July 4, 1776, one can see that slavery existed under the auspices of Great Britain for 135 years (1641 to 1776) and under the auspices of the United States for 89 years (1776 to 1865). Why should American taxpayers be called upon to pay for the actions of Great Britain? Is it right to demand that United States citizens pay for something that happened before the United States even existed? But, of course, this is exactly what political-correctness promoters are demanding, that is, payment for something that happened before any living American or the American nation was born.

It is most amazing to hear the clamorous rhetoric condemning slavery that happened more than two hundred years ago. Yet, today slavery exists in several African nations (see chapter 9), and little or no denunciation of those countries or their flags is heard. Even after the tragedy of September 11, the United States maintains the most cordial of relationships with Saudi Arabia, a nation that ended slavery almost one hundred years *after* it was ended in the South. Contrast the treatment of the South with that of Saudi Arabia as it relates to the issue of slavery. Which nation is most often condemned, ridiculed, and scorned due to its history of slavery? Why is the South an object of scorn while African nations such as Mauritania and Sudan, where slavery still exists today, are seldom condemned? Why is Saudi Arabia protected by American blood but never scorned for its sixty-two years of twentieth-century slavery?

These questions deserve some thought. If we are to continue as a free people, we must reject the victimization thesis of the left-of-center powerbrokers of today. Like the Marxists, America's political-correctness police of today will become the KGB storm troopers of tomorrow.

SUMMARY

Although most people think of slavery in the New World in terms of Southern slavery, as has been shown there is much more to the history of slavery than just slavery in the South. The foundation of Southern slavery was laid in the days of the Ancient World. Even before African slaves became a part of the South, slavery was an ongoing institution in the New World. The driving force behind African slavery in the New World was the desire by Europeans for sugar.

The need for a large labor supply by the sugar plantations in the Caribbean made the Trans-Atlantic African slave trade possible. Long before cotton became a viable crop for export, the demand for sugar stimulated the massive movement of slaves from Africa to the New World. Under the influence first of Portugal, then Spain, the Trans-Atlantic slave trade began.

Early in the history of slavery in the New World, several breaches of the law of unintended results led the way to African slavery in Dixie. First, Queen Isabella, desiring to relieve the distress of the Native American slaves in Hispaniola, ordered the sending of African slaves to the New World. Not only did this effort not assist the Native American population, but worse still, it made African slavery the cornerstone of every European colony in the New World. About two hundred years later, a Northerner, Eli Whitney, invented the cotton gin in an effort to find a less labor-intensive method of extracting cotton fiber from its seed. The unintended result of this invention was the creation of a cotton empire in the South. This empire eventually resulted in the enslavement of some four million Africans. Only forty years after the invention of the cotton gin, in an effort to foster immediate abolition of slavery, the Radical Abolitionists began an attack upon Southern slaveholders and the South. This attack, unlike earlier efforts to end slavery, was viewed by most Southerners as a personal attack by one section of the United States against another. Even more upsetting to Southerners, the Radical Abolitionists had changed the terms of the debate against slavery. What was once a debate on ridding the nation of a poor political choice (i.e., slavery) was changed to an attack against the "sin" of slavery. By redefining slavery as a sin, the abolitionists made compromise and gradual emancipation (something the North had taken full advantage of) impossible. Thus, we see another example of an unintended result. More than merely academic curiosity, this unintended result made freedom less attainable and war a future reality.

As previously demonstrated, from the sugar plantations of the Caribbean and Latin America; the fields, factories, and infrastructure projects of the North; and the rice and cotton plantations of the South; the need for labor was the driving force behind the institution of slavery. Slavery existed across the racial spectrum: white, red, and black. In the absence of the mechanical advantage of the internal combustion engine, numerous types of unfree labor were utilized. Early in the seventeenth century, white slavery and indentured servitude were used in an attempt to supply the needed labor to turn the wilderness of America into a prosperous society. Even when substituted with Native American slavery, the supply of white labor was insufficient to meet the needs of early colonists. Thus, Africa became America's ready source for dependable labor.

The commerce in African slaves was not an invention of Europeans desiring laborers for their colonies. Rather, it was a continuation of an old process that goes back to ancient times. As repulsive as we of this age find that nefarious commerce to be, it must be remembered that from the seventeenth through the early nineteenth century, little or no odium was attached to the slave trade.

By the mid-nineteenth century, the Southern states of America had become the home of the largest segment of slave population in the New World. Yet, slavery was common to all of the original thirteen colonies of America. The need for a reliable labor supply was the driving force for slavery both in the North and in the South. As long as the need for labor was acute, abolitionism and arguments of morality had little effect on ending slavery. With an adequate supply of white laborers to meet the needs of society, the ending of slavery was possible.

The movement to abolish slavery began in the South and North early in the eighteenth century. By the early nineteenth century, most societies for the elimination of slavery were in the South. Southern slaveholders were in the forefront of the movement to end slavery. Both Northerners and Southerners worked together for the elimination of this institution. With the rise of Radical Abolitionism in the second decade of the nineteenth century, the mood of the country radically changed. From mutual respect and cooperation, the North and South began to view each other as deadly enemies. This change was due in large part to the antics of the Radical Abolitionists who had changed the nature of the debate on how to end slavery. From the second decade of the nineteenth century until 1860, America was stampeded into a bloody conflict. This conflict, along with the slave revolt in Hispaniola (Haiti and the Dominican Republic) are the only instances in the Western Hemisphere of slavery being ended by war.

Even though New England was the one area of colonial America that was least involved with the institution of slavery, it stands out as the area of America most involved with the nefarious slave trade. This point needs to be made, not to demean New England, but rather to point out how much each section of the United States owes the institution of African slavery for its well being. The South is often criticized because "so many" slaves lived in Dixie. Yet, those who launch such criticism fail to criticize New England and the North because "so many" slaves were brought to the New World by Yankee ships.

At this point, a couple more myths about slavery can be exposed:

MYTH: American slavery is a Southern institution.

REALITY: True, the most common form of slavery within the knowledge of most Americans is the antebellum slavery of the cotton-field variety. Nevertheless, as demonstrated, American slavery extended throughout the North and the South. Pious Puritans, Quaker Friends, as well as Southern planters were avid slaveholders. Slavery was abolished in the North only after it was no longer needed. It could not be abolished on moral or ethical grounds until after it was replaced by free white labor. As will be explained in subsequent chapters, leading members of Northern society noted that slavery in the North was not abolished because people believed it to be immoral, but because of its adverse effect upon white laborers.

MYTH: The South was a defender of slavery.

REALITY: No myth about the South gets more play than the myth that the South was a defender of slavery. Yet, the South was an early opponent of the African slave trade and of slavery itself. Southerners such as Thomas Jefferson spoke out against the institution. Jefferson was not alone in his anti-slavery views. From early in the history of the republic down to the eve of the War for

Southern Independence, men such as St. George Tucker of Virginia in 1796, Governor Gerard C. Brandon of Mississippi in 1828, and Robert E. Lee in 1861, spoke out against slavery and/or the slave trade. Unfortunately for the Southern abolition movement, there were two factors working against them. First, like the early abolition efforts in the North, as long as the demand for labor was high and the supply of free white laborers low, appeals to the sense of moral outrage of the man in the street had little effect in promoting the end of slavery. Second, with the advent of Radical Abolitionism in the North, efforts to end slavery in the South were given a death blow. Even in the face of these obstacles, men such as Jefferson Davis and other Southerners still pursued the idea of gradual emancipation. No, the South was not wedded to the idea of slavery. Slavery existed in the South just as it had existed under very similar circumstances in the North. The South has always insisted that the whole truth about the institution of slavery be told and not just that portion that panders to the Radical Abolitionists' myth.

CHAPTER 3

Abolitionism Versus Christianity

In denying that slave-holding is in itself sinful, I do not defend slavery as an institution that ought to be perpetuated. . . . I desire to see every slave free; not nominally free, as are the colored people in Ohio.[1]

N. L. Rice

A Debate on Slavery

To the average church-going American, nothing could sound more absurd than the idea that the movement to end slavery was anti-Christian. As previously demonstrated, early in this movement representatives from all sections and social groups in America participated in the anti-slavery effort. The biblical world-view of early Americans led the way to ameliorate the evils associated with slavery or to end slavery itself. Even slaveholders, being motivated by Christianity and a sense of humanity, were active in these efforts. Both Northern and Southern emancipationists viewed slavery as a social evil much akin to a tyrannical system of government. Being republicans, they viewed despotic government as a poor social choice but *not* as a sinful choice. An individual who supports a despotic government may be participating in an unwise form of government, yet not be participating in a sin. This is a key point to remember when considering the life of early emancipationists. Early slaveholders, who pointed the way to the abolition of slavery by freeing their slaves, were viewed as men who were no more responsible for the institution of slavery than non-slaveholders. Thus, the movement for ending slavery moved forward.

As has been shown, with the onset of the Radical Abolitionist movement, slavery was redefined as one of the most hideous and hateful sins known to mankind. Those associated with slaveholding were held up to the nation and to the world as the personification of evil. By the time of the rise of Radical Abolitionism, the slavery kingdom in America for the most part existed in the South. Concomitantly with the rise of a new definition of slavery, there was a rejection of orthodox Christianity in the North and the advent of the South as America's Bible Belt.[2] At that time, the orthodox Bible-believing South was beginning to see itself portrayed as a den of sinfulness by heretical Northern Unitarians and Transcendentalists. Obviously, the movement to end slavery, as well as many other societal reforms, was in response to the effects of Christianity. But, equally important, the rise of Radical Abolitionism, with its non-biblical definition of slavery as a sin in itself, had dire consequences not only for the ending of slavery, but also for the union among the American states.

Unfortunately the non-biblical view of slavery, as espoused by the Radical Abolitionists, dominates the discussion of slavery in most churches in modern America. As a result, the views of the Radical Abolitionists are taken as *the* American view of ending slavery. Therefore, the more commonly held view of the early emancipationists of the North and South is characterized as a "pro-slavery" argument. The work and effort of early Christians toward ending the slave trade, improving the condition of existing slaves, and advancing the idea of gradual emancipation are scoffed at and otherwise ridiculed as halfway measures that tended to prolong the *sin* of slavery. From approximately 1820 until the eve of the War for Southern Independence, the Radical Abolitionists' view increasingly gained influence in the North. Since the War, that same view has also gained sway over the pulpits and academic centers of the South. Therefore, the work and the effort of early Southern emancipationists are virtually unspoken of by modern churchmen. Even worse, when note is given to the work of the early emancipationists, they are too often condemned as (using the Radical Abolitionists' terminology) "defenders of slavery."

This view of slavery as a "sin" was debated at length in Cincinnati, Ohio, in 1845. The question of the debate was "Is Slave-Holding In Itself Sinful, And The Relation Between Master And Slave, A Sinful Relation?" Representing the views of the Radical Abolitionists, Rev. J. Blanchard, pastor of the Sixth Presbyterian Church, Cincinnati, Ohio, spoke in the affirmative. Representing the views of the traditional emancipationists, Dr. N. L. Rice, pastor of the Central Presbyterian Church, Cincinnati, Ohio, spoke in the negative. The debate took place in one of the largest public rooms in Cincinnati and took several days to complete. If slavery is as horrible a sin as Radical Abolitionists maintain, it should be rather easy to prove the point. Yet, in more than twenty-four hours of debate, the Radical Abolitionists' view could not be maintained. This fact should give cause for modern Christians, who are inundated with the Radical Abolitionist view of slavery as a sin, to stop and question this now-prominent point of view. Why did it take the Church more than nineteen hundred years to determine that this most contemptible practice is "sinful"? More important, what are the counter-arguments that Christians, starting with the Apostle Paul and including New England cleric Cotton Mather, as well as American pastors such as Dr. N. L. Rice of Cincinnati, Ohio, and R. L. Dabney of Virginia, used to refute the assertion that slavery itself is a sin?

Although modern Christianity has incorporated the Radical Abolitionists' view of slavery into its theology, there is a large pre-twenty-first-century view of slavery that is not acknowledged by the modern Church. In actuality, the pre-twenty-first-century Christian view of slavery has been suppressed by the modern Church. Therefore, in the spirit of openness, Dr. Rice's pre-twenty-first-century argument that slavery is not a *sin in itself* will be given below in an abbreviated form. In the following account some of the more important points and arguments made by Dr. Rice, from his speech in opposition to the view that slavery in itself is a sin, will be presented. Rev. Blanchard, a proponent of the Radical Abolitionists' view, had been chosen by a group of ten Radical Abolitionists in the city of Cincinnati to speak in defense of their point of view of slavery.[3] Modern Christianity's arguments that slavery *is* a sin in itself runs parallel with those of Rev. Blanchard.

Again, it must be remembered that the theme of the debate was not whether or not sinful acts took place within the system of slavery, but rather whether slavery in itself and the relationship between slave and master was a sin. It should also be pointed out that Dr. Rice was not defending slavery. Dr. Rice, like many Southerners, was an open opponent of slavery. Like the early American abolitionists (i.e., emancipationists), Dr. Rice understood that ending slavery was a difficult task that would take both time and Christian charity to accomplish. Nevertheless, to this day, Radical Abolitionists (or their modern counterparts, liberals) will describe Dr. Rice's defense of the biblical view of slavery as a defense of slavery itself.

In typical form, Rev. Blanchard, a Radical Abolitionist, opened the debate with many charges against slavery itself. Some of the charges leveled against slavery were that: (1) slaves are not citizens of any country, (2) slaves are not allowed to marry, (3) slave children are born out of wedlock, and (4) children of slaves are not born into families. As Dr. Rice took note, Rev. Blanchard used all his time in opening the debate and yet did not once address the theme of the debate (i.e., the *biblical* issue)—is slavery in *itself* sinful. Dr. Rice's opening remarks are as follows:

> I am happy to meet Mr. Blanchard on the present occasion, not as an *individual,* but as the chosen *representative* of the abolitionists of this city, selected by *ten* of their most respectable men. We have the right to conclude, that now full justice will be done to their cause; that if the claims of abolitionism can be sustained, it will now be done. I rejoice that the debate, as published, will be circulated both in the slave-holding and in the free States—that now at length the abolitionists will have the opportunity of spreading their strongest arguments before the slaveholders, as well as before the public generally.
>
> It is important that the audience keep distinctly before their minds the question we have met to discuss, to wit: Is slave-holding in itself sinful, and the relation between master and slave a sinful relationship? I was truly surprised to hear the gentleman speak *forty minutes* without reaching the question, and *twenty* more without defining what he means by *slave-holding!* I had expected to hear from a gentleman so long accustomed to discuss this subject, at least something in the way of argument, during the first hour, but it is passed, and the definition is not completed!
>
> I am perfectly aware of the prejudices I must encounter in the minds of some of the audience, from the fact that I stand opposed, in this discussion, to those who claim to be *par excellence* the friends of liberty, and particularly of the slave. To remove such prejudices from the minds of the candid, I will state precisely the ground I intend to occupy; and, if I mistake not, before this debate shall close, it will be considered at least a debatable question, whether the abolitionists are entitled to be considered the best friends of the slaves.
>
> 1. The question between us and the abolitionists, is not *whether it is right to force a free man with no crime, into slavery.* The gentleman has indeed presented the subject in this light. He has told you, that I am about to justify those who, at a future

day, may enslave our children. Such, however, I need scarcely say, is not the fact. In the slave-holding, as well as in the free States, it is admitted and maintained, that to reduce a free man into a state of slavery, is a crime of the first magnitude. Far from defending the African slave trade, we abhor and denounce it as piracy. We therefore, maintain, that American slavery ought never to have existed. But the slave-holding States have *inherited* this evil; and the important and difficult question now arises—*how shall the evil be removed?* The present owners of slaves did not reduce them to their present condition. They found them in a state of slavery; and the question to be solved is—how far are individuals bound, under existing circumstances, to restore them to freedom? For example, it would be very wicked in me whether by force or fraud, to reduce a rich man to poverty, but how far I am bound to enrich a man reduced to poverty by others, is a very different question.

2. The question before us is not whether the particular laws by which slavery has been regulated in the countries where it has existed, are just and righteous. What has the present discussion to do with Aristotle's description of slavery, which the gentleman has given us? Or what has it to do with the laws by which in the Roman empire slavery was regulated? Does the gentleman really expect me, in proving that slave-holding is not in itself sinful, to defend the slave laws of Rome? It is impossible not to see, that those laws have nothing to do with the question he stands pledged to discuss. Still he entertains us with Aristotle's definition of slavery, and with Gibbon's account of slavery in the Roman empire. Many of those laws, it is readily admitted, were unjust and cruel in a high degree. But by the same kind of logic it would be easy to prove, that the *conjugal* and *parental* relations are in themselves sinful. *I do not place the relation of master and slave on an equal footing with those relations; but I do maintain that the gentleman has no right to use an argument against the former, that would bear with equal force against the latter.* The Roman laws gave the father power over the life of his child, and the husband power over the life of his child, and the husband power to degrade and tyrannize over his wife; and the same is true of almost all pagan countries. But shall we denounce the conjugal and parental relations as in themselves sinful, because they were regulated by bad laws? Those relations, we contend, are lawful and right; but the particular laws by which in many countries they are regulated, are unjust. So

the fact that many of the laws of Rome concerning slavery were cruel, does not prove, that the relation is in itself sinful. The gentleman's argument proves too much, and, therefore, according to an admitted principle of logic, proves nothing.

Many of the laws by which in our country slavery is regulated are defective, and ought to be amended; or unjust, and ought to be repealed. . . . The laws may be most unjust, and yet the relation may not be in itself sinful.

3. The question is not whether masters may treat their servants cruelly, either by failing to give them abundant food and raiment, by inflicting cruel chastisement, by separating husbands and wives, parents and children, or by neglecting to give them religious instructions. A master, a father, or a husband, may be cruel. There is no relation in human society, that may not be abused by wicked men. But is the master *obliged* to treat his slaves cruelly? Must he of necessity starve them, or abuse them? Is he compelled, because he is a master, to separate husbands and wives? Or to neglect their religious instruction, and leave their minds in pagan darkness? No—he may treat them with all kindness, providing abundant food and raiment; he may sacredly regard the marriage relation among them; he may have them carefully instructed in the truths of the glorious gospel; and yet he may sustain to them the relation of *master.*

Were I to employ my time in searching for them, I could furnish thousands of examples of inhuman cruelty in connection with the conjugal and parental relations, in the free States, as well as elsewhere. Will the gentleman denounce these relations because they are abused? because wicked men take advantage of them to tyrannize over the weak? True, cruelty is often found in connection with slavery; but it is equally true that many slaveholders treat their slaves with uniform kindness, as rational, accountable, immortal beings. We are not discussing the question whether cruelty of any kind is right.

4. The question before us is not whether it is sinful to speculate in human beings. The slave-trader is looked upon by decent men in the slave-holding States with disgust. None but a monster could inflict anguish upon unoffending men for the sake of accumulating wealth. But since Mr. B. feels so deeply on account of the multiplication of slave-gangs in Kentucky, it may be well for him to know, that this is one of the sad effects of the doctrine and practice of the abolitionists. They have sought to make the slaves discontented in their condition; they have succeeded in decoying many from their masters, and running

them to Canada. Consequently masters, for fear of losing their slaves, sell them to the hard-hearted trader; and they are marched to the South. Thus they rivet the chains on the poor slave, and aggravate every evil attending his condition. Such is human nature, that men provoked by such a course of conduct as that of the abolitionists, will, in many instances, resort to greater severity; and upon those who thus provoke men, rests in no small degree the responsibility of increasing the suffering of the slaves.

5. The question before us, is not whether it is right for a man to treat his slaves as mere *chattels personal*, not as sentient beings. The Scriptures condemn cruelty not only toward man, but toward irrational animals. "A righteous man regardeth the life of his beast." A man ought to be excluded from the church, who would treat his horse inhumanly. Even the civil law would punish him for such cruelty. Yet it is not a sin to own a horse.

Christianity prescribes the duties of both masters and servants. The servant is required to render obedience to his master with all fidelity "as unto Christ;" and the master is required to treat his slaves with all kindness, even as rational, accountable, immortal beings. Cruelty toward slaves, would be a just ground for his exclusion from the privileges of the church. On this subject the law of the Presbyterian church is clear and explicit. Sessions and Presbyteries were enjoined by the General Assembly of 1818, to prevent all cruelty in the treatment of servants; and to subject those chargeable with it to the discipline of the church. Let the abolitionists prove, that any member of our church has been guilty of cruelty toward his slaves, and I pledge my word, he will be disciplined. Let it be tried, and if it be ascertained, that the Presbyterian church will not exclude men from her pale, who are guilty of such conduct, then I will denounce her.

6. The question is not whether a great amount of sin is in fact committed in connection with slave-holding. This is admitted. Wicked men act out their wickedness in every relation in life. Wicked husbands in ten thousand instances treat their wives most cruelly; and ungodly parents inflict great suffering on their children. No wonder, then, that in this relation a great amount of sin is committed. But the question is not how much men can sin in this relation, but whether the relation is in itself sinful, whether a man is to be denounced as a heinous sinner, simply because he is a master. Abolitionists dwell upon,

and magnify the sins of men committed in this relation; but the relation may, and in multitudes of instances does exist without the oppression and cruelty of which they speak. Consequently the sin is not in the relation itself.

7. Nor is the question before us, whether slavery is an evil, a very great evil, which should be removed as speedily as it can be done by the operation of correct principles. This I cheerfully admit. But there are many evils and great evils in connection with human society, which cannot be immediately removed. Whilst, therefore, I admit that slavery is an evil, I utterly protest against upturning the very foundation of society in order to abolish it. Shall we do evil that good may come? The question, I repeat, is not whether slavery is an evil, but whether we are to denounce and excommunicate every individual who is so unfortunate as to be connected with it.

8. The question before us does not relate to the duty or the policy of Kentucky or any other State concerning slavery. There is a broad distinction to be made between the duty of a State as a body politic, and the duty of individuals residing in the State. I might maintain, that it is the duty of the State of Kentucky immediately to adopt a plan of gradual emancipation, and yet contend, with perfect consistency, that so long as slavery is continued by the civil government, individuals may own slaves without sinning. The duty of the State is one thing; the duty of individuals quite another. Moreover, I might maintain what I firmly believe to be true—that slavery is a commercial evil in Kentucky, and that her true policy would be to rid herself of it as soon as possible—without at all admitting, that every individual who sustains the relation of master, is a heinous sinner.

9. In a word, we are not met to discuss the merits of any *system of slavery* Roman, Spanish, English, or American. . . . The question stated by the challengers to this discussion, and the question the gentleman stands pledged to debate, is—whether slave-holding is in itself sinful, and the relation between master and slave a sinful relation.

Let it be distinctly understood, that if slaveholding is in itself sinful; it is sinful under all possible circumstances, and must be instantly abandoned without regard to consequences. Blasphemy, for example, is in itself sinful; and therefore it cannot be justified by any possible circumstances.

In denying that slave-holding is in itself sinful, I do not defend slavery as an institution that ought to be perpetuated [emphasis added]. I am opposed to slavery; I deplore the evils connected with it. Most sincerely do I desire its removal from our land, so soon as it can be effected with safety to the parties involved in it. Most heartily do I desire to see every slave free; not *nominally* free, as are the colored people of Ohio, but truly free, as are many now in Liberia, who were once slaves. I go for gradual emancipation, and for colonization; but I will not agree to denounce and excommunicate every individual, who under existing circumstances, is a slave-holder. I maintain, that circumstances have existed, and do now exist, which justify the relation for the time being.

I oppose abolitionism, not because it tends to abolish slavery, and improve the condition of the slave, but because, as I firmly believe, it tends to perpetuate slavery, and to aggravate all its evils. That such is its tendency, that such have been its effects, I think I can prove to every unprejudiced mind.

If the doctrine for which I contend, were held only by slaveholders, or by men residing in slave-holding communities, I might be led strongly to suspect, that by early prejudices, my judgement had been unduly biased; but when I remember, that it has been held, and is now held by the great body of the wisest and best men; that every commentator, critic and theologian of any note, however opposed to slavery, interprets the Scriptures on this subject just as I do; I cannot hesitate as to whether my views are correct. Sustained by such names, I go forward fearlessly in their defense.

[T]he gentleman tells us that the slaves have no families; that their children are born out of wedlock, and are illegitimate, because the civil law does not recognize their marriage. This, however, is not true. The marriage of slaves is as valid in the view of God's law as that of their masters. Marriage is a Bible institution. Will the gentleman point us to the portion of Scripture which prescribes any particular ceremony as essential to its validity?

By way of exciting our sympathies, he told us that the slaves have no *patronymics,* but like dogs and horses, are called Sally, and Bill, and Tom, &c. Will the gentleman inform us what was Abraham's *sirname?* Or what were the *patronymics* of Isaac and Jacob? He can find multitudes of slaves named Abraham, and Isaac, and Jacob. Indeed, he will find amongst them the names of all the twelve Patriarchs. I presume they are not suffering for lack of names.

I do not remember that the gentleman offered one argument

> to prove slave-holding in itself sinful, unless he intended his appeal to the Constitutions of Ohio, Indiana, and Illinois, to be so considered! [Yet], they are not the rule of our faith, or of our morals.

At this point, Dr. Rice explained how his opponent had attempted to appeal to the sympathies of the audience rather than making biblical arguments to support the Radical Abolitionists' theory that slavery in itself is sinful. As he pointed out, rehashing accounts of slave abuse will no more prove slavery a sin in itself than rehashing accounts of wife abuse proves that marriage is itself sinful. Remember, Dr. Rice was a proponent of the abolition of slavery. By making the preceding point, he was demonstrating the absurdity of appealing to emotion instead of fact when considering matters of great importance. In the absence of any biblical arguments that slavery is in itself sinful, Dr. Rice pointed out that no recognized biblical scholar in the preceding nineteen hundred years had ever agreed with the Radical Abolitionists' view of slavery and sin. Like Judge Saffin of Massachusetts (see Chapter 2), the traditional Christian view of slavery was that sinful acts may take place within any institution, and those acts must be condemned. Whether it was Judge Saffin's 1701 tract in defense of the biblical view of slavery, Dr. Rice's arguments in 1845, or any number of Southern theologians' views on slavery, sinfulness was condemned, but not the holding of slaves. Dr. Rice continued:

> The question before us is not to be decided by appeals to sympathy, but by scriptural argument. Yet if the gentleman is determined to rely on such appeals, I hope to be able to present sufficient number of instances of cruelty in connection with the parental and conjugal relations, to demonstrate the utter fallacy of all such logic. Or if from it the conclusion be drawn, that slave-holding is in itself sinful; the conclusion that these relations are sinful, will follow, of course. To this result the audience, especially the younger portion, I presume, will be slow to come.—They must come to it, however, or pronounce all the gentleman's arguments from the cruelty of wicked men, destitute of weight.
>
> We profess to be the friends of the slave; and we are prepared to prove, that those who adopt substantially our views, have done and are doing incalculably more to improve their condition, than the abolitionists; that whenever slavery has been abolished, it has been effected, not by the principles of

> modern abolitionism, but by the principles we advocate. We take the Bible of God as our guide; and to its plain teachings we confidently appeal. The question is not, as already remarked, whether the oppressed shall find in Christianity an asylum; but shall we condemn those whom God has not condemned? Shall we denounce and excommunicate persons of such character as were admitted to fellowship by the inspired Apostles of Christ? Shall we preach the gospel to slaves, and thus secure to them happiness here and glory hereafter; or shall we run a few of them to Canada, where their condition, instead of being improved, is made worse, and where they will rarely, if ever, hear the sound of the gospel? If I believed the doctrine so zealously propagated by the gentleman and his abolitionist brethren, tended to abolish slavery, and improve the condition of the slave, I should be slow to oppose it. But most full am I convinced, that its tendency is precisely the reverse; and, therefore, as the friend of the slaves I oppose it.[4]

In the first hour of his debate, Dr. Rice stated that he was not defending the institution of slavery but standing in opposition to the efforts of Radical Abolitionists. As a representative of the traditional emancipationist's view of gradual abolition of slavery, Dr. Rice viewed Southern slaveholders as individuals who had inherited a system of labor much the same as Northern slaveholders had done in an early age. To foster the elimination of slavery in the South, Dr. Rice stressed calm rhetoric and Christian charity as opposed to the strident rabble-rousing of the Radical Abolitionists.

As was established in Chapter 2, the gradual abolition of slavery in the North took place only when the need for slavery no longer existed. With slavery no longer necessary, the influence of Christianity and the gentle persuasion of society made the elimination of slavery possible in the North. But, as Dr. Rice pointed out, with the advent of the intemperate attacks upon the South by the Radical Abolitionists, the elimination of slavery was made more difficult and less likely to be achieved. Dr. Rice stated, "I do not believe [slavery] to be in itself sinful, though it is a great evil, and, therefore, I can consistently go for its *gradual removal*."[5] By agitating the issue, the Radical Abolitionists, with their demand for immediate emancipation and condemnation of Southerners as vile sinners, halted all progress towards ending slavery. According to Dr. Rice, "For this unfavorable change, we are indebted to the ceaseless agitations of Abolitionists."[6]

One other point that Dr. Rice kept going back to during this debate is the lack of biblical authority his opponent was willing to assert in the maintenance of the theory that slavery is a sin. As Dr. Rice pointed out, there are many good biblical reasons for Christians to be opposed to slavery. But the debate was not whether Christians should be opposed to slavery; the point of the debate was whether slavery in itself is a sin. Thus, in the following brief exerts from Dr. Rice's second and third defense of his view of slavery, he set forth several biblical arguments to prove that slavery is not a sin. It is at this point that modern abolitionists (i.e., liberal politically correct theologians and academics) will assert that men such as Dr. Rice were defending slavery. Rather than using the Bible to defend slavery, Dr. Rice was attempting to point out the error of Radical Abolitionists. He asserted that they were responsible for curbing the long-standing movement in the South for ending slavery. This then is the reason Dr. Rice felt it necessary to point out that the Bible regulates and therefore ameliorates the evils associated with slavery, but does not condemn it as a sin.

For those adhering to orthodox Christian faith, using extra-biblical authorities to create a new class of "sin" would be nothing less than heresy. Theologians such as R. L. Dabney of Virginia would point out that once man-made philosophies become the judge of morality rather than the Bible, a whole host of ills can befall Christianity. Dabney noted, "He who discards this criterion [the Bible] makes man a reasonless brute, and the world an atheistic chaos."[7] In 1879, Dabney even went so far as to predict the rise of modern feminism, the sexual revolution, and the banning of the Bible from public schools as a result of America's adoption of the Radical Abolitionist creed.[8] Since his death, all the ills predicted by Dabney have been fulfilled. Therefore, the points being made by Drs. Rice and Dabney should not be lightly dismissed.

Subsequently during Dr. Rice's defense of the traditional view of emancipation, he chided his antagonist for not offering biblical arguments to prove that slaveholding in itself was a sin. In response to his antagonist's lack of biblical authority to prove slavery in itself to be a sin, Dr. Rice proceeded to prove that God regulates slavery in the Bible. According to orthodox Christianity, God cannot associate with sin; therefore, the regulation of slavery proves that it is no sin. Dr. Rice stated:

> Let me call your attention to one striking fact. Many odious charges, as you know, were brought against the apostles of

Christ: and yet, though slavery existed in its most odious form throughout all parts of the Roman Empire, *they never were charged with being Abolitionists.* Now I ask, and I put it to the candor of the brother opposed to me, and to the common sense of every man that hears me, if they had preached and acted as modern Abolitionists do, is it possible that no such charge would have been made by any one of the innumerable slave-holders with whom they came in contact? The apostles, it will not be denied, were as faithful in preaching what they believed to be truth, as our abolition friends, yet not a word of reproach was cast on them by any slave-holder, as if they had preached abolitionism. How is this fact to be accounted for?

My first position is this: God did recognize the relation of master and slave among the Patriarchs of the Old Testament; and did give express permission to the Jewish church to form that relation.—But God who is infinitely holy, could not recognize a relation in itself wrong, or give men permission to form such a relation. Therefore the relation of master and slave is not in itself sinful.

I presume the brother will not maintain, that God can ever, under any circumstances, give men permission to commit sin. The question, then, is whether God did give permission to the Jews to form the relation in question? If he did, and it is in itself a sinful relation, then he did give them express permission to commit abominable sin. I affirm that he did give such permission, and will proceed to prove it from the clear and unequivocal declarations of the Bible.

1. God recognized the relation of master and slave among the patriarchs.

My first proof is, that Hagar was the female slave of Abraham and Sarah. The Abolitionists tell us that the word *"servant"* in our English version of the Bible, does not mean *slave.* This word is derived from the Latin word *servus,* the literal and proper meaning of which, as every Latin scholar knows, is *slave.* The Romans had two words which they used to signify slave; one was *servus,* the other *mancipium.* In the passage, however, where Hagar is first named, *Gen. xvi, I,* she is called "an handmaid"—and in the 2d, 3d, 5th, 6th, and 8th, verses she is called Sarah's "maid." The Hebrew word *shifha* translated "maid" signifies a female slave.

2. The Septuagint version, which is a translation of the Hebrew Scriptures into the Greek language, and which was made by Hebrews, renders the word in the Hebrew by *paidiske* which, my brother will scarcely deny, means a female slave.

> 3. But that Hagar was a *slave* is proved beyond contradiction by the language of the apostle Paul, in Galatians, 4th chapter, and 22d and following verses. "For it is written, that Abraham had two sons, the one by a bond-maid, the other by a free woman. . . ."
>
> My second proof, that God recognized the relation of master and slave among the patriarchs, is drawn from the 17th chapter of Genesis, which contain the institution of circumcision. We read the 12th and 13th verses. "He that is eight days old shall be circumcised among you, every man child in your generation, he that is born in the house, or *bought with money* of any stranger, and he that is not of thy seed. He that is born in thy house, and he that is *bought with money,* must needs be circumcised." Does not this divine provision prove, that at that time Abraham had servants, who were Bought with his money, as well as such as were born in his house?—and were not servants bought with money slaves? If not, what were they? Who would so describe a hired servant? And can we believe, that, if slave-holding were in itself sinful, God could have entered into a covenant with Abraham, requiring him not to liberate his slaves, but to circumcise them?

The preceding is just a *small* example of the biblical arguments laid out by Dr. Rice in defense of his position that slavery is not, in itself, a sin. It must be stated once again that Dr. Rice was not a defender of slavery; he was a vocal advocate of gradual abolition of slavery. His biblical defense as given here was merely an effort to point out the groundless accusations made by Radical Abolitionists that slavery in itself is sinful. Let us recur to Dr. Rice's earlier statement as to his views of slavery. "In denying that slave-holding is in itself sinful, I do not defend slavery as an institution that ought to be perpetuated. I am not a pro-slavery man. I am opposed to slavery."[9]

The same biblical arguments as advanced by Dr. Rice, a Presbyterian minister, were restated in 1863 by John H. Hopkins, D.D., LL.D., the Episcopal bishop of the Diocese of *Vermont.* In a letter requesting permission to publish Bishop Hopkins's defense of biblical slavery, Episcopalians from Philadelphia, Pennsylvania, noted, "We believe that false teachings on this subject have had a great deal to do with bringing on the unhappy strife between two sections of our common country, and that a lamentable degree of ignorance prevails in regard to it."[10] In his response to the request by the gentlemen of Philadelphia, Bishop Hopkins, like Dr. Rice, made it known that he desired to see slavery ended. Nevertheless, he did not approve of the un-biblical methods being employed by the Radical Abolitionists. Bishop Hopkins stated, "I should rejoice in the adoption of any plan of gradual abolition which could be accepted peacefully by general consent, I can not see that we have any right to interfere with the domestic institutions of the South, either by the law or by the *Gospel*."[11] Bishop Hopkins spoke out against those who, using extra-biblical sources, would assume the authority of God and proclaim something as sinful that the Bible did not. Hopkins stated: "I shall not oppose the prevalent idea that slavery is an evil in itself. A *physical* evil it may be, but this does not satisfy the judgement of its more zealous adversaries, since they contend that it is a *moral* evil—a positive *sin* to hold a human being in bondage."[12]

It is important for the modern reader, imbued with more than 135 years of radical abolitionist propaganda, to remember that the arguments given by ministers of the gospel such as Dr. Rice and Bishop Hopkins were not in defense of slavery. The Radical Abolitionists in the nineteenth century and modern liberal politically correct commentators would condemn anyone opposed to their radical approach for ending slavery as a "defender of slavery." As pointed out numerous times, men such as Dr. Rice and Bishop Hopkins were not defending slavery, which they detested, but were defending the *truth* about the institution of slavery. Although these ministers were ardent anti-slavery men, the fact that they opposed the Radical Abolitionist view is enough to cause them and their arguments to be anathematized by the modern Church. As will be subsequently demonstrated, this narrow-minded view about ending slavery is just as prevalent in the modern Church as it was in the mid-nineteenth century. Yet, the Radical Abolitionist view was not the view of Christianity for more than nineteen hundred years. In the defense of his view that slavery was not sinful in itself, Bishop Hopkins stated, "I stand upon the ground which the Church of God has occupied from the beginning."[13] Here then is an important *theological* point. If the word of God (i.e., the Bible) is the exclusive rule for righteous living, how can one tolerate the use of extra-biblical arguments to create a sin where it has not existed for more than nineteen hundred years? Even pro-slavery men took note of this error in Radical Abolitionism. "If ever the abolitionists succeed in thoroughly imbuing the world with their doctrines and opinions, all religion, all government, all order, will be slowly but surely subverted and destroyed."[14]

It may be shocking for modern readers to learn, but Joseph R. Wilson, the father of President Woodrow Wilson, spoke in defense of the biblical view of slavery and in opposition to the Radical Abolitionists' views. In a letter to men inquiring to obtain permission to publish a sermon preached by Dr. Wilson titled *Mutual Relation of Master and Slaves as Taught in the Bible,* Dr. Wilson stated: "It is surely high time that the Bible view of slavery should be examined, and that we should begin to meet the infidel fanaticism of our infatuated enemies upon the elevated ground of a divine warrant for the institution [slavery]. . . . My sermon is, therefore, placed at your disposal."[15]

Returning to the great slavery debate in Cincinnati, Ohio, in 1845, we will now look at Dr. Rice's final points which summarized his position that slaveholding in itself is not a sin.

> The gentleman, by way of proving that the Jews had no slaves, refers us to the law of Moses against man-stealing. But who denies that stealing men was made a capital offence under the Jewish law? No man, surely, who reads his Bible; but that law never forbade the purchase of a bond-servant from a heathen master. On the contrary, as I have proved, the law gave express permission to do so. . . .
>
> Mr. Blanchard attempts to prove, that there were no slaveholders in the Christian church, because in the constitution of Christianity "there is neither barbarian, Scythian, bond or free." And, strangely enough, the gentleman seems to understand this language literally! Just as if it would not prove as conclusively, that there were no *females* in the early church, as that there were no *slaves* there! Who denies (what that text imports) that in the privileges of the Christian church and in the blessed hopes of the gospel, there are no distinctions—that at the table of the Lord the richest man takes his seat by the poorest of the poor? But a king is a king still, though his meanest subject is on a par with himself in the things of religion. The equality of all men on the great platform of Christian privilege and hope, does not prevent great inequalities in their civil condition. I go for both—for defending their equality in Christian privileges, whilst I would not interfere with the order of society in things touching this life. The equality of a Jew and his slave in their right to the passover, did in no wise destroy their relation to each other as master and slave.

The gentleman has repeatedly asserted the sinfulness of slave-holding in itself, on the ground, that the master takes the labor of the slave *without wages.* Now, on this subject, what says God's law? That law, as I have proved, expressly required that the wages of a *hired servant (sakir)* should be promptly paid; but it says not a word about the wages of the bond-servant (*eved*) bought from the heathen. How shall we account for this fact? The reason is obvious, if the doctrine for which I contend is true; but the thing is wholly unaccountable, if Mr. B.'s principles are correct. The law did not require wages to be paid to the bond-servant, because the master had already paid for his labor what, under the circumstances, it was worth, and because the master was bound to provide his slave food and raiment, and shelter, in sickness and health, until death. This support was the servant's wages—quite as much, by the way, as most men obtain for their labor.

The gentleman asserts, that the word *doulos* does not mean slave. This is merely *assertion*; but we call for *evidence.* I called upon him to tell us what word in the Greek language does mean slave, if this word does not. He has not given us the information. A similar question was asked concerning the Hebrew *eved*; but the gentleman could find no other word signifying *slave.* Indeed he told us, virtually, that there is no word either in the Hebrew or Greek language, which does definitely signify slave! A statement contradicted by every Greek Lexicon, by classic usage, by Bible usage, and by all Greek and Hebrew scholars. Stuart, McNight, Barnes, and a host of others, commentators, critics and theologians, say unhesitatingly, that the literal and proper meaning of *doulos,* is slave.

The faith of the abolitionists induces them to pursue a course widely different from that pursued by the apostles of Christ, in regard to prevailing sins, particularly in regard to slavery. Abolitionists stand at a distance, and denounce and villify all slaveholders; the apostles never did so. On the contrary, they preached the gospel both to masters and slaves, enjoining on each the faithful discharge of their respective duties. Abolitionists seek to render the slaves discontented, and to induce them to leave the service of their masters; the apostles pursued an opposite course. In a word—the apostles, though assailed with many odious charges, were never represented as abolitionists, or as seeking to interfere with the relation of master and slave. They, in their epistles and discourses, so far as they are recorded in the Bible, never denounced the relation itself as sinful. They sought to reform men, not by abusing and denouncing them in papers, pamphlets and public meetings, but by going amongst them, and kindly reasoning with them. The course of the abolitionists is precisely opposite to this. Now if it be true, as the apostle James teaches, that men show *their faith by their works*—it follows, that since the works of abolitionists are widely different from those of the apostles, and opposed to them, their faith is equally different from the faith of the apostles.

I have not asked you to depend upon my assertions, touching these important points, but have referred you to a number of the best commentators, critics, and theologians, such as Poole, Henry, Horne, Bush, Barnes, Stuart, McNight, Doddridge, and others; and I have challenged the gentleman to produce one respectable commentator, critic, or theologian, who agrees with him in his views of the scriptures quoted, or who gives a different exposition of them, from that which I have given. *He has not done it, because he cannot* [emphasis added].

You have heard his replies, so far as he has attempted to reply to these arguments; and *you have observed how carefully he, from the very commencement of this debate, shunned the Bible* [emphasis added], because he knew, if he went into a scriptural argument, we should be troubled with *eved* and *doulos,* lexicons, commentators and critics; and he very much feared I would confuse the minds of the people in this way!!!

[Mr. Blanchard rose to explain. I said I did so because if you took the brother from the slaveholders' texts in the Bible, you put him out of his tract.]

The gentleman is right. It is true, that I cannot discuss great moral and religious questions, without the Bible—the only infallible rule of right. *On such subjects my "tract" takes me directly to the "Blessed Book," the fountain of truth* [emphasis added].

I repeat, I did not ask you to depend on my assertions concerning the meaning of that book, I gave the gentleman standard authorities in great abundance. Poole, Henry, Scott, Gill, and many other eminently, wise and good men, who, if they were here now, would be denounced and excommunicated, because they were not abolitionists! But the gentleman, though bold in his assertions concerning the Bible, has not one sound scholar to agree with him.

If Poole, and Henry, and Scott, and Gill, and Horne, and Dick, and Chalmers, and Cunningham, and Woods, and Stuart, and Tyler, and Spring, and Wayland, and Bacon, and the whole Church of Scotland, are ignorant of the Bible, and all in error concerning the facts there recorded about slavery and slave-holders; I am quite content to be denounced in such company; and I am clearly of opinion, that if they, and such as they have failed to understand the Bible on this subject, we cannot expect much light from the gentleman and his coadjutors.

I repeat what I have said before, that I oppose abolitionism, not because it tends to abolish slavery, and improve the condition of the slave, but because it tends to perpetuate it, and aggravate all its evils. Never as I firmly believe, will slavery be abolished by your abolition lectures, your newspaper and pamphlet denunciations of slaveholders, without regard to the character or circumstances; or by attempting to exclude them from the Christian church. In New York, New Jersey, Pennsylvania, Connecticut, it has been abolished, but not by the principles of abolitionists. So long as the system continued, masters and slaves were members of the same churches, and sat at the same table of the Lord. Ministers of the Gospel, faithful to their high commission, such men as many who are now denounced by abolitionists as pro-slavery, proclaimed the Gospel both to masters and slaves; and through its elevating and purifying influence upon the public mind, slavery was gradually abolished. And thus it must be abolished, if abolished at all, in the present slave-holding States.[16]

With more than twenty-four hours of debate, and including no less that sixteen different speeches by each contender, this subject was well discussed. More to the point, it should be obvious that both sides in this debate had good points to make and were sincere in their beliefs. Unfortunately, in today's politically correct environment, only one side of this great debate is allowed a hearing. In academia, in the media, and in the churches and the synagogues throughout America, anyone who dares to question the Radical Abolitionists' view of slavery as a "sin" will reap more abuse and odium than those who take the name of the Lord in vain. As a matter of fact, a minister could be caught in the arms of a harlot and not receive the condemnation one would receive who dares to preach a sermon such as the one preached by President Woodrow Wilson's father in 1861.[17] If this scenario had been true for the entire history of Christianity, no one would have reason to question it. For almost two thousand years, the Church had not responded to the subject of slavery as a sin, as has been done for the last 150 years. The question is, why? Were the Puritan and Pilgrim clerics of New England, who countenanced both slavery and the slave trade, blinded by sinful passions? Were there no biblical scholars worthy of the subject until the advent of the Radical Abolitionists? Were Southerners, living in the Bible Belt of the antebellum South, so tainted by the odious "sin" of slavery as to make their profession of Christianity null and void?

More than just a theological oddity, this subject strikes at the heart of Radical Abolitionism and, therefore, at the political consequences of the Radical Abolitionists' efforts. Modern American political theory places the Radical Abolitionists at the pinnacle of the defenders of the downtrodden. Yet, as Dr. Rice, Bishop Hopkins, and many others have pointed out, rather than being a friend of the slave, Radical Abolitionism damaged the efforts of ending slavery on equitable grounds.

If the only damage done to America by the Radical Abolitionists was that of prolonging slavery or making its abolition impossible outside of an armed conflict, that in itself would be tragic enough. But, the loathsome influence of these radicals extends, through history, to us today. As Dr. Rice pointed out, the Radical Abolitionists did not allow the Bible to stand in their way when defining a subject as sinful. If no Bible verse could be found to make slavery a "sin," then man's feelings were called upon to elicit the needed approval to label slavery as sinful. Thus, the use of extra-biblical authorities has been introduced into the modern Church. This influence is seen even in some of the most "conservative" churches in America today. As an example of the radicals' influence in a "conservative" church, let us consider the 150th Annual Southern Baptist Convention.

RADICAL INFLUENCE IN THE SOUTHERN BAPTIST CONVENTION

In the life of humanity 150 years is but a mere "drop in the bucket." But what a "drop" the last 150 years has been for the Southern Baptist Convention. Now let it be known from the outset, that at the time of the writing of this book, the author was a Southern Baptist. He was nurtured in a Southern Baptist home, his father was a Baptist deacon for more than forty years, and his grandparents were also good Southern Baptists. Instilled from an early age in the most fundamental and orthodox Christian doctrines by many good Baptists, the author was totally unprepared for the action of the One Hundred and Fifty Year Assembly of the Southern Baptist Convention in 1995. The passing of the so-called Racial Reconciliation Resolution by the assembled delegates defamed and otherwise slandered the good name of Southern Baptists of the past 150 years. The resolution is nothing more than liberal double-speak for an act of cultural genocide against the South.

Today, in this most "enlightened" age, no people in America can be hated with complete impunity except Southerners. Southerners are the only people in America without "official" status and therefore no history worthy of remembrance, no heritage suitable for sharing, and no symbols deserving protection; putting it bluntly, Southerners "ain't got no rights." Southerners can thank the conquering Yankee, the liberal establishment, and Southern scalawags for their plight.

The infamous Baptist resolution makes no less than four errors: two historical errors, one political error, and one major biblical error. The historical errors stem from the wholehearted attachment that the Baptist delegates gave to the "Yankee myth of history." The duped delegates regurgitated on cue the abolitionist (i.e., liberal) propaganda about the institution of African servitude and life in the Old South.

Historical Errors

ERROR # 1: "Our relationship to African-Americans has been hindered *from the beginning* [emphasis added] by the role that slavery played in the formation of the Southern Baptist Convention."

TRUTH # 1: From the very beginning of Baptist churches in the South, black and white Christians have worked and worshiped together much closer than anywhere in the world. For example, in 1786 in Simpson County, Mississippi, one of the first Baptist churches in that state was established by thirteen men—twelve white and one black. In 1858 the congregation had grown to more than 175 members—one hundred white and seventy-five black. The first pastor of the oldest surviving Baptist church in Louisiana was a black free man of color, and yet the church was, and is to this day, a white Baptist church. Noted Southern historian Francis Butler Simkins observed in his textbook on Southern history the close and respectful relationship between the races in the Old South. Simkins stated:

"The Baptists did this less by deliberate missionary efforts than by accepting Negro members on a basis of Christian brotherhood that seems strange in the twentieth-century South. There were many instances in which gifted Negroes were allowed to preach to congregations of both races."[18] According to this historian, true Christian love was displayed more often during the times of slavery than in modern times of freedom. (What a condemnation on both Yankee-induced "freedom" and the modern liberal mind-set.)

The very idea that a Christian slave master could have a positive influence on his slave is to the modern mind unthinkable. (Never mind that such was the example taught by the Apostle Paul and first-century Christianity.) Let us consider the life of Rev. John Jasper. Born a slave, John Jasper lived with his Baptist master. It was through the life and example of his Christian master that John's eyes were opened to the good providence of God, and he professed his belief in Jesus Christ and later became a minister of the gospel. As a slave, Rev. Jasper earned the respect of many, including wounded Confederate soldiers to whom he often preached.[19] After the War he preached for both black and white people for more than fifteen years. Until his death, he always spoke kindly and with brotherly love of his Christian master. Before Rev. Jasper died, he said that the first thing he wished to do when he got to heaven, after seeing Jesus, was to call on his "dear old marster."[20] What a shame! Southern Baptists should be celebrating the victories of God's grace, even under the most strange of relationships (strange to modern man), rather than degrading the memory of God-fearing men such as Rev. John Jasper and his Christian master.

ERROR # 2: "Southern Baptist forbears defended the 'right' to own slaves, and either participated in, supported, or acquiesced in the *particularly inhumane* [emphasis added] nature of American slavery."

TRUTH # 2: Two points jump out at the reader of this bit of liberal "feel-good" sophism. As it is stated here, one is left with the view that only Southerners defended the "right" to own slaves. Not only has slavery existed since the dawn of time in every civilization and race known to mankind, but every American state and/or colony practiced slavery *as long as it was needed* in that state or colony. The very first colony in America to protect the "right" to own slaves was Massachusetts (*not* South Carolina). As black historian W. E. B. DuBois demonstrated, during the so-called Civil War more than a thousand slaves were brought to the Western Hemisphere under the protection of the *United States* flag. These slaves were sold, as were 94 percent of all slaves brought to the New World, in Latin America, *not* the American South. Even after the defeat of the South in 1865, slavery existed in the New World until 1888. This resolution also conveniently overlooks the thousands of slaves owned by fellow African-Americans in the United States. To all of this should be added the fact that the first colony that attempted to stop the African slave trade was the *Southern* colony of Virginia.

Now let us look at the charge that Southern slavery was "particularly inhumane." Most Americans' view of slavery in the South is based upon fictional accounts of the antebellum South. This view is drawn from the works of fiction ranging from *Uncle Tom's Cabin* and *Roots* to the *Gone With the Wind* account. Although interesting to read, fiction is fiction and should never be substituted for truth. The most recent factual study of the life of slaves in the Old South was done by Dr. Robert W. Fogel. Fogel's study of Southern slavery and Western railroads was so complete and impressive that it won for him the 1994 Nobel Peace Prize. Yet, Fogel's work has proven that slavery in the Old South was not the evil and harsh system so often portrayed by the liberal establishment. In his book *Time on the Cross,* Fogel demonstrated that nowhere in the Western Hemisphere were slaves better treated and cared for than in the South. What is more shocking is that he showed that slaves of the South were treated better than the free blacks in the North. Fogel's study paralleled the study done by the Work Projects Administration during the Great Depression commonly known as the "slave narratives," in which oral histories of former slaves were recorded and published. In this work, 60 to 80 percent of all respondents had only positive things to say about their masters and their life during slave days. The work of a Nobel Prize-winning scientist and the very words of the last living slaves in America refute the Southern Baptist Convention's resolution.

Political Error

ERROR # 3: "Racism has led to discrimination, oppression, injustice, and violence."

TRUTH # 3: Typical of standard liberal logic, the resolution places all blame for the evils of modern society upon the people of European culture (i.e., white people). While most Southerners believe in a society in which merit, not race, is the only limiting factor in a person's advancement, liberals hold to and promote the most vicious forms of discrimination. Yes, discrimination today is based upon skin color, but the color discriminated against is white, not black. Minority set-asides, reverse discrimination, forced busing, all are aimed not at black people, but at white people. Where are the Baptist ministers demanding the end of this form of discrimination? Black conservatives such as senior Hoover Institution fellow Dr. Thomas Sowell and black conservative talk show host Ken Hamblin have warned Americans about the deleterious effect of pursuing this liberal course. The liberal agenda of welfare, reverse discrimination, and slavery-victimization rhetoric has led to more racial division and conflict than anything since the end of the civil rights struggle. Even black Supreme Court Justice Clarence Thomas has spoken out against this liberal agenda. When will the Southern Baptist Convention and its ministers stop and listen to the voices of reason?

For every action there is a counter reaction. When Southern Baptists "admit" to the guilt of racism and slavery, the intended result is of course better race relations. But, in politics, what one seeks is not always what one gets. Rather than increasing good will, black militants and their liberal allies are now using the "guilt of slavery and racism" resolution to demand more minority set-asides, affirmative action, and reparations. Yes, now at last, we have the likes of "Rev." Jesse Jackson, "Rev." Al Sharpton, and "Rev." Louis Farrakhan all in the same political bed with Southern Baptist ministers!

Congress has before it H.R. 891, a bill that would establish a commission to study how reparations (this could literally and figuratively be called *black* mail) would be given to African-Americans, due them from white Americans because of the "guilt of slavery and racism." All mainstream liberal organizations such as the NAACP and the ACLU have jumped on the reparations bandwagon. The only result of kowtowing to black militants and other liberals is a further decrease in positive relationship between the two cultures. When it comes to good race relations, liberalism is more deadly than cancer. To quote Ken ("The Black Avenger") Hamblin, "Liberalism, Public Enemy # one; Cancer, Public Enemy # two!"

Biblical Error

ERROR # 4: Throughout the resolution, the unspoken idea and/or point that begs to be made is that slavery is sinful. Many passages of scripture are quoted to show that all people were "equal" and that God's plan was for man (and woman) to live on a footing of absolute equality. According to the resolution, slavery denies the existence of absolute equality of humankind, and therefore slavery must be a sin. The main thrust of the liberals' argument is that since slavery is a sin, no one should complain when he or she is ordered to pay his fair share for the horrors of that most sinful of institutions. This logic, or lack of it, follows the lies of earlier liberals known as abolitionists. Confronting this fallacy about slavery, the following letter was submitted to several local newspapers. The author is not arguing that no sin took place within the institution of slavery but rather that there is no biblical justification for charging the institution of slavery in itself to be a sin. The body of the following letter is printed below.

TRUTH # 4: Only God can define what is a sin.

In an effort to defend the good name of Southern Baptists of the nineteenth century, the following letter was submitted to a North Louisiana daily paper in 1995. The letter was rejected for publication no less than three times. It was also rejected by the official newspaper of the Louisiana Baptist Convention:

> An innocent man in the Greek play "Antigone" is given a death sentence and laments, "It is a grievous thing when the right judge, judges wrong." The recent slanderous attack upon the good name and honor of deceased Southern Christians by the Southern Baptist Convention, with their apology for the "sins" of slavery and racism, brought forth a similar sense of agony in many Christians.
>
> One stands astonished by the hypocrisy of modern Baptist Churchmen who dare condemn Christians of the 19th century, yet, no century has produced more death and destruction than the 20th century. Never has this nation seen a people with less civility or respect for law and moral standards than in this 20th century. Never have illegitimacy, murder, rape and divorce been as high as it is today in the 20th century. Compared to our ancestors of the last century, we of the 20th century live in

a virtual Sodom and Gomorrah. Yet, Southern Baptists can find nothing better to do than to desecrate the graves of our sainted dead. "Honor thy Father and Mother." I will honor my Christian Father, who is interred alongside his Father and Grandfather (a Confederate Soldier). I will not stand silent as the sycophants of liberal political correctness desecrate the graves of my people.

If slavery is such a diabolical sin it should be easy to find a clear-cut "thus saith the Lord" repudiation of slavery. I defy the minions of political correctness to come forward and reveal such a text. While they rush to and fro, I direct the reader's attention to Leviticus 25:44-46. In Leviticus, the LORD gives to Israel HIS law on slavery. God's law on slavery not only made provision for the Hebrew slave, who was subject to the law of Jubilee, but also the "stranger" or non-Hebrew slave which would be the property of the Hebrew forever. The listing of slaves along with other property is seen in the Ten Commandments.

A search of the New Testament will not find one verse that unequivocally condemns slavery as a sin. During the life of Christ, the cruel, pagan, Roman system of slavery brought people from all over the world under its control. Yet, during his ministry, Jesus Christ never condemned slaveholders nor the system of slavery. Christ nor his Apostles saw fit to condemn slavery as sinful.

In the New Testament we read Paul's Epistle of Philemon where the Apostle returns a runaway slave to his master with a request that the slave be received back with love. If ever there was needed a time for the Holy Spirit to move Paul to condemn slavery here was that opportunity. Yet, nowhere is the slave master nor the institution of slavery condemned as "sinful."

The Biblical argument for slavery given here is neither Baptist nor Southern. The New England Puritan cleric Cotton Mather, among other Yankees, used Biblical arguments to defend the New England system of slavery and the slave trade. Today, due to liberal education our people, most of all Southerners, know little about the history of slavery under the Puritans of Massachusetts.

What will be the response of our Churchmen when they are met with a demand for an apology for all the years of patriarchy, i.e., male dominance in church and family, or an apology for the homophobic attitude of the church? If current events offers us any guide, get ready for a full scale apology to the feminists and the sodomites. When one starts down the path of rewriting Holy Scripture, all types of apostasy are possible.

The Sunday after the local paper carried a slanderous attack upon my Southern ancestors, by several local Baptist ministers, I had the pleasure of worshiping in a church where Southern Pride and respect for our people are commonplace. The most often seen flag in that church is the Confederate Flag, twice each year the church is the focal point for Southern Heritage celebrations, and the Pastor is a resolute proponent of Southern Independence. That Sunday and each Sunday thereafter, I look at the congregation and see more racial and cultural diversity in that church than is found in the average Baptist Church. These Christians have no trouble worshiping with people of various races or different cultural background; yet, they display love and respect for their Southern heritage and would never defile the honor of their Southern ancestors. I trust that one day Southern Baptist will learn how to love in this manner.

Deo Vindice,
Walter D. Kennedy

Southerners never like to "talk bad" about churches or ministers. This is just plain good manners that their parents taught them. But, when a long train of abuse continues from the misguided, even if they profess to be ministers of the gospel, Southerners must stand up and demand an accounting. I do not believe that most Baptist ministers and laymen are intentionally attacking Southern families. For the most part, the attack is made because they have not taken the time to study the Southern view of the cause and effects of the War for Southern Independence. Nevertheless, the results from a political point of view are the same—a continuing eroding of the rights of Southerners. Six weeks after local Baptist ministers acquiesced in the attack on Southern culture, it was not surprising at all when black militants and liberals in a city twenty-five miles from the author's home demanded the removable of the Confederate battle flag in that city. After all, it had already been admitted that the "sin" of slavery and racism is common to all Southerners in the area. The sad point is that all Southerners know that the cultural bigots will not stop at the removable of a battle flag. The liberal elite has already said that they will stop at nothing until all vestiges of the South are "gone with the wind."

Like many modern Southerners, the author has spent the greater part of his life fighting for equal opportunity for all.

Nevertheless, we Southerners now find ourselves condemned by liberals and their sycophants as racists. Today the South embraces the belief in the Jeffersonian idea of "equality of opportunity." We Southerners have not changed our views; we continue demanding equal treatment for all Americans—even Southerners. This is something liberals and their sycophants cannot tolerate. Today, it is not the racial bigots that berate and castigate those of us who believe in true Jeffersonian equality, but the liberals and their scalawag dupes. These liberals are nothing less than cultural bigots who will stop at nothing but the total destruction of the South.

SUMMARY

The discussion in this chapter is not about whether slavery is or is not a sin. In America today, that would be somewhat of a moot question. Regardless of how one feels about the biblical issue of slavery, it must be recognized that both parties in this debate were making some rather good arguments. This being the case, it behooves modern society not to quickly adopt the view of Radical Abolitionism to the exclusion of other *anti-slavery* views. Leaders such as Dr. Rice of Ohio and Bishop Hopkins of Vermont were both anti-slavery men, but both opposed the antics of the Radical Abolitionists. Likewise, important men in the South also had different views on how and when slavery was to end. At great personal expense, Robert E. Lee freed his slaves long before the advent of the War for Southern Independence. Others, such as Jefferson Davis, believed that the slaves should be educated and made ready for freedom. On Davis's plantation the idea of educating the slave for freedom was put into practice.[21] Jefferson Davis, Robert E. Lee, Thomas Jefferson, and George Washington, among a score of others, represent the numerous Southern slaveholders who believed in some system of emancipation. Due to the adoption of the Radical Abolitionists' view of slavery, today all these honorable men are subject to being slandered and abused as "defenders of slavery."

The puerile demand to judge people of the eighteenth and nineteenth centuries by the knowledge, experience, and standards of the twentieth and twenty-first centuries is inexcusable. For example, using the medical knowledge of the eighteenth and ninetheeth centuries, smallpox was treated by placing stones in bed with the victim; heart problems were treated by bleeding the patient; and the use of anesthetics (crude as they were) for amputating soldiers' limbs, was considered harmful to the morale of the army. This being the case, should we condemn all physicians of the eighteenth and nineteenth centuries? Furthermore, using the extra-biblical method of the Radical Abolitionists, could we not find abundant proofs of undue pain, suffering, and death at the hands of these physicians to warrant the invention of a new species of "sin"? In the same fashion, we could condemn the great document of English liberties, the Magna Carta. When this document was written, it afforded little freedom to the common man in England. The Magna Carta did limit the power of the king vis-à-vis the English nobles. Therefore, using today's standards, we can truthfully say that the Magna Carta is a hoax and fraud upon the common peoples' liberties. These assessments of physicians and the Magna Carta are just as juvenile and ridiculous as the modern liberal politically correct demand to condemn all anti-slavery advocates who did not agree with the radical approach to abolition. Equally true, the history of Christianity during its first nineteen hundred years demonstrates that slavery was not viewed as a sin in itself; therefore, to condemn Christianity by twentieth- and twenty-first-century views is also juvenile.

Not only did the Radical Abolitionists adversely affect the nature of the abolition struggle of the nineteenth century, they have had an adverse impact on both church and state today. Because of the adoption of the radical view of slavery, everything Southern—flags, heroes, monuments, plantations, and holidays—are all subject to condemnation. The struggle for Southern independence has also been redefined to coincide with the views of modern followers of the Radical Abolitionists. No longer are Southern armies characterized as fighting to defend home and family from an invader; now they are depicted as fighting to promote slavery—that most odious of all sins.

In dealing with the issue of Radical Abolitionism and Christianity, several myths have been exposed:

MYTH: Slavery is and has always been a sin in itself.

REALITY: According to the only constitution that true Christianity recognizes, the Holy Bible, there are no unequivocal passages that condemn slavery as a sin in itself. What is true is that the pagan system of slavery in which the whole person was owned by a master was disallowed. Under the biblical system of slavery, only the labor of the individual was secured for the master; the slave's body, soul, and spirit always belonged to God. This concept, as seen in both the Old and the New Testaments, provided the starting point for the amelioration of the evils of slavery and eventually, the complete abolition of it. It should be noted that the biblical system of slavery and its eventual abolition were denigrated by the Radical Abolitionists as a "defense of slavery."

MYTH: The passage in the Bible that condemns "man stealing" is proof that Southern slaveholders were sinful.

REALITY: Man stealing, according to the laws of every Southern and Northern state was a crime. The liberation of a slave in Louisiana, *by the authorities in Louisiana,* because, as a free man of color in New York, he had been kidnapped and sold into slavery proves the point.[22] Buying a person already a slave, having been taken in war, as punishment of crime, or one who had sold himself into slavery, is not man stealing. The taking of slaves in this manner was common practice by both the Hebrews in the Old Testament and the Puritan Fathers of New England. According to the law of Moses and common jurisprudence in the several American states, man stealing is the reduction of a free person into slavery, not the buying of lawful slaves. At one time, prior to the advent of Radical Abolitionism, this was the commonly held view of both the North and the South.

MYTH: The Golden Rule, "Do unto others as you would have them do unto you," makes holding a person in slavery sinful.

REALITY: If the Golden Rule is enforceable upon the master of a slave, it is also enforceable upon a slave. Therefore, according to the Golden Rule, a slave must view his master's betterment before his own. How can taking away a valuable asset (slave property) better his master? If both master and slave live by the Golden Rule, all the evils of pagan slavery are destroyed. But even more benefits can result if the Golden Rule is correctly followed. The good will established by these two men, while following the Golden Rule, makes it possible for the slave to gain his freedom. This was the plea of the early American emancipationists; a plea that was given a death blow by Radical Abolitionism.

MYTH: The view of slavery as a biblically sanctioned institution was a Southern idea, held by very few religious leaders.

REALITY: As has been demonstrated in Chapters 1 and 2, the view of slavery held by Southerners in the mid-nineteenth century was held by the vast majority of Christians up until that time. Early New England clerics were some of the strongest advocates of biblical slavery. Even as late as 1863, an Anglican bishop, John Hopkins of Vermont, was defending this biblical view of slavery. Anglicans, Presbyterians, Baptists, and Methodists all at various times were defenders of this view. In the state of Maryland, the largest slaveholders were a group of Catholic priests of the Jesuit order. In Louisiana, the largest Roman Catholic state in the Union, Catholics were just as involved with the institution of slavery as their Protestant neighbors. Nevertheless, Catholic religious leaders were no more condemning of slavery as a sin than their Protestant counterparts.

CHAPTER 4

African-Americans, Free Born and Slave

Slave and free, black and white, lived close to one another, and their relationship led to a wide spread reputation for "better treatment."[1]

Eugene D. Genovese
Roll, Jordan, Roll
The World the Slaves Made

No prophet in early times could have told that kindliness would grow as a flower from a soil so foul, that slaves would come to be cherished not only as property of high value but as loving if lowly friends.[2]

Ulrich B. Phillips
Life and Labor in the Old South

No study of American slavery would be complete without a look at the relationships that developed in American society between the two races in the eighteenth and nineteenth centuries. Following the traditions of the Radical Abolitionists when looking at race relationships in early America, most investigators look only at the relationship between master and slave in the South. While it is true that by the nineteenth century the vast majority of slave and free blacks lived in the South, there were still some slaves in the North as well as a growing body of free blacks at that time. In the following text, the lives and conditions of free people of color and slaves in both the North and the South will be examined.

The quotations by Genovese and Phillips given at the beginning of this chapter may make it appear as if these authors are attempting to paint a "moonlight and magnolias" picture of slavery. But, be reassured, they are not blind to the abuses that took place within the institution. Southerners are much aware of the evils associated with the institution of slavery and the need to abolish slavery. Also, they are quite aware of the paradox that exists in a society which holds men in bondage and yet proclaims itself to be a nation of liberty. But if an individual is sincere in his desire to pursue truth, he must be willing to follow the trail of facts wherever it goes. The complete and true story of American slavery in general and Southern slavery in particular is far beyond the comprehension of the average modern American. Tutored by the liberal (and therefore politically correct) theory of American history, most Americans have been exposed to only one view of slavery. That view is taken from fiction, not from jures up images of bullwhips, broken families, abusive overseers, and maniacal masters? This is the *Uncle Tom's Cabin* and *Roots* version of fictionalized history. "Fictionalized history" is an oxymoron, but it is the sanctioned view of slavery that is enforced by the established order in modern American society.

In the following brief overview of African-American life in early America, some of the myths about slavery as well as black freedom in both the North and the South will be exposed. Again the reader will notice that the facts about living conditions for black Americans in both sections of the United States and the mythology advanced by the victors of the War for Southern Independence are at odds with each other.

AFRICAN-AMERICAN LIFE IN THE NORTH

As was demonstrated in Chapter 2, early in American history slavery existed in every colony and state of the North. This fact in itself flies in the face of conventional wisdom, which views the North as a land of *freedom.* Early in the history of New England, the enslavement of Native Americans was justified by none other than Rev. Cotton Mather. As his fellow countrymen were making slaves of Native Americans and selling them in the Caribbean islands, Rev. Mather stated: "We know not when or how these Indians first became inhabitants of this mighty Continent, yet we may guess that probably the Devil decoy'd these miserable Savages hither, in hopes that the Gospel of the Lord Jesus Christ would never come here to destroy or disturb his Absolute Empire over them."[3] It should be noted that the Native American slave trade had as one of its by-products the purchase of African slaves. Native Americans captured near the colony of Massachusetts did not make good slaves; therefore, they were sold in the Caribbean, and more profitable African slaves were bought. Thus, African slaves were introduced into New England, whereupon is demonstrated the genesis of the Intra-American slave trade.

When confronted with the evidence of the North as a society of slave traders and slaveholders, Southerners are often rebuked with the assertion that because of their sense of humanity, Northerners freed their slaves and ended the slave trade. Yet, the claim of humanity and brotherhood for the downtrodden Northern slave does not hold up under historical scrutiny. Speaking on the question of why the North abolished slavery, John Adams stated, "Argument might have some weight in the abolition of slavery in Massachusetts, but the real cause was the multiplication of labouring white people, who would no longer suffer the rich to employ these sable rivals so much to their injury. The common people would not suffer the labor, by which alone they could obtain a subsistence, to be done by slaves. If the gentlemen had been permitted by law to hold slaves, the common white people would have put the slaves to death, and their masters too perhaps."[4] Was it the feelings of fraternal equality that Adams was describing when he said that the good people of Massachusetts would have killed the slaves if necessary? Without any sophism about liberty, equality, and fraternity, it becomes clear why the North ended slavery. It was not the desire for "liberty, equality, and fraternity" that prompted Massachusetts to abolish slavery; it was for the economic advantage of white men that slavery was abolished there. Fifty years after John Adams explained why slavery was abolished in Massachusetts, Frenchman Alexis de Tocqueville made the following observation about the abolition of slavery in America: "It is not for the good of the negroes, but for that of the whites, that measures are taken to abolish slavery in the United States."[5]

Rather than being a land of freedom and opportunity for African-Americans, the North was a place of bondage for most blacks and second-class citizenship for those few who were freed. Long before Virginia or South Carolina passed laws defending a master's right in his slave property, Massachusetts became the first American colony to do so in 1641.[6] As demonstrated in Chapter 2, slavery and the slave trade existed in the North as long as it was needed. Puritans, Quakers, Anglicans, and Catholics all participated in the institution of slavery in the North. Some of the most prominent men of New England were involved in the institution of slavery. Benjamin Wadsworth, president of Harvard College, was allowed to pay for a slave on an installment plan;[7] Peter Faneuil, a prominent Bostonian who gave the city Faneuil Hall, was engaged in the slave trade;[8] Benjamin Franklin advertised slaves for sale in his newspaper; and Josiah Franklin, Benjamin's brother, sold slaves at his tavern.[9] These are but a few examples of New Englanders who profited from the institution of slavery.

In 1636, the *Desire,* America's first slave ship, was built at Marblehead, Massachusetts.[10] The following year, 1637, it went on a trading voyage in which it conveyed slaves from the Pequod Indian tribe—two women and fifteen boys—to be sold in the Caribbean. These Native Americans became slaves after being captured by colonists during a recent battle near Fairfield, Connecticut.[11] On the return trip from the Caribbean, the *Desire* brought back to Boston commodities of cotton, tobacco, and Negro slaves. As historian George F. Dow asserts, "[I]t was not long before negro and Indian slaves were owned in all of the New England settlements."[12] From this meager beginning in 1637, the number of slaves in the Boston area increased to more than 4,489 by the year 1754.

In the year 1644, New England advanced into the big league of slave trading. At that time New England, along with most other European powers, entered into the commerce of the Trans-Atlantic African slave trade. That year, a group of Boston merchants financed a slaving venture to the coast of Africa. The success of this endeavor was the stimulus for other Boston merchants to move into the lucrative business.[13] Rhode Island proved to be Massachusetts's staunchest rival in this enterprise. As late as 1758, this ad was printed in the *Boston Gazette*:

> Just imported from Africa, and to be sold on board the brig *jenney,* William Ellery, Commander, now lying at New-Boston, A Number of likely Negro Boys and Girls, from 12 to 24 years of Age; Inquire of said Ellery on board said Brig, where constant attandance is given.
>
> *Note.* The above Slaves have all had the Small-Pox. Treasurer's Notes, and New England Rum will be as Pay.[14]

From early in colonial history right up to the advent of the War for Southern Independence, the North was engaged in the African slave trade. After 1842 the United States Navy maintained a fleet off the coast of Africa to police its merchant fleet for slavers. On April 21, 1861, the American slaver *Nightingale* was captured off the African coast. The *Nightingale,* affectionately known as the "Prince of Slavers," was built in Portsmouth, New Hampshire, fitted out for the slave trade in Salem, Massachusetts, and its captain was from New York. When captured by the U.S.S. *Saratoga,* the *Nightingale* was flying the United States flag, and had more than nine hundred slaves on board.

One of the last American vessels to be captured in the slave trade was the *Erie,* Capt. Nathaniel Gordon of Portland, Maine, commander.[15] It should be noted that these vessels were not bringing slaves into the South. Not only did the Constitution of the Confederate States not allow the importation of African slaves, but the Union Navy had an effective blockade which ended any illegal importation of slaves into the South. As black historian W. E. B. Dubois noted, during the War for Southern Independence several thousand African slaves were brought into the Western Hemisphere. These Africans, like 94 percent of all African slaves, were destined for Cuba or South America, not Dixie.[16]

According to historian George H. Moore, Massachusetts was the first colony not only to institute positive laws for the protection of a master's right in his slave property but, using the biblical foundation, identified those classes of people who were subject to the classification of a slave in that state. The law describes the following groups of people as slaves:

> 1. Indian slaves—their captives taken in war.
> 2. Negro slaves—their own importations of "strangers" obtained by purchase or exchange.
> 3. Criminals—condemned to slavery as a punishment for offences.
>
> Thus stood the statute through the whole colonial period, and it was *never expressly repealed* [emphasis added]. Based on the Mosaic code, it is an absolute recognition of slavery as a legitimate status, and of the right of one man to sell himself as well as that of another man to buy him. It sanctions the slave-trade, and the perpetual bondage of Indians and negroes, their children and their children's children, and entitles Massachusetts to precedence over any and all the other colonies in similar legislation. It anticipates by many years anything of the sort to be found in the statutes of Virginia, or Maryland, or South Carolina, and nothing like it is to be found in the contemporary codes of her sister colonies in New England.[17]

As demonstrated in Chapter 2, according to many historians, New England's slave codes, punishments, and other evils which are normally associated with Southern slavery were different from its Southern counterpart only in the numbers of slaves and slaveholders within each region's society.

According to the Congressional Record, March 26, 1884, a Southern congressman from North Carolina saw fit to remind the folks of Massachusetts how much they were responsible for slavery in the Americas:

> Massachusetts is a State more responsible under heaven than any other community in this land for the introduction of slavery into this Continent, with all the curses that have followed it; that it is the nursing mother of the horrors of the middle passage, and that after slavery in Massachusetts was found not to pay, her slaves were sold down South for a consideration, and then their former owners thanked God and sang the long metre Doxology through their noses, that they were responsible no longer for the sin of human slavery.[18]

As has been abundantly demonstrated, the North played a large part in the institution of slavery in America. But, more than just black slaves lived in the North. What was life like in the North for a free person of color? Alexis de Tocqueville, in *Democracy in America,* noted the conditions of the free people of color in the North:

> The prejudice of the race appears to be stronger in the States which have abolished slavery, than in those where it still exists; and nowhere is it so intolerant as in those states where servitude has never been known. . . . If oppressed, they may bring an action at law, but they will find none but whites amongst their judges; and although they may legally serve as jurors, prejudice repulses them from that office. The same schools do not receive the child of the black and of the European. In the theatres, gold cannot procure a seat for the servile race beside their former masters. . . . The negro is free, but he can share neither the rights, nor the pleasures, nor the labor, nor the afflictions, nor the tomb of him whose equal he has been declared to be; and he cannot meet him upon fair terms in life or in death.
>
> Thus it is, in the United States, that the prejudice which repels the negroes seems to increase in proportion as they are emancipated, and inequality is sanctioned by the manners whilst it is effaced from the laws of the country.[19]

In 1834, a Frenchman, Michael Chevalier was sent by the Minister of the Interior of France to study various public works in the United States. So intriguing did Chevalier find American society that he extended his stay and toured every section of the United States. His observations and impressions of America were published in 1839 in a book titled *Society Manners & Politics in the United States.*[20] Chevalier's impression of life in the North for free blacks supports the view described by his fellow countryman, Alexis de Tocqueville. According to Chevalier, "[T]o the men of the North . . . the negro is a Philistine, a son of Ham. In the States without slaves, as well as in those which slavery is admitted, the elevation of the black seems impossible. . . . The man of color is a Pariah; he is denied lodging at the inns; at the theatre or in the steamboats he has a distinct place allotted him far from the whites."[21]

It should be remembered that this description of life for African-Americans is being made by an impartial foreign observer visiting the North. In observing Northern society as it relates to African-Americans, Chevalier noted that although many forms of *de jure* (legal) discrimination had been eliminated, nevertheless, *de facto* (actual) discrimination in the North was just as effective in keeping the African-American from exercising privileges normally reserved for white people.

> In Massachusetts and most of New England the blacks are legally citizens, and, as such, have the right of voting; they do not, however, at present exercise this right, either because they are prevented from doing so, or because their names are designedly omitted on the list of tax-payers. . . . The constitution of Connecticut, formed in 1818, excludes them from this franchise. In New York, real estate of the value of 250 dollars, and the payment of taxes is made the electoral qualification of blacks. [The new constitution of Pennsylvania, formed in 1838, restricts the right of suffrage to the whites, although it was extended to blacks by the old constitution—Transl.] The Western States, in which slavery does not exist, do not admit blacks to vote.[22]

The second-class treatment afforded resident African-Americans in the North extended also to officials of predominantly black nations visiting there. Chevalier gives the following account of the treatment of a black foreigner upon his visit to the North.

> A young Haytian, who had received a good education in France; having arrived in New York, he could not get admittance

> into any hotel, his money was refused at the door of the theatre, he was ordered out of the cabin of a steamboat, and was obliged to quit the country without being able to speak to any body. At Philadelphia, I heard of a man of colour who had acquired wealth, a rare thing among that class, who used sometimes to invite whites to dine with him, and who did not sit at table, but waited upon his guests himself. At the dessert, however, upon their pressing him to be seated with them, he would yield to their urgency. At the end of 1833, in one of the New England States, and I think it was in Massachusetts, a man of color being on board a steamer with his wife, wished to get her admitted into the ladies' cabin; the captain refused her admission. A suit was, therefore, brought against the captain, by the man, who was desirous of having it decided by the courts, whether free people of color, conducting themselves with propriety, could enjoy the same privileges with whites in a State, in which they were recognized as citizens by the law. He gained his cause on the first hearing, but was cast on appeal.[23]

To many foreign observers, "Negrophobia" seemed to be the generally held view throughout the North in the nineteenth century. So prominent was this Northern-held view of Africans that it calls into question the vaunted idea of Northerners fighting for freedom and equality. Indeed, the willingness of many white people of the North in opposing the *institution* of slavery had little, if anything, to do with concern for the freedom and the welfare of Africans. The prime motive in the elimination of slavery in Northern society had much more to do with the benefits that abolition would bring free white workers than with any benefit abolition would bring the slave population.[24] In actuality, slavery was abolished in the North to protect the white population from competition with slave labor. Even the elimination of the slave trade was based more on the needs of white citizens than on a desire to assist the unfortunate Africans. For example, the elimination of the importation of slaves into New Jersey was accomplished in order "that white labor may be protected."[25] Likewise, Connecticut prohibited the importation of slaves into that state because "the increase of slaves is injurious to the poor."[26] As can be seen, pecuniary interests, and not "liberty, equality, fraternity," had more to do with the abolition of slavery in the North. By pointing out the role that self-interest played in the abolition of slavery in the

North, the author does not mean to diminish the role that religion and the sense of humanity played in the abolition of slavery. Often in the discussion of slavery in America, Southerners are challenged by those who portray the North as "freedom loving" and "humanitarian"; therefore, the South must be regarded as the antithesis of freedom and humanity. Since no Northern state adopted a system for the abolition of slavery that granted immediate freedom to slaves, each slaveholder's right in the property that he held was protected. Some states, such as New Jersey, maintained slavery by redefining it as "apprenticeship." Thus, as late as 1860 the Federal census listed slaves in New Jersey.[27]

Most Northern states adopted a system of emancipation for slaves that allowed the Northern slaveholders to liquidate their slave property without suffering the loss of their assets. For example, the laws for abolition of slavery stated that any slave born in a particular state after a certain date, and after attaining the age of twenty-one years, would be free. Therefore, slaveholders with a pregnant slave could send her out of the state before the birth of her child. The child not being born in the state then could not claim freedom under the act of emancipation. Some slaveholders granted their slaves freedom with the stipulation that they remain under the care and direction of their former master over an extremely long indentureship. Therefore, the former slaveholder granted "freedom" to his slave, yet retained the services of the slave while freeing himself of all the liabilities of owning slaves. Many slaves were kidnapped or otherwise lured away from the North and sold into slavery by unscrupulous Northern slave traders. All in all, the pretentious gift of freedom for the African-American of the North proved to be a highly decorated box with little of substance therein.

George Fitzhugh, a staunch defender of Southern slavery, even noted the degraded condition occupied by the freed African-Americans of the North. Fitzhugh stated:

> In the United States the situation of the free blacks is becoming worse every day. The silly attempts of the Abolitionists to put them on a footing of equality with whites, has exasperated the laboring whites at the North, and excited odium and suspicion against them at the South. The natural antipathies of race have been fanned into such a degree of

> excitement, that the free negro is bandied from pillar to post—from North to South and South to North, till not a ray of hope is left him for a quiet, permanent residence any where, so long as he remains free. Illinois and California will not permit him to enter their dominions—Ohio places him under severe conditions, and is now moving to expel him altogether, and Virginia also proposes to send him back to Africa. Mobs in our Northern cities drive him from his home and hunt him like a wild beast. . . . The white laborers of the North think the existence of negroes at the North as free, or at the South as slaves, injurious to themselves. They do not like the competition of human beings who have all the physical powers of men, with the wants only of brutes. Free Soilism pretty well represents and embodies this feeling. It is universal at the North, because the hostility to negroes—the wish to get rid of their competition is universal there. It excludes free negroes from California as well as slaves, showing that the Wilmot Proviso is directed against the negro race—not against slavery.[28]

Note how Fitzhugh views the actions of the Free Soil movement. These pious Northerners were archenemies of slavery within any territory of the United States. Yet, it was not just slavery that they wanted to keep out of the territories, it was also the African-American. Thus we see the exclusion from California of the African-American as attempted by the Wilmot Proviso. (The reader is directed back to Chapter 2 and the discussion about the Fire-Eaters of Mississippi. It will be remembered that "Old Copperas Breeches" also condemned the exclusion of slaves, Africans, and Southerners from California.)

The overall condition and health of free African-Americans in the North can be judged by the rate of growth of their population. While most groups in Northern society were expanding, what was the condition of black society? According to Federal census records, in New York the rate of growth in the black population constantly decreased from 1790 until 1830. The African-American population of New York decreased from just over 7.5 percent of the population to just under 2.5 percent from 1790 to 1830.[29] The same decline in African-American population is seen in every Northern state during this time. According to Edgar J. McManus, author of *Black Bondage in the North,* two factors account for this decrease: (1) Since free African-Americans were no longer taxable property, they may have been somewhat undercounted; and, (2) The movement of slave property, by legal or illegal means, tended to decrease the African-American population in the North, while increasing it in the South. This tendency was noted by Frenchman Alexis de Tocqueville:

> From the time at which a Northern State prohibits the importation of slaves, no slaves were brought from the South to be sold in its [Northern] markets. On the other hand, as the sale of slaves was forbidden in that State, an owner was no longer able to get rid of his slave (who thus became a burdensome possession) otherwise than by transporting him to the South. But when a Northern State declared that the son of the slave should be born free, the slave lost a large portion of his market-value, since his posterity was no longer included in the bargain, and the owner had then a strong interest in transporting him to the South. Thus the same law prevents the slaves of the South from coming to the Northern States, and drives those of the North to the South.
>
> Thus the abolition of slavery does not set the slave free, but it merely transfers him from one master to another, and from the North to the South.[30]

According to de Tocqueville, the African-Americans of the North had to contend not only with those who would sell them into Southern slavery, but also with a death rate that was higher among them than it was among the white population of the North.

> There is a very great difference between the mortality of the blacks and of the whites in the States in which slavery is abolished; from 1820 to 1830, only one out of forty-two individuals of the white population died in Philadelphia; but one negro out of twenty-one individuals of the black population died in the same space of time. The mortality is by no means so great amongst the negroes who are still slaves.[31]

De Tocqueville describes free African-Americans in the North as leading "a wretched and precarious existence." Notice de Tocqueville's assertion that the death rate for free African-Americans in the North was higher than the death rate for those who remained in slavery in the South. Free Northern African-Americans with a death rate higher than slaves in the South and leading a wretched and precarious existence! Where is the vaunted land of Northern freedom? One is left perplexed. With Northern freedom working such dire results on the lives of African-Americans, is there any wonder that so few Southern slaves and free people of color chose the North as a home rather than remaining in the South?

The strong sense of racial superiority by white people of the North contributed to an ever-decreasing quality of life for African-Americans in the North. The passage of a law forbidding interracial sexual contact in 1705 by the state of Massachusetts is just one example of this sense of racial superiority in the North. The purpose for passing this law is self-evident. The law stated that it was being passed for "the better preventing of a spurious and mixt issue."[32] The abolition of slavery in the North did little to reduce, and in many ways actually increased, the racial prejudice faced by African-Americans. As many historians have pointed out, whether in the North or South, white people have very seldom changed their society solely for the benefit of African-Americans. Although willing to end slavery, Northerners in the early nineteenth century found it very difficult to change existing societal mores as it related to African-Americans. As long as both slavery *and* the African-American could be eliminated, the North moved forward with its system of gradual emancipation. That which the North so eagerly took advantage of (gradual emancipation and elimination of the Negro from its society), the South was never allowed to do.

FREE AND SLAVE AFRICAN-AMERICANS IN DIXIE

Regardless of how long slavery existed in the North or how extensive a role slavery played in the history of the North, it was in the South that African-American slavery really had its greatest impact. Both free people of color and slaves called Dixie home. In many ways, the life of free and slave in the South differed little from life in the North. In both regions of America, slavery existed for the economic benefit of society at large. In both regions, slavery was an acceptable practice as long as it was deemed an economic necessity. In both sections of the country there was a growing desire to see the institution eliminated. Unfortunately for the South, the size of the slave population and the relentless demand for slave labor to prop up the local economy made abolition of slavery more difficult. This unfortunate fact set the stage for America's greatest and saddest struggles. Without a doubt, the one thing that antebellum Americans did agree on was the innate inferiority of the African race.[33] This fact in itself made the abolition of slavery more difficult to achieve.

For the most part, after Reconstruction and until the mid-twentieth century, the institution of slavery in the South was viewed more as a paternalistic system than as a solely oppressive system. That is not to say that during this time the negative aspects of Southern slavery were ignored. Rather, while applauding the abolition of slavery, most Americans acknowledged the difficulty faced by Southern slaveholders as they attempted to end slavery. During this same time, Americas also noted the positive contributions that slavery offered the slave. Since the advent of the modern civil rights revolution around 1950, the commonly held view of Southern slavery has moved from one of benign acceptance to one of malignant hatred. This change in attitude is reminiscent of the movement of the Radical Abolitionists of the early nineteenth century as they denigrated everything Southern, not just Southern slaveholders. The most obvious expression of this neo-radical abolitionist view today is seen in the condemnation of the Confederate flag because of its supposed connection with slavery. (This subject will be discussed in more detail in Chapter 7.)

Although the benign view of slavery has fallen into disfavor with modern scholars, at one time this view was held and promoted by some of America's most notable personalities. For example, Woodrow Wilson had this to say about the treatment of slaves in the South:

> Domestic slaves were almost uniformly dealt with indulgently and even affectionately by their masters. Among those masters who had the sensibility and breeding of gentlemen, the dignity and responsibility of ownership were apt to produce a noble and gracious type of manhood, and relationships really patriarchal. "On principle, in habits, and even on grounds of self-interests, the greater part of the slave-owners were humane in the treatment of their slaves,—kind, indulgent, not over-exacting, and sincerely interested in the physical well-being of their dependents,"—is the judgement of an eminently competent northern observer who visited the South in 1844. "Field hands" on the ordinary plantations came constantly under their master's eye, were comfortably quartered, and were kept from overwork both by their own laziness and

> by the slack discipline to which they were subject. They were often commanded in brutal language, but they were not often compelled to obey by brutal treatment.[34]

At the turn of the century, Woodrow Wilson, a future president of the United States, viewed Southern slavery as, more or less, a paternalistic institution—an institution in which the slave was treated not just as an instrument of labor but as a person with needs and feelings. Unfortunately, anyone in today's liberal politically correct society who dares to promote such a view of slavery in the South will be stigmatized as a "defender of slavery."

It must be reasserted once again that those who hold views different from the existing liberal norm of today, are not *ipso facto* defenders of slavery. Many slaveholders of the Old South, who were in favor of the abolition of slavery and who at great personal expense to themselves emancipated their own slaves, are condemned as "defenders of slavery" by contemporary liberals. Likewise, today when Southerners demand a fair treatment of the issue of slavery (i.e., acknowledgment of the many good relationships and experiences that took place within the institution of slavery), they are stigmatized as "defenders of slavery" by the liberal establishment. To determine whether there was, indeed, a system of Southern paternalism as it related to the system of slavery, let us look at the historical record.

John Randolph of Roanoke was the earliest and foremost leader of the "Southern Rights" movement. A Southern State's Rights man years before John C. Calhoun embraced the cause, Randolph advocated a conservative, strict constructionist view of government. Randolph often styled himself a lover of liberty and not a lover of democracy; he would say of himself, "I love liberty, I hate equality."[35] It should come as no surprise to modern readers that this "hater of equality" was a slaveholder. Yet, this "hater of equality" managed to do what Jefferson, also a slaveholder, who penned the immortal words "all men are created equal," could not do. Randolph, the owner of more that four hundred slaves, freed his slaves, while Jefferson never did so.[36] How is it that the archetypical conservative Southern aristocrat became an abolitionist, while the egalitarian Jefferson never managed to do so? First, one must understand that Jefferson's concept of equality is not the commonly held view of that term as understood by this present generation. Also, the economic factors of each man played a role in his ability to emancipate his slaves. Nevertheless, it should be obvious that just because a man (like Randolph) has strong traditional and State's Rights views does not mean that he can not also be an advocate of the abolition of slavery. This is not the view currently held and enforced by the liberal establishment.

In 1814, much of Randolph's land was ravaged by floods. At that time, his paternalistic feelings toward his slaves were revealed in a letter to a friend:

> With a family of more than two hundred mouths looking up to me for food, I feel an awful charge on my hands. It is easy to rid myself of the burden if I could shut my heart to the cry of humanity and the voice of duty. But in these poor slaves I have found my best and most faithful friends; and I feel that it would be more difficult to abandon them to the cruel fate to which our laws would consign them, than to suffer with them.[37]

During his terms in Congress, Randolph, the stepson of St. George Tucker, one of Virginia's most distinguished jurists and abolitionists, worked to maintain the abolition of the African slave trade and to keep slavery out of those areas of the United States where it had been proscribed. Although an opponent of slavery and the slave trade, his voting record in Congress always followed the State's Rights view of the Constitution. Therefore, Randolph voted against any bill that came before Congress that tended to increase the Federal government's power (i.e., power not delegated to it by the Constitution) even if the bill tended to decrease slavery or the slave trade. Thus, some commentators have asserted that Randolph was voting to defend slavery. Nothing could be further from the truth. Randolph and other Southerners were voting in *defense of the Constitution.* As John Randolph, John C. Calhoun, Jefferson Davis, and a host of other Southerners would proclaim, there is no virtue in trampling upon the principles of the Constitution in the pursuit of a worthy cause. To do so is only to fall victim to the notion of letting the ends justify the means. Trampling upon the Constitution in order to emancipate slaves, and thus destroying the protection of freedom from Federal tyranny, would only promote the evil of bondage to *all* Americans. British politician, orator, and author Edmund Burke warned that in pursuing a worthy goal by unjust means one would "deprecate the value of freedom itself."[38] Preventing this deprecation of freedom was the major motivating factor for Randolph, Calhoun, Davis, and other Southerners.

Not only did Southern and English statesmen oppose the view that the ends justify the means, so did a noted Northern jurist. Chancellor James Kent, in *Commentaries on American Law,* noted that "[n]o nation had a right . . . to procure an eminent good by means that were unlawful; or *to press forward to a great principle, by breaking through other great principles that stood in the way*" [emphasis added].[39] It should be instructive to the skeptical that the above-mentioned statement by Kent was made because America would not allow its maritime vessels to be boarded by foreign navies in search of slave traders. Even in pursuit of the worthy goal of ending the slave trade, the sovereign rights of America upon the high seas could not be sacrificed. This view was upheld by the Congress and the president of the United States; therefore, one must ask, were they "defending slavery"? Even John Quincy Adams of Massachusetts got involved in the issue of protecting the maritime rights of America, and thus allowing the continuation of many slave-trading ventures.[40] Can it be maintained that John Q. Adams was a defender of the African slave trade? The clear answer to this questions is no. What was being defended was the principle that the ends do not justify the means. This is the lesson which Burke, Kent, Adams, and a host of other notable statesmen were endeavoring to teach the world. That which was true in the early history of America is true today: Often in the mad rush to "do good," the very foundation of American liberty is endangered.

It was against the incessant push for change by the radicals of the North that Southerners such as John Randolph took their stand. Randolph saw in the North's never-ending demand for change, the leading edge of the floodtide of revolution. This is the very revolution that the Radical Abolitionists set loose upon America, a revolution that bears bitter fruit to this day.

Yet, this man, John Randolph of Roanoke, who resisted the radical change in society and the trampling upon constitutional rights in the pursuit of a worthy objective, was an enemy of slavery. Not only an enemy of slavery, he was a friend to his slaves. Randolph was the archetypical paternalistic Southern slaveholder. Prior to his death and at great expense to himself, Randolph made preparations for his slaves' emancipation. Upon his death, his slaves were granted their freedom and given homes in Ohio, bought and paid for by John Randolph. Unfortunately for his former slaves, the good freedom-loving people of Ohio would not allow Randolph's former slaves to live there.[41] Yet, it is constantly proclaimed by the liberal establishment that Northerners, unlike their Southern neighbors, believe in equality and freedom for African-Americans.

Paternalism was a natural outgrowth of the institution of slavery as it existed in the South during the antebellum period. Unlike the slave/master relationship in the Caribbean, in the antebellum South the slave and master lived, worked, died, and were buried within sight of each other. This close working relationship in the South led to the slaveholder knowing more about the needs of his slaves than did the absentee masters of the Caribbean plantations. The care given to their slaves by Southern slaveholders is demonstrated by the phenomenal growth rate in the population of African-Americans during the antebellum period. From the introduction of slavery in the South until the advent of the War, around 400,000 Africans were imported into the South. From this modest number (remember that more than 20,000,000 Africans were taken from Africa to the New World), the African-American population in the United States grew to more than 4,000,000. The fact remains, that of all the slave cultures within the New World, it was only in the American South that African-Americans reproduced themselves at such a phenomenal rate.[42] In order to maintain a reliable labor force in South America and the Caribbean, it was necessary to maintain a continuous flow of new slaves from Africa. Although there was some demand for the renewal of the importation of slaves from Africa, the South never needed to resort to that necessity.

The closeness of the slave/master community on the plantations of the Old South was not solely the product of Southern altruism. After all, the one major problem in maintaining a slave society was keeping the slaves docile. How does one maintain an orderly life not only for the slaves but also for the master class if one is holding people in a work force against their will? The South, with its biblical world-view answered that question by creating a system of labor in which the slave would be well treated. This was not a one-sided effort. Both the slave and the master had much to gain by fostering a paternalistic system of forced labor. The master would gain not only the favor and loyalty of his slaves, but also a group of contented workers. The slaves would gain a lenient master who would be considerate of their lives and wellbeing, one to whom the slaves could appeal for assistance in times of trial. In essence, both master and slaves found a way to ameliorate the harsher elements of the institution of slavery.[43] Thus, each participant in the institution of slavery enlisted self-interest to make life within the slave/master relationship more tolerable. One thing is for sure, the paternalism of the Old South was a tacit recognition of the humanity of the slave. This tacit recognition of the slave's humanity, coupled with state laws that recognized the slave's dual identity as property and as a person, is proof positive of paternalism within the institution of Southern slavery.[44] Thus, as many Southern slaveholders would attest, slaves were more than just property. Each Southern state recognized the humanity of the slaves by passing and enforcing laws for the benefit of the life of those in bondage. The rediscovery of this more humane aspect in the slave/master relationship has led some historians to assert that the slave was more than just an object of white oppression. Rather than being an object of the white man, the slave, in many ways, can be described as a subject in his own right.[45] In other words, the slave played a more important role in antebellum society and had more input into the functioning of that society than either the liberals or the racists would have the nation believe.

Nothing is more revealing about the nature of the slave's life than the stories told by the former slaves themselves. During the Great Depression, the Federal government paid journalists to search out and record the accounts of the lives of America's last living slaves. Most of these folks were well into their seventh or eight decade when questioned about life during slavery. One of the most remarkable consequences of these accounts is the high number of former slaves who had positive recollections about their life as slaves and their relationship with their former master. These positive statements about slavery by former slaves have been criticized by many liberals. Allowing for some overstatement due to the passage of time, the words of these former slaves will be taken at face value. The following quotations from them will help to demonstrate how well the paternalistic attitude between slave and master worked.

> Ole Marster dead an'gone an Ole Mistis too, but I 'members 'em jus'lak dey was, when dey looked atter us whenst we

> belonged to 'em or dey belong to us, I dunno which it was. . . . De times was better fo'de war . . . I goes to church an' sings an' prays, an' when de good Lord teks me, I'se ready to go, en I specs to see Jesus an' Ole Mistis an' Ole Marster when I gits to de he'benly land'![46]

Even after the War, many slaves stayed on the plantations with their masters. Although not always the case, often a master who was on good terms with his slaves before freedom was the recipient of the good will and affection of his slaves after freedom. Former slave Ezra Adams noted:

> De slaves on our plantation didn't stop workin' for old marster, even when dey was told dat dey was free. Us didn't want no more freedom than us was gittin' on our plantation already. Us knowed too well dat us was well took care of, wid plenty of vittles to eat and tight log and board houses to live in. De slaves, where I lived, knowed after de war dat they had abundance of dat somethin' called freedom, what they could not eat, wear, and sleep in. Yes, sir, they soon found out dat freedom ain't nothin' 'less you is got somethin' to live on and a place to call home. Dis livin' on liberty is lak young folks livin' on love after they gits married. It just don't work.[47]

Former slave Simon Phillips of Alabama noted:

> People has the wrong idea of slave days. We was treated good. My Massa never laid a hand on me the whole time I was wid him. . . . Sometime we loaned the massa money when he was hard pushed.[48]

From Texas, former slave Felix Haywood offers an insight into why slaves did not rise up and kill their masters during the War:

> If every mother's son of a black had thrown 'way his hoe and took up a gun to fight for his own freedom along with the Yankees, the war'd be over before it began. But we didn't do it. We couldn't help stick to our masters. We couldn't no more shoot them than we could fly. My father and me used to talk 'bout it. We decided we was too soft and freedom wasn't goin' to be much to our good even if we had a education.[49]

The assertion by this former slave is substantiated by white Louisianian Kate Stone who wrote, "We would be practically helpless should the Negroes rise, since there are so few men left at home. It is only because the Negroes do not want to kill us that we are still alive."[50] The feelings of love and respect granted to the master's family by his bondsmen was the outgrowth of years of loving care extended by the master's family toward the slaves. On March 8, 1801, Oliver Hering wrote the following to Mary Helen Hering Middleton:

> The pleasure of pleasing those poor people who labour for our advantage is a great argument with me in favor of living among them and will I doubt not compensate you for the trouble & fatigue of a 60 miles journey over bad roads. . . . I used to fancy myself the Father of a large Family in whose affection & fidelity I lived with the most perfect confidence.[51]

In a letter dated May 16, 1824, Mary Helen Hering Middleton wrote to Oliver Hering expressing her belief that their slaves lived in better conditions than the poor workers of England. Mrs. Middleton wrote, "It has often struck me that the slaves there are much better off in many respects than the poor in England who are doomed to labour and to starve."[52]

While editing the South Carolina Slave Narratives, Belinda Hurmence noted that former slaves often reported life during slavery in a rather stereotypical pro-Southern manner. While questioning the validity of such an image of life under slavery, she nevertheless noted that the more she studied the narratives, the more this view was reinforced. She even noted that there was little if any indignation displayed by former slaves toward their former masters.[53] Again, this conclusion flies in the face of accepted knowledge about the institution of slavery "down South." Yet, the words of many historians and the very words of former slaves dispute the theories of modern liberal politically correct society. Indeed, life under slavery was trying and not one the author would wish to be visited upon any person or group of people. This is true not only because of the deprecation of the slave as an individual, but more important because of the deprecation of freedom itself. As Jefferson Davis noted, "The idea of freedom is captivating, that of slavery repellent to the moral sense of mankind in general."[54] As sad as the consequences would be if an individual were reduced to slavery, the consequences would be even sadder if freedom were cheapened within a society by the acceptance of the system of slavery.

Southern paternalism was a system that bound master to slave just as surely as it bound slave to master. The master was obligated to see to the needs of his "people" from cradle to grave. No doubt, one reason why so many slaves remained loyal to their "white folks" during and after the War was their desire for the security that their masters provided.

As McManus noted, the average slave who escaped from the South to the North was a young, aggressive male, under forty years of age.[55] There was a tacit agreement between the slave and master which stated that in exchange for the slave's service to his master during his productive years, the master would take care of the slave in his old age. This was a form of antebellum social security. A slave above the age of forty, having spent his life working for a good master, had much to lose by fleeing the plantation. As Phillips notes, "[T]o the slave himself, or to the community, the master was responsible for maintenance throughout life and for needful medical services. . . . The aged and infirm must be cared for along with the young and able-bodied, to maintain the good will of their kinsmen among the workers."[56] When told by his master that he was now a free man and no longer his slave, Toby, an old slave, remarked to his master, "You brought me here from Africa and North Carolina and I goiner' stay wid you as long as ever I get sompin to eat. You gotter look after me!"[57] Thus is seen at work within the system of Southern paternalism, the need of the master to maintain the good will of his work force, as well as the need of the slave to be able to exercise some form of control over his life. Obviously, it was the self-interest of both the master and the slave that drove this relationship. While acknowledging that this Southern system of paternalism had its faults and blatant failures, the author cannot allow the neo-Radical Abolitionist view to stand unchallenged.

While the Southern plantation is often viewed as the only home for slaves "down South," only 12 percent of all slaveholders in the South were members of the planter class. In other words, more slaveholders were small holders of slaves than were rich plantation owners. At the time of the War for Southern Independence, 75 percent of Southern families did not own a slave. Out of a total white population of 8 million people, only 385,000 were slaveholders. Of those who did own slaves, 50 percent owned only one to five slaves, 38 percent owned from five to twenty slaves, and 12 percent owned twenty or more slaves, which was the minimum for classification as a planter.[58]

Claiborne Parish, Louisiana, provides a small glimpse into the life of slaves on some of the smaller slaveholding estates in the South. The slaves of that area made up approximately 47 percent of the population. A record of slave accounts at Old Germantown store yields quite a bit of information about the lives of the slaves on these small farms. The fact that slaves often worked and earned money for their own use is often scoffed at by liberals. Liberals assert that slaves could not own property; yet from the records of Germantown, it is possible to determine just how much property these particular slaves actually owned and how much freedom they enjoyed.

From early 1850, local slaves bought and sold items at the Germantown store. They maintained their own accounts with the store and bought freely from the owners.[59] After working for their masters, the slaves were allowed free time to work and earn their own money. Many of the products of the slaves' own labor were used to purchase items at the Germantown store. Many slaves were hired by the store owners and paid the same wages that white laborers were being paid. Slaves sold many different items to the store such as eggs, vegetables, corn, charcoal, and handmade articles like horse collars; they even worked as shoe repairmen. No doubt there was an active trade going on between white people and slaves in the area. Many slaves went into partnership with other slaves to produce goods for sale. For example, one partnership yielded 527 bushels of corn grown and sold; another partnership yielded more than 1,107 pounds of cotton. Again, it must be pointed out that this produce was the property of the slaves who worked the fields that their masters had given to them. But there was more than just selling going on.

Records of the Germantown store provide enlightenment as to what items were being purchased by the slaves. Due to the fact that a master was obligated to maintain the basic necessities of life for his slaves, all the money the slaves made in their free time could be considered "discretionary" income. Therefore, few items such as work clothes or basic foodstuffs are recorded as being sold to the slaves. The food that was purchased could be listed as snack items such as gingerbread, candy, molasses, cheese, raisins, honey, and sugar. Although reading and writing was not routinely taught to the slaves, sales of slates, ink, pencils, and pens has also been noted.[60] Items listed as being bought by slaves fell into the following categories: food, sewing materials, clothing, household articles, and other miscellaneous articles. It should be noted that the clothing items consisted of luxury items such as a fine silk bonnet, white gloves, goatskin boots, a silk hat, and patent leather shoes.[61] These luxury items were purchased by the slaves with money they had earned and with the approval of their masters.

Even whisky and tobacco were bought by slaves at Germantown. But even more surprising, the slaves bought knives of all descriptions as well as gunpowder and percussion caps. This fact surely debunks the liberal concept of the downtrodden oppressed slaves of the Old South. In the nineteenth century, knives were equivalent to the modern-day Saturday night specials. Slaves making their own money and buying knives, gunpowder, percussion caps (needed for the firing of arms), and writing materials—this list does not fit the description of Southern slavery in *Roots* or *Uncle Tom's Cabin.*

While decrying the idea of human bondage, the author must insist upon reporting the *whole* truth about the life of slaves in the Old South. Even partisan defenders of Southern slavery such as U. B. Phillips admitted, "That cruelties occurred is never to be denied."[62] Cruel people, whether slaveholders from the South or slave traders from the North, committed hideous acts. According to the traditional Southern view of slavery as explained by Woodrow Wilson, for the most part, Southern slavery was a mild and paternalist system. As Wilson stated, "For public opinion in the South . . . was as intolerant of the graver forms of cruelty as was the opinion of the best people in the North."[63] Both Woodrow Wilson and U. B. Phillips agreed that depictions of Southern slavery as seen in *Uncle Tom's Cabin,* although stirring to the emotions of Northerners, were far removed from reality.[64] During a visit to Charleston, South Carolina, Bostonian Charles Eliot Norton wrote of his observations about slavery in the South:

> The slaves do not go about looking unhappy, and are with difficulty, I fancy, persuaded to feel so. Whips and chains, oaths and brutality, are as common, for all that one sees, in the free as the slave states. We have come thus far, and might have gone ten times as far, I dare say, without seeing the first sign of Negro misery or white tyranny.[65]

Even foreign observers of Southern slavery noted how well slaves were treated. Louis F. Tasistro of Great Britain had this to say about the ease of life for the slaves:

> To say that they are underworked and overfed, and far happier than the labourers of Great Britain would hardly convey a sufficiently clear notion of their actual condition. They put me much more in mind of a community of grown-up children, spoiled by too much kindness, than a body of dependants, much less a company of slaves.[66]

In life and in death, slaves became an integral part of their extended families, both black and white. The closeness that developed between these two divergent classes of people is displayed in many old cemeteries in the Old South. The epitaph on the tombstone of one old faithful slave reads:

John
A Faithful Servant
And True Friend;
Kindly, and Considerate:
Loyal, and Affectionate:
The Family He Served
Honours Him In Death:
But in Life, They Gave Him Love:
For He Was One of Them.

No better view of Southern paternalism could be given than the words of Solomon Northup. A free man of color, Northup was born in New York. After being kidnapped, he was sold into slavery in Louisiana by unscrupulous Northerners. For twelve years, Northup lived as the slave of several Louisiana masters, having the dubious distinction of serving both a good master and an evil master. The benefit of having a paternalistic master was not lost on Northup, who later stated:

> During my residence with Master Ford I had seen only the bright side of slavery. His was no heavy hand crushing us to the earth. *He* pointed upwards, and with benign and cheering words addressed us as his fellow-mortals, accountable, like himself, to the Maker of us all. I think of him with affection, and had my family been with me, could have borne his gentle servitude, without murmuring, all my days.[67]

It should be noted that "Master Ford" of whom Northup spoke so appreciatively was a Baptist preacher. According to Northup, "[T]here never was a more kind, noble, candid, Christian man than

William Ford."[68] This is the type of man the Radical Abolitionists and the modern liberals condemn as an evil racist slaveholder. Yet, Rev. Ford's slave could only bless his master's name.

The idea that a Southern family would consider a black man, slave or free, as "one of them," or that a slave would refer to the memory of his master with affection, is a difficult concept to grasp by modern Americans. The idea that such a relationship ever existed is scoffed at and ridiculed by the liberal establishment. White Southerners who maintain this idea are tarred as "moonlight and magnolia" racists, and black Southerners who accept this view are castigated as modern-day "Uncle Toms." Historian U. B. Phillips summed up the many-faceted nature of Southern slavery in these words, "The slave regime was a curious blend of force and concession, of arbitrary disposal by the master and self-direction by the slave, of tyranny and benevolence, of antipathy and affection."[69]

As demonstrated, there is much more to the story of slavery "down South" than the all too often reported accounts of chains and bullwhips. Unfortunately, the incessant efforts of the liberal establishment to publicize only the negative aspects of slavery is driving race relations in America toward animosity and violence. A little balance in reporting of historic fact could go a long way toward restoring respect between black people and white people in America.

By reporting the story of Southern paternalism as it deals with the issue of slavery, the author is not suggesting that slavery was an enviable status. No authority cited in this work ever suggested that Southern slavery was a noble institution. Most authorities cited herein went on record as opposing the institution of slavery; nevertheless, they also understood the complexity of freeing the slaves. Also, they recognized and applauded the sincere efforts of many slaveholders to improve the lot of their slaves. Sadly for race relations in modern America, only the Radical Abolitionists' views are allowed free access to the marketplace of ideas and the public mind.

BLACK SLAVEHOLDERS AND FREE PEOPLE OF COLOR IN THE SOUTH

As if the foregoing account of Southern paternalism and slavery was not shocking enough for those holding politically correct views of slavery, the author will now proceed with a short review of black slaveholders and free people of color in the Old South. The truth can be shocking, but that shock is not anything new in the history of the South. Union soldier John William Deforest of the Twelfth Connecticut informed his Yankee relatives of his amazement at seeing so many "colored" slaveholders in Louisiana. Deforest wrote:

> You would be amazed to see the swarming mulattos and quadroons and octoroons who possess this region and call themselves Americans. Some of the richest planters, men of really great wealth, are of mixed descent. When we march through a town the people who gather to stare at us remind me of the Negro quarters of Philadelphia and New York . . . *These are not former slaves, observe, but the former masters* [emphasis added].[70]

This was not the situation the Yankees expected to find "down South." Nor is this truth about African-Americans as slaveholders understood today. When confronted with the truth about African-Americans owning slaves in America, the sycophants of political correctness often will scoff as if to say, "Don't bother me with facts; my mind is made up."

When faced with mounting evidence to support the fact of African-American slaveholders, the politically correct crowd will assert that black slaveholding was done only to protect relatives who were slaves (i.e., slaveholding for benevolent reasons only). In his work on the subject of African-American slaveholders in South Carolina, Larry Koger demonstrates that the desire to save relatives from slavery was neither the sole nor the primary reason for African-Americans owing slaves. Koger points out that in urban areas more female slaves were owned by African-Americans than male slaves; whereas, in rural areas more male slaves were owned by African-Americans than in urban areas. In urban areas, domestic help, provided by females more than by males, was at a premium. In rural areas, where more "man" power was needed, male slaves were at a premium; demonstrating that the need of labor, not kinship, was driving African-American slave ownership.[71] Free people of color paid great deference to the fact that they were of a different color than their slaves.[72] The difference in skin tone and color between slaves and free people of color is an indicator that African-American slaveholders were not purchasing their close relatives. As the Union Army was approaching Charleston, South Carolina, African-American slaveholders still maintained control of their slaves. They did not relinquish this control until they were ordered to do so, freeing more than 240 slaves, *after* the war was over.[73] If African-Americans owned slaves only to save their brothers or sisters from evil white slaveholders, why did they have to be forced to free their slaves after the war had ended? Koger concludes that African-American slaveholders owned slaves for the same reason that white slaveholders did so—the desire for profits.[74]

According to the historical record, African-Americans owned fellow African-Americans throughout the United States. Of course, the largest segment of African-American slaveholders resided in the South. For example, according to the 1830 census, more that ten thousand slaves were owned by African-Americans in the states of South Carolina, Louisiana, Virginia, and Maryland. As if not to be left out, in the same year eight African-Americans in New York City owned seventeen slaves.[75]

The majority of African-American slaveholders owned only a small number of slaves and used them in their own business or hired them out for income. Nevertheless, there were some very prosperous African-Americans who owned enough slaves to be classified as "planters." One example is Auguste Donatto of St. Landry Parish in Louisiana, who owned a five-hundred-acre plantation and at least seventy slaves. In South Carolina, William Ellison also owned seventy slaves on his plantation.[76] As has been discussed, only 12 percent of Southern slaveholders owned twenty or more slaves, thus meeting the requirement of a planter. Donatto and Ellison were two among many African-Americans who met this requirement.

Hidden away in North Louisiana in a section of Natchitoches Parish was the home of the state's largest area of non-white slaveholders. The creoles of color in the Cane River area of the parish were well established and prosperous by the advent of the War for Southern Independence. These folks were not a ragtag band of vagabonds. They were the owners of fine homes; their children were tutored by well-established educators; their houses were graced with furnishings of taste and quality; and they owned slaves. The quality of the homes and plantations in the area was noted by a steamboat captain: "The plantations appeared no way different from the generality of those of white Creoles; and on some of them were large, handsome, and comfortable houses."[77] According to a study by Gary B. Mills, no less that seven plantation homes once existed within the 15,000 acres of the Cane River area, worked by more than 379 slaves, and valued at close to $1,000,000.[78] The census records of 1850 reveal that the average farm of the free people of color in this area was worked by nine slaves—the same number as in the rest of the parish.[79] Thus it would appear that the slave-holding free people of color were just as prosperous as their white neighbors. The work of Mills parallels the work of Koger, who reported that the benefits of American slavery extended to free people of color in South Carolina. These African-Americans would, on rare occasions, advance into the slaveholding plantation class.[80] Whether in Natchitoches Parish, Louisiana, Charleston, South Carolina, or New York City, African-Americans owned slaves for the same reasons their white counterparts owned slaves—profits.

Nowhere in the Old South did free people of color compose as large a part of society or have as much influence within that society as in New Orleans, Louisiana. Free people of color in Orleans Parish comprised 23 percent of the population in 1810, 17 percent in 1817, and 24 percent in 1830. Although society was divided along color and racial lines, a warm relationship was maintained by many people across that line. A good example is the life of free man of color, Andrew Durnford of Louisiana. During his life he and John McDonogh, a white man, were very close. McDonogh even kept a special room in his home for his colored friend. In business and pleasure they were strong allies.[81] As shocking as this relationship may be to those raised on the theory of Southern white animosity toward African-Americans, the fact that this free man of color owned slaves and maintained a close relationship with many of them is also perplexing. An exceptionally close relationship existed between Durnford and his slave Noel. David O. Whitten, Durnford's biographer, noted that this close relationship was based on friendship and trust between the master and the slave.[82] Indeed, the whole truth about slavery in the Old South can be most discomforting to liberals and their sycophants.

With the assistance of his white friend, in 1828 Durnford established himself as proprietor of St. Rosalie Plantation. St. Rosalie was located on the Mississippi River approximately thirty-three miles South of New Orleans. Within three years, Durnford had increased his holdings in both land and slaves. In 1831 his holdings had increased to twenty-one slaves. With hopes of increasing his sugar production, he wrote to McDonogh in New Orleans inquiring about the purchase of more slaves: "Be so good my dear sir to say if there is plenty of Negroes in town and horses. I fear that Negroes will sell high in six months or a year, therefore I hope ere this you have met with a bargain for me."[83] The necessity of providing labor for his plantation was so acute that Durnford bought more slaves, hired slaves from other planters, and employed Irish laborers.[84] The idea of a "colored" person hiring a white laborer in the antebellum South does not fit into the politically correct concept of that age. Nevertheless, as so often done in this study of slavery, it must be pointed out that what passes for fact and the actual truth about American slavery are often at odds.

Not only did Durnford seek the assistance of his white friend in the purchase of slaves but also, in 1834, he undertook a trip east for the purpose of buying additional slaves. This trip would take an African-American slaveholder from Louisiana, along with a portion of his sugar crop, and a faithful slave, to Philadelphia, Pennsylvania, and then to Virginia. For those who maintain that African-Americans only bought slaves to rescue relatives from bondage to white slaveholders, this trip by Durnford must be a disappointment. No one can maintain, nor do his records support, the idea that Durnford, of French and African decent, went to Virginia to purchase his brothers, sisters, or even cousins. He went east to buy slaves: a clear and simple fact. Even though the prices were not the bargain he had hoped for, Durnford did buy several slaves: "I have bought a woman with two children for the sum of 625$ one of about 4 years old the other a couple of months's both boys." While reading Durnford's report about his slave-buying trip to Virginia, one does not note a sense of regret about buying women and children. The one regret that this African-American slaveholder did express was his shock at the high prices he had to pay for slaves: "People is higher than ever. . . . Blacks are getting higher every day, even the Negro traders are surprised at the prices demanded."[85] In his letters home, Durnford expressed much anxiety about the prices for slaves and the problems of transporting them from Virginia to New Orleans. Also, he made note of the physical exhaustion he was suffering as a result of his slave-buying activities: "My thighs is all blistered riding round or within twenty miles of Richmond."[86] Durnford's efforts at securing a sufficient labor supply for his plantation were well rewarded. By the time of his death, this African-American plantation owner had accumulated large land holdings, worked by more than seventy-seven slaves.[87]

As many historians will point out, Louisiana and South Carolina were the states with the largest numbers of free people of color who were slaveholders. Yet, they were not the only Southern states with African-American slaveholders. In Natchez, Mississippi, we find the example of another African-American slaveholder, William Johnson. It is believed that Johnson was the son of Amy Johnson and her master William Johnson, for whom the younger William was named. In 1814, William Johnson, Sr., manumitted Amy according to the laws of the state of Louisiana. As was true in most slaveholding states, even Massachusetts, a master could not free a slave unless he could assure the general public that the freed person would not become a burden upon society. This law served to protect not only society at large but also the slave. Once a man bought a slave, he was obligated to maintain that slave in sickness and health, as well as in youth and old age. A master was not allowed to free himself of his responsibility of caring for his slave just because of old age or sickness. Many Northerners noted this major difference between the labor systems in the South and in the North:

> As slavery pays in a pecuniary sense, it is easy for the Southron to believe it is justified by Divine authority. On the other hand, we of the North *couldn't* make it pay, so we are convinced that it is "the sum of all villainy." Our plan is more profitable; we take care of no children or sick people, except as paupers, *while the owners of slaves have to provide for them from birth till death* [emphasis added].[88]

At the time that William Johnson, Sr., manumitted his slave Amy, he posted a legal notice of intent in which he stated that, "for divers good causes and considerations me thereunto moving . . . [I therefore] released from slavery, liberated, manumitted, and set free my Negro woman Amy."[89] Johnson was also obligated to make a statement that the said Negro woman Amy would be capable of providing for herself and that he would be responsible for her care if she should ever "be in want owing to sickness, old age, insanity, or any other proven infirmity."[90] Being denied the right to free a slave child by Louisiana law, William Johnson, Sr., applied for the right to manumit Amy's son William from the Mississippi legislature. In order to manumit the slave child in Mississippi, William Johnson, Sr., had to prove that he resided in Mississippi and that he was debt free. This being the case, in 1820 he petitioned the state legislature in the following manner:

> Your Petitioner humbly prays your Honorable Body to permit him to make that disposition of his property most agreeable to his feelings & consonant to humanity . . . that Liberty to a human being which all are entitled to as a Birthright, & extend the hand of humanity to a rational Creature, on whom unfortunately Complexion Custom & even Law in This Land of freedom, has conspired to rivet the fetters of Slavery.[91]

Both houses of the Mississippi legislature, after some minor amendments, passed a bill allowing for the manumission of the minor William Johnson. On February 10, 1820, the following bill was signed into law by Mississippi governor George Poindexter:

> An Act To Emancipate William, A Person of Color
>
> Sec. I. *Be it enacted by the Senate and House of Representatives of the state of Mississippi, in general assembly convened,* That the mulatto boy named William, son of Amy, a free woman of color, and the slave of William Johnson of Adams County, be, and he is hereby emancipated and set free from slavery, saving however the rights of creditors, and on the express condition that the said William Johnson, enter into and security in the sum of one thousand dollars, to be filed in the office of secretary of state, and made payable to the governor for the time being, and his successors in office, conditioned that the said boy William, shall never become a public charge, and that the said William Johnson shall educate and maintain said child, according to the provisions of the second section of this act.
>
> Sec. 2. *And be it further enacted,* That the said William Johnson shall educate, or cause to be educated, and maintain or caused to be maintained, said child until he arrive at the age of twenty-one years.
>
> E. Turner,
> *Speaker of the House of Representatives,*
> James Patton,
> *Lieutenant-Governor and President of the Senate.*
> Approved, February 10, 1820
> George Poindexter, Gov.[92]

At the tender age of eleven, William became a free person of color and took the name of the man who had freed him, William Johnson. Obviously, young William took advantage of the education offered him in his manumission act. By the time he was twenty-one years old, he already was a small business owner in Port Gibson, Mississippi, and in Natchez, Mississippi. Very few accounts of the life of a free man of color are as complete as the account left by William Johnson. Johnson made a habit of keeping a daily record of both his business and social life from 1835 until his death in 1851. This record is a gold mine for those who are seeking an understanding of life in the Old South for a free man of color.[93] During his life Johnson became a well-known and respected businessman and slaveholder. Johnson's views on subjects such as buying and selling slaves, slave punishment, and runaway slaves are all freely written down.

As an African-American, Johnson never appeared to regret living and profiting from the system of chattel slavery. Over his lifetime, Johnson owned no less than thirty-one slaves. At his death he owned fifteen slaves, whose value varied from $25 (Old Rose), to $1000 (Jim), for a total valuation of $6,075. Johnson bought his first slave in 1832, and for the next twenty years was the master of numerous slaves. During his life as a slaveholder, it can be determined that he sold three slaves for a profit, six died as his slaves, one ran away, and at least fifteen were living at his death.[94] Many a bitter tear has been shed by liberals for slaves who are flogged by a white overseer. Yet, as will be shown, even an African-American slaveholder was not beyond using the whip on his wayward slave. Johnson gives the following account of his discovering his slave, Steven, whom he had hired out, in Natchez and not at work:

> Steven was in town and I Knew if he was in town that Early that he must have runaway from Mr. Gregory where I had hired to haul wood in the swamp. It was after Breakfast and I got on my Horse and wrode up the street and I found him in the Back St. near P. Bakers—Gave him a tap or two with my riding whip and then Brot him to my shop and in a few minutes after I got to the shop Mr. Vernon Came to inform me that Steven had took a watch from one of his men and that he had been seen to have it and that he had taken it yesterday as he passed there. I Commenced a Search on his person and I

> found it in his Coat Pocket. I gave it to Mr. Vernon and was Glad that he Came So Soon for it. I then made him get on a horse and go on down to Mr. Vernons place and there I made his Driver Give him a good Flogging with his Big whip.[95]

Johnson was so matter of fact about the two floggings given his wayward slave that in the very next sentence he proceeds to describes a hunting trip he took that very same day. Of course, hunting requires firearms. Another myth is hereby exposed. The fact that an African-American could and did own any form of weapon runs counter to the accepted view of life in the Old South. Yet, Johnson, at numerous times, recounts his adventures and prowess as a sportsman in Mississippi.

Of the many stories related by Johnson in his diary is the story of how a slave saved the life of his mistress. Johnson informs us that when Mr. J. Ross Wade's residence burned, one child was killed in the fire and the mistress of the house was burned, but her life was saved by her faithful slave.[96] Thus is shown that the facts of history contradict the accepted myth about Southern slavery as enforced by the victor of the War for Southern Independence.

Just as Andrew Durnford, a fellow free man of color in Louisiana had done, Johnson, an African-American in Mississippi, hired a white man to oversee his rural holdings.[97] Here again we see a non-traditional view of antebellum society. According to liberal historians, white people were loathe to work under the direction of an African-American; yet, we see in these two cases African-American slaveholders hiring white people to work for them. Regardless of whether it was buying slaves, punishing slaves, seeking runaway slaves, or profiting from slave labor, the African-American slaveholder had views very similar to those of white slaveholders in both the North and the South.

SUMMARY

"Evidence can be presented to support almost any generalization—favorable or unfavorable—concerning the treatment of slaves."[98] That which historian Francis B. Simkins noted to be true in 1959 is just as true today. The one major difference between the present age and 1959 is that the generalization favorable to the South is seldom if ever acknowledged. When discussing the nature of Southern slavery in today's politically correct society, the only view that is accepted is that of mistreatment of slaves in its most vile form and racially based oppression. Anytime researchers or historians attempt to show that in many (if not most) cases slaves were treated more like family members than objects for mistreatment, they are immediately slandered as "defenders of slavery." This cultural bias of the politically correct society is in sharp contrast to the opinion of a noted Southern historian who stated, "Kindliness and patience, frequently extended even to a tolerance of slackness in every concern not vital to routine."[99] Most slaveholders' desire for the good treatment and management of their slave holdings had little to do with a sense of altruism. Rather, they understood that a healthy and happy slave population would translate into more profits. "Masters wished to preserve the health and life of their slaves because a sick Negro was a liability and a dead Negro was worth nothing."[100]

Many Northerners reported on what they considered to be a scandalous situation in which black and white children and adults were in too close proximity. One such observer, Frederick L. Olmsted, noted this close relationship: "Negro women are carrying black and white babies together in their arms; black and white children are playing together; black and white faces are constantly thrust together out of doors, to see the train go by."[101] As has been pointed out throughout this work, nineteenth-century Americans firmly believed in the principle of Negro inferiority. Nowhere was this view more strongly held than in the North. Up until the second decade of the nineteenth century, this view supported the system of slavery in the North. After the elimination of Northern slavery, the view of Negro inferiority became the foundation for the numerous laws which denied Northern black citizens equality before the law. Just as true, in the South this view was used to rationalize the institution of slavery and then discriminatory law thereafter. There seems to be two major differences between how the North and the South dealt with the race issue during the nineteenth century. By and large, the North was a white society with only a few black citizens; whereas, in the South, blacks were, in some places, almost one-half of the population. Moreover, in the North very few white people associated with black people. In the South, as Olmsted and others have noted, the relations between black and white citizens were too close to suit the prejudices of Northerners.

In this chapter the author has demonstrated that slavery was not just a white Southern institution. Indeed, Northerners owned slaves and participated in the African slave trade. He also pointed out that the institution of slavery was not solely a white-versus-black institution. African-Americans also owned black slaves, both in the North and in the South. One final point must be restated, only a small number of Southerners owned slaves.

When faced with the reality of Northerners owning slaves and Northern participation in the African slave trade, the country is often assured that no *general* blame should fall upon all Northerners because so few Northerners were involved. When faced with the reality of African-Americans owning slaves, the country is likewise assured that no *general* blame should fall upon all African-Americans because so few African-Americans owned slaves. But when Southerners proclaim that only a few Southerners owned slaves, they are told that the blame for slavery in America rests upon all Southerners, and the Confederate flag should be purged from society to boot. Is this not a prime example of cultural bias? Why are Northern heroes and Northern culture spared condemnation for their association with slavery and the slave trade, while Southern heroes and culture are condemned? Why are African-American slaveholders given a "pass" for their association with the institution of slavery, while Southern slaveholders and non-slaveholders alike are condemned? Is this not an example of cultural bigotry? Why is it that in America, African-American slavery and Northern slavery can be overlooked, but not Southern slavery? Why is it that some in America can praise the movement to end slavery in the North, but condemn that very same movement in the South as "defending slavery?" The point should be clear: In today's politically correct society, the only prejudice that is sanctioned is anti-South prejudice. Liberals love to hate the South, and they will not let a few historical facts get in the way of their preconceived notions.

MYTH: Southerners who support the notion of a benevolent slaveholding society are merely defending slavery.

REALITY: There is more to the idea of a benevolent slaveholding society in the Old South than the so-called moonlight and magnolias notion of slavery "down South." The retort that by defending the *truth* about the institution of slavery, one is not defending the institution of slavery is not a twenty-first-century sentiment. As pointed out in Chapter 3, in 1845 Dr. N. L. Rice made the same plea to the people of Ohio when he was defending the view that slavery in itself was not a sin. Dr. Rice was a vocal opponent of slavery, yet, he defended the truth about the institution of slavery while working for its elimination. General Robert E. Lee was so much opposed to slavery that he freed his slaves long before the War for Southern Independence, yet, he fought for his state and the South during the War. President Jefferson Davis believed that slavery would have a natural end and that the slaves had to be educated to make them "fit for freedom and unfit for slavery." Southern historian Francis B. Simkins noted that both good and bad relations existed between slaves and masters in the Old South. If a person is seeking the truth about the institution of slavery in America, why should he ignore the good and only report the negative? Defending the truth about the institution of slavery is not tantamount to defending slavery itself. Unfortunately, with the adoption of the politically correct view about slavery (i.e., the Radical Abolitionists' view), only the negative view is reported, and anyone who strays from the "party" line about slavery is viewed as a "defender of slavery."

MYTH: The North provided a haven of freedom and of opportunity for African-Americans.

REALITY: The myth of the North as a land of freedom and opportunity for African-Americans runs opposed to every known fact about race relations in the North at that time. This myth is based upon the modern assumption that slavery was abandoned in the North because it offended Northerners' humanitarian views. Yet, as John Adams pointed out, slavery was eliminated because Northern white workers did not wish to compete with slave labor. It was for the benefit of white workers and not African-Americans that slavery was eliminated in the North. Also, as proven, Northern states spared no effort in preventing an increase in the numbers of free African-American citizens in the North. This fear of increasing numbers of African-Americans in their states became even greater after Abraham Lincoln's Emancipation Proclamation. In a message to Congress in 1862 Lincoln took note of this fear: "But why should emancipation South send free people North? And in any event cannot the North decide for itself whether to receive them?"[102] These are just a few examples which prove how inhospitable the people of the North were to their fellow African-Americans.[103] Northerners, Southerners, and even Europeans all noted that even though the North had abandoned slavery, it still clung to the notion of Negro inferiority. With the notion of Negro inferiority firmly ensconced in the psyche of the North, how could one expect African-Americans to be treated other than as second-class citizens?

While some African-Americans did leave the South for the North, many other free people of color, even some who had the means to leave, stayed in the South. If the North was such a wonderful land of opportunity, and the South was such a land of racist white people, why did the vast majority of free people of color choose to stay in the South? The truth is plain and simple. While both sections of the United States, North and South, had embraced the dogma of Negro inferiority, the South, even with its institution of slavery, was just as appealing and in some cases more appealing as a home for many free people of color. As has been noted, the laws of many Northern states did not allow Negro immigration. No, the North was not a haven for African-Americans, and neither was the South the scourge to the African-American that it has been portrayed.

MYTH: The existence of the Underground Railroad proves that the people of the North had a strong desire to assist the African-American slaves in the South.

REALITY: While the existence of the Underground Railroad cannot be denied, one must put its effect on African-Americans into perspective. During the life of the Underground Railroad (approximately forty years), it is estimated that about 75,000 slaves escaped slavery via the Underground Railroad. In just *one year* alone, the Yankee slave traders brought about 74,000 slaves from Africa to the Americas. If some are going to offer up unlimited praise for Northerners stealing slave property from the South at a rate of 75,000 in forty years, how much more should they condemn Northerners for stealing Africans from Africa at a rate of 74,000 a *year?* Granted, while this rate of 74,000 Africans was a peak year for the ever-aggressive Yankee, his trade in Africans existed from 1640 until 1860 or 220 years. Very seldom does one hear about the numbers of Northern African-Americans who were kidnapped by Northerners and sold into slavery "down South" or in South

American countries. If the number of free Northern African-Americans who were sold *into slavery* were deducted from the number of African-Americans freed as a result of the activity of the Underground Railroad, the number of freed African-Americans would be even less than 75,000 in forty years.[104] The Underground Railroad stands as a monument to Yankee hypocrisy. While enriching themselves by engaging in the infamous African slave trade for more than two hundred years; while abolishing slavery in a manner which caused slavery and the African-American to disappear in their states; while making their society as inhospitable to free people of color as possible, while making money on slave-grown produce from the South, the same slave-grown produce that they were condemning Southerners for producing with slave labor; Northerners enticed slaves from their Southern masters, the same Southern masters to whom they had sold these slaves, and placed the newly freed slaves into a society which treated them as pariahs.

MYTH: African-American slaveholders only owned slaves who were related to them in order to free them from slavery to white men.

REALITY: As shown in this chapter, in most cases, African-Americans owned slaves for the same reason white Americans owned slaves; both in the North and in the South, slaves were owned for the financial benefit of their masters. While there is little doubt that there are some cases in which relatives were bought in order to free family members from slavery, the historical record does not support this theory in a majority of cases. The written records of many free people of color demonstrate the desire for social advancement as the main reason for acquiring slaves. The two Southern states where the largest numbers of free people of color owned slaves were South Carolina and Louisiana. In both cases, we have looked at the record of African-American slave ownership and noted that the need to provide labor was the main objective of slave ownership by African-Americans. Not only have the reasons for slave ownership by African-Americans been demonstrated, it has been demonstrated that African-American slaveholders dealt with their slaves just as their white counterparts had done. Slave punishment, hunting down runaway slaves, and dealing with the long-term care of slaves were just as time-consuming and demanding for the African-American slaveholder as any other slaveholder. In the purchase of slaves and the management of slaves, little difference can be seen in the relationship between master and slave regardless of the color of the master. Despite what the politically correct comrades maintain, slavery was not solely a white-versus-black institution in the Old South.

CHAPTER 5

Slavery Versus Secession

Secession was no new thing to Mississippians. New Englanders had even talked of it back in the War of 1812. Then came the tariff and the Abolitionists; and embattled Mississippians joined others of the South against the measures and men that threatened the Southland.[1]

John K. Bettersworth
MISSISSIPPI: A History

As late as 1959, Southern historians such as John K. Bettersworth were insisting that the War for Southern Independence was more than just a war to defend slavery. Nevertheless, with an ever-increasing chorus from the end of that war until the present, the South has been denigrated as the defender of slavery. In 1866, George H. Moore, while discussing the history of slavery in Massachusetts, described the Confederate States of America as the "Slaveholders Confederacy."[2] Having been thoroughly indoctrinated in the victors' view of the South and of the War, most Americans view slavery as the paramount issue of the War for Southern Independence; therefore, every other issue which may have been a factor in the causation of that war is viewed as underpinning the main focus of the War. The victor and his sycophants have established, in the minds of many people, the idea that any issue that is brought forth by Southerners in defense of Southern Independence is done so, ultimately, in an effort to defend slavery. According to America's liberal establishment, State's Rights, strict construction of the Constitution, and secession are issues that have an irretrievable connection with the defense of slavery. This theoretical connection therefore makes secession, *ipso facto,* an evil political theory.

Is there a connection so deep and so interrelated between secession and the defense of slavery as to make the idea of secession totally repulsive to freedom- loving Americans? Was secession nothing more than a mad scheme concocted by wicked Southern slaveholders to protect their slave property? Is secession a philosophy that stands in opposition to the idea of American civil liberty and civil rights? Those who have never been exposed to the *complete* truth about American political philosophy believe the answer to these questions is yes. Yet, as has been demonstrated throughout this work, what is advanced by the victors of the War for Southern Independence and the *actual* truth about those questions are at odds with each other. Therefore, let us proceed in the examination of the issue of slavery by looking at the one political issue that has come to be connected with the defense of slavery more than any other issue—secession.

"When in the Course of human events, it becomes necessary for one people to dissolve the political bands which have connected them with another, and to assume among the powers of the earth, the separate and equal station to which the Laws of Nature and of Nature's God entitle them. . . ." Most Americans will recognize the preceding words as the first sentence of the Declaration of Independence. What most Americans will not understand is that they are reading one of the grandest *secession* documents ever written. The famous Fourth of July declaration was a joint resolution by the several states proclaiming their separate status as independent states.[3] Note that a dissolution of the "political bands" between the people of the colonies and the central government in London is announced. The words "dissolve the political bands" are nothing less than the announcement of the secession of the colonies from the central government of Great Britain. This right is not something granted or allowed by any government. It is, as the declaration asserts, a God-given right; a right granted by the "Laws of Nature and of Nature's God." Probably the most revolutionary phrase in the entire document states *"that to secure these rights, Governments are instituted among Men, deriving their just powers from the consent of the governed, That whenever any Form of Government becomes destructive of these ends, it is the Right of the People to alter or to abolish it, and to institute new Government. . . ."* Two important points are asserted here by the Founding Fathers in this phrase: (1) The institution of government does not originate from the divine right of kings; that is, kings are not granted the right to rule their subjects by some supernatural decree but rather by the express consent of the governed. (2) The right of the people to

alter or *abolish* the government they live under *is* granted them by divine decree. Therefore, the act of altering or abolishing government, being a God-given right, is not an act of sedition or treason. Nor can it be bartered away by the owner, nor taken away by another party.

The idea that the people at the local level (i.e., the state) have the right to form and/or reform the type of government they live under is well established in early American history. For example, the forming or reforming of government (secession) took place at least three times between 1775 and 1795. The first such secession movement took place when the various colonies directed their representatives to vote for a unanimous Declaration of Independence. Here we see the people of the several states, acting on their own authority, withdrawing their consent to be governed by the central government in London. The second instance occurred with the adoption of the Articles of Confederation. Under the terms of this article, the states, while maintaining their independence and sovereignty,[4] removed themselves from the society of nations and confederated with other American states for their mutual benefit. The third instance of a secession movement occurred with the adoption of the Federal Constitution. In order to accede to the new form of government under the Constitution, the several states had to first adopt a new form of government, thereby seceding from the government that had been established under the Articles of Confederation. From what has just been discussed, it should be obvious that secession is neither "un-American" nor a system designed solely for the defense of slavery; rather, it is a uniquely *American* political philosophy. Remember that at the time of each of the aforementioned "secession" movements, slavery and/or the African slave trade existed in each state, just as slavery, but *not* the African slave trade, existed in the Confederate States of America in 1861.

While agreeing with the concept of early American secession movements, some political commentators will maintain that the idea of secession from the Union by an American state was abandoned after the adoption of the United States Constitution. These same commentators maintain that the principle of secession was revived by evil slaveholders as a means of defending the institution of slavery in the South. To test the preceding theory, let us look at the life and writings of several constitutional scholars from both the North and the South. From the South let us look to the writings of St. George Tucker of Virginia. St. George Tucker, one of America's Founding Fathers, attended the Annapolis Convention which was responsible for calling the Philadelphia Constitutional Convention. He is noted as editor of America's first edition of Blackstone's *Commentaries on the Laws of England.* During the American War for Independence, Tucker served as the colonel of a company of Virginia militia at the battle of Guilford Courthouse in North Carolina and was wounded at the battle of Yorktown. After the war he served as Professor of Law at William and Mary College at which time he wrote commentaries on both the Constitution of Virginia and the Federal Constitution. In 1803, Tucker was appointed judge of the Virginia Supreme Court, and subsequently was appointed as a district Federal judge for Virginia. From the North, let us look at the work of William Rawle of Pennsylvania.

Rawle, although not a member of that august body of men known as the "Founding Fathers," was a friend of both Benjamin Franklin and George Washington. When Benjamin Franklin organized the Society for Political Inquiries, Rawle was invited to join. It was at this time that Rawle became friends with the newly elected president, George Washington. President Washington appointed Rawle as district Federal judge for Pennsylvania in 1791, a position he held for eight years. During that time it became his duty to prosecute those individuals responsible for the Whiskey Rebellion in Western Pennsylvania. In 1792 Rawle became an honorary member of the Maryland Society for Promoting the Abolition of Slavery. In 1818, he was elected president of that society and remained its president until his death in 1836. In 1825 Rawle wrote *A View of the Constitution of the United States of America,* one of the first textbooks on the United States Constitution.

In studying the works of Tucker and Rawle, we will endeavor to determine if indeed they advanced the theory that secession ended after the adoption of the Federal Constitution. We will also investigate the charge that secession was a pro-slavery scheme. As will be demonstrated, these men were both opposed to slavery and in favor of the right of secession.

A noted scholar on the life of Tucker and Calhoun, Dr. Clyde N. Wilson gives the following account of Tucker's views of the right of secession:

THE CONFEDERATE FLAG

The First National Flag

The Second National Flag

The Third National Flag

The Confederate Flag: During the life of the Confederate States of America, three national flags were adopted. The First National Flag was known as the "Stars and Bars"; the Second National Flag was known as the "Stainless Banner" or the "Jackson" flag; the Third National Flag was adopted a few weeks before the surrender of the Confederate military forces.

Battle flag more often associated with the Army of Northern Virginia

Battle flag more often associated with the Army of Tennessee and the Confederate Navy

The Battle Flag of the Confederacy: Commonly known as the "Rebel flag" or the "Confederate flag," this flag was adopted by various units of the Confederate military. As is noted, many different styles of Confederate flags were used during the war, but, today, the rectangular Saint Andrews cross is more commonly identified with the Southern cause than any other emblem.

UNUSUAL CONFEDERATE FLAGS

General Leonidas Polk's Corps flag, Army of Tennessee

Flag of the Choctaw Brigade

Missouri battle flag, Army of the Trans-Mississippi

General William D. Hardee's battle flag, Army of Tennessee

Unusual Confederate Flags: These flags are typical of the many different styles of Confederate battle flags carried by the men of the South during the War for Southern Independence.

Battle flag of Co. F, 5th South Carolina Volunteer Infantry, King's Mountain, South Carolina

"Like Our Ancestors—We Will Be Free." The motto on this Confederate battle flag points to the real issue between the Federal government and the Southern states. This flag was carried by the men from King's Mountain, South Carolina. Their ancestors defeated the British invaders at the Battle of King's Mountain during the American War for Independence.

Ku Klux Klan protesting,
Ruston, Louisiana, 1995
Photograph courtesy of the *Ruston Daily Leader,* Ruston, Louisiana

Logo, Citizens Councils
Collections of Old Capitol Museum, Mississippi Department of Archives and History, Civil Rights Exhibit

Photograph courtesy of the Library of Congress, Washington, D.C.

These photographs demonstrate that the United States flag has been and still is being used by various hate groups in America. Is this reason for banning it? The misuse of symbols should be condemned, not the flag—whether United States or Confederate States.

Photograph in author's collections, Jim Whittington, artist

William Rawle: An example of a Northern abolitionist who, uniting with his Southern counterparts, worked for the abolition of slavery. His textbook on the United States Constitution was highly acclaimed by Northerners. It stated the case for the right of secession of a state from the Union.

Photograph courtesy of the Earl Gregg Swem Library, The College of William and Mary

St. George Tucker: A veteran of the War for Independence, a noted jurist, and an individual instrumental in the adoption of the Constitution, Tucker was an early proponent of the abolition of slavery. Tucker was also critical of laws that discriminated against free people of color. A Virginian, Tucker was a firm advocate of the right of the people of the sovereign states to withdraw from the Union at their volition.

Photograph courtesy of the Mississippi Department of Archives and History

Malmaison: The plantation home of Chief Greenwood Leflore. From the cupola of his mansion LeFlore, a slaveholder and an opponent of secession, flew the United States flag during the War for Southern Independence.

Photograph courtesy of the Mississippi Department of Archives and History

Chief Greenwood Leflore: Of French and Choctaw decent, Leflore was a prominent member of the Choctaw tribe, member of the Mississippi legislature, planter, and slaveholder. Leflore is another example of a pro-Union, non-white slaveholder.

Photograph courtesy of The Library of Congress, Washington, D.C.

The Prince of Slaves: Abd Rahman Ibrahima, while in the process of capturing fellow Africans to sell as slaves, was captured by an enemy tribe and sold into slavery. His life as a prince, a prisoner of war, and a slave, and his return to freedom, is an excellent rebuff to those who maintain that Africans never participated in the enslavement of fellow Africans.

Photograph courtesy of The Peabody Essex Museum, Salem, Massachusetts

The Prince of Slavers: The Nightingale, *built in Maine and sailing from Salem, Massachusetts, with a New York captain, was captured off the coast of Africa in 1861. It had more than nine hundred slaves on board with a death rate of eight slaves per day. The* Nightingale *is an example of New England's continued involvement with the slave trade. Also note the American flag flying from the* Nightingale. *The United States flag was often used by slave traders to protect their ships from being inspected by French and English warships.*

> Tucker takes for granted the option of secession. If the Constitution draws its authority from the consent of the sovereign—which is the people of the several states—then the sovereign may withdraw that consent (not, of course, something to be done lightly). The people's consent to the Constitution is not a one-time event that forever after binds them to be obedient to the federal government. A state's right of withdrawal remains always an open option against a government overstepping its bounds, and is affirmed in the nature of the Constitution itself and in the right of revolution propounded by the Declaration of Independence.[5]

Tucker, pursuing the philosophy of 1776, notes that the ultimate power of government resides with the people and not with a king or with government itself. This power, often referred to as "sovereignty" in Tucker's words, "resides only in the people; is inherent in them; and unalienable from them. . . . Legitimate government can therefore be derived only from the voluntary grant of the people, and exercised for their benefit."[6] For Tucker, the very foundation of American civil liberty rests upon having a government that exists by the consent of the governed. Eliminate the right of the people to consent to the form of government they live under, and all civil liberties (civil rights) are subject to governmental abuse.[7] If people at the local level have no way to negate the abuse of the central government, then abuse is almost guaranteed. Tucker explains why he is an advocate of the principle of voluntary consent:

> When a government is founded upon the voluntary consent, and agreement of a people uniting themselves together for their common benefit, the people, or nation, collectively taken, is free, although the administration of the government should happen to be oppressive, and to a certain degree, even tyrannical; since it is in the power of the people to alter, *or abolish it* [emphasis added], whenever they shall think proper; and to institute such new government as may seem most likely to effect their safety and happiness. But if the government be founded in fear, constraint, or force although the administration should happen to be mild, the people, being deprived of the sovereignty, are reduced to a state of civil slavery. Should the administration, in this case, become tyrannical, they are without redress. Submission, punishment, or a successful revolt, are the only alternatives.[8]

Here Tucker points out something most modern Americans no longer understand. As long as the people retain the right to alter or abolish their government, they remain free. Even if the government is in some ways tyrannical, they, the people, hold the ultimate check on governmental abuse; therefore, the people remain free. Even if a government is installed that is only mildly abusive of the people's liberties, if the people do not have the privilege of an ultimate check on that government, they are, according to Tucker, in a state of civil slavery. Tucker points out that "if government be founded in fear, constraint, or force . . . the people . . . are reduced to a state of civil slavery." This is the very point that defenders of State's Rights have warned their fellow Americans. When Abraham Lincoln demanded the use of troops to enforce the "rights" of the Federal government, he in effect destroyed the very foundation of American civil liberties (i.e., government by the consent of the governed). *Conquest* has replaced *consent* as the foundation of American government. If this is the case, what are the implications for the people of America, both North and South?

> [T]he nature of a government, so far as [it] respects the freedom of the people, may be considered as depending upon the nature of the bond of their union. If the bond of union be the voluntary consent of the people, the government may be pronounced to be free; where constraint and fear constitute that bond, the government is no longer the government of the people, and consequently they [the people] are enslaved.[9]

Tucker goes on to state that a free government is not dependent upon so-called checks and balances, but it is dependent upon the people's retaining of the ultimate control of their government. According to Tucker, freedom cannot exist when the right of the people to alter or abolish their government is withdrawn.

> [N]o people can ever be free, whose government is founded upon the usurpation of their sovereign rights; for by the act of usurpation, the sovereignty is transferred from the people, in whom alone it can legitimately reside, to those who by that act have manifested a determination to oppress them.[10]

What a condemnation of Lincoln's war policy. As has been maintained by many Southerners, Lincoln's war was not so much a war against slavery or even against the South: Lincoln's war was a war against free government in America. The most tragic surrender at Appomattox was not Lee's army, but the right of "we the people" to alter or abolish our government. From that time forward, regardless of how mild our government may be, we have ceased to be free.

Now let us return directly to the question of secession. Tucker addresses this issue by looking at the actions of the states as they seceded from the "confederacy" under the Articles of Confederation by acceding to the new Federal Constitution. Even though the government under the Articles of Confederation was denoted as being "perpetual," various states withdrew from that government to form a new government under the Constitution. Tucker notes that even though the government under the Articles of Confederation was denoted as being perpetual, the people of the states possessed the ultimate authority to determine how they were to be governed. Tucker states:

> [T]he seceding states were certainly justified upon that principle; and from the duty which every state is acknowledged to owe to itself, and its own citizens by doing whatsoever may best contribute to advance its own happiness and prosperity; and much more, what may be necessary to the preservation of its existence as a state. . . . That whenever any form of government is destructive of the ends of its institution, it is the right of the people to alter or abolish it, and to institute new government. Consequently whenever the people of any state, or number of states, discovered the inadequacy of the first form of federal government to promote or preserve their independence, happiness, and union, they only exerted that natural right in rejecting it, and adopting another, which all had unanimously assented to, and of which no force or compact can deprive the people of any state, whenever they see the necessity, and possess the power to do it. . . . We may infer that right has not been diminished by any new compact which they may since have entered into, since none could be more solemn or explicit than the first, nor more binding upon the contracting parties. Their obligation, therefore, to preserve the present constitution, is not greater than their former obligations were, to adhere to the Articles of Confederation; each state possessing the same right of withdrawing itself from the confederacy without the consent of the rest, as any number of them do, or ever did, possess. . . . It then becomes not only the right, but the duty of the states respectively, to throw off such government,

> and to provide new guards for their future security. To deny this, would be to deny to sovereign and independent states, the power which, as colonies, and dependent territories, they have mutually agreed they had a right to exercise, and did actually exercise, when they shook off the government of England, first, and adopted the present constitution of the United States, in the second instance.[11]

How can anyone read these words of a noted Founding Father of this Republic of Republics, these United States, and dare assert that secession is un-American? It must be pointed out here that Tucker unequivocally states that the obligation to preserve the government under the Constitution is no greater than the obligation to preserve the government under the Articles of Confederation. If the people of the sovereign states had the right and power to abolish the government under the Articles of Confederation, they also retain that same right under the Constitution. Tucker makes it plain and clear, secession is a right of "we the people" of the sovereign states. We are the final authority on how we are to be governed, not the Federal Supreme Court, Federal Congress, or the president. We the people of the sovereign states have the ultimate authority, and therefore the ultimate check, upon abuses of our civil liberties by the Federal government. All of this was true at the time of Tucker's writings. Unfortunately, Lincoln and the armies of Northern aggression changed everything.

We have now addressed the first question, *viz,* Was the right of secession abandoned after the adoption of the Federal Constitution? According to St. George Tucker, a noted jurist and Founding Father, the answer is—no. We now press on to the next question: Was the right of secession a theory dreamed up by slaveholders to protect their slave property? Again, let us look to the writings of St. George Tucker for the answer to this question from a Southern point of view.

"Whilst America hath been the land of promise to Europeans, and their descendants, it hath been the vale of death to millions of the wretched sons of Africa."[12] These are not the words of a Northern "bleeding-heart" abolitionist pining away for the liberation of Southern slaves. These are the words of one of the South's staunchest defenders of the right of secession, St. George Tucker. Tucker first proposed the gradual elimination of slavery in a 1796 pamphlet titled *A Dissertation on Slavery: With a Proposal for the*

Gradual Abolition of It, in the State of Virginia. This pamphlet was incorporated as an appendix in his edition of Blackstone's *Commentaries on the Laws of England,* published in 1803.

Tucker was one of many eminent Southerners, such as George Washington, Thomas Jefferson, Patrick Henry, James Monroe and others, who were vocal opponents of slavery. His credentials as an abolitionist began with his publication of the aforementioned tract in 1796. Here we see an early advocate of the right of secession also securing for himself a place as a vocal opponent of both the African slave trade and of slavery itself. As noted historian Clyde N. Wilson states:

> Like many of the great Southerners of the early republic, Tucker considered Negro slavery an undesirable element of the American body politic, and hoped for its eventual elimination, though, like Jefferson, and later Lincoln, he felt that emancipation would best be followed by removal of the freed people from American society.
>
> Perhaps the most important things about Tucker's essay for later times are the following: it shows the potential in the South for constructively addressing the most difficult issue in American society before the time when it became necessary to defend against outside control; and, it demonstrates that Tucker's state rights understanding of the Constitution is not merely a rationalization in defense of slavery, a misunderstanding that is a mainstay of conventional accounts of American history.[13]

Indeed, as Dr. Wilson notes, the State's Rights view of the Constitution is often seen as merely a "rationalization in the defense of slavery." Defenders of the strict construction (State's Rights) view of the Constitution are often ridiculed as using "code words" for the defense of slavery. In other words, the defense of the state's right of secession is viewed as only a stratagem in the defense of the institution of slavery. Yet, when we look at early Southern history, we see that those who worked for the abolition of slavery also believed in the State's Rights concept of American government. Although vilified by today's liberal establishment, the concept of limited government with the right of self-government in the hands of "we the people" of the sovereign states was never a theory promulgated for the defense of slaveholders. As demonstrated, both Southern slaveholders and Southern abolitionists held to the State's Rights concept of American government.

Tucker opened his anti-slavery pamphlet with a denunciation of the existence of slavery in a country supposedly founded upon the principle of equal freedom. Not only did Tucker condemn the institution of slavery, he also condemned the unequal application of civil liberties according to "particular complection." This fact alone would mark St. George Tucker as an American political philosopher 150 years ahead of his time. Tucker states:

> The genial light of liberty, which hath shone with unrivalled lustre on the former [Europeans in America], hath yielded no comfort to the latter [Africans in America], but to them hath proved a pillar of darkness, whilst it hath conducted the former to the most enviable state of human existence. Whilst we were offering up vows at the shrine of Liberty, and sacrificing hecatombs upon her altars; whilst we swore irreconcilable hostility to her enemies, and hurled defiance in their faces; whilst we adjured the God of Hosts to witness our resolution to live free, or die, and imprecated curses on their heads who refused to unite with us in establishing the empire of freedom; we were imposing upon our fellow men, who differed in complexion from us, a *slavery,* ten thousand times more cruel than the utmost extremity of those grievances and oppressions, of which we complained. Such are the inconsistencies of human nature; such the blindness of those who pluck not the beam out of their own eyes, whilst they can espy a moat, in the eyes of their brother; such that partial system of morality which confines rights and injuries, to particular complexions; such the effect of that self-love which justifies, or condemns, not according to principle, but to the agent.[14]

From the very beginning of his treatise, Tucker is willing to take a very unpopular stand on two related subjects. He not only condemns slavery and the slave trade in America, but also condemns the denial of civil liberties to those of "particular complexions." These were bold statements for anyone in the early part of the nineteenth century. Continuing his attack on the institution of slavery, Tucker makes sure that his readers understand that slavery and the slave trade were not unique to the South. Tucker is not to be numbered among the self-deprecating Southern scalawags who never miss a chance to condemn the South while praising the North. Tucker understands that the institution of slavery is a universal curse and not something particular to the South.

As Tucker notes, the institution of slavery had an early beginning in America, and the result of that beginning would have ramifications for later generations of Americans. He also explains why slavery was more successful in the South than in the North:

> The climate of the northern states [being] less favourable to the constitution of the natives of Africa than the southern, proved alike unfavourable to their propagation, and to the increase of their numbers by importants. As the southern colonies advanced in population, not only importations increased there, but Nature herself, under a climate more congenial to the African constitution, assisted in multiplying the blacks in those parts, no less than in diminishing their numbers in the more rigorous climates to the north. . . . The great increase of slavery in the southern, in proportion to the northern states in the union, is therefore not attributable, *solely,* to the effect of sentiment, but to natural causes.[15]

In his treatise against slavery, Tucker describes three forms of slavery: (1) *Political slavery.* Political slavery exists when a nation has been conquered by another nation. Tucker states that the "subjection of one nation or people, to the will of another, constitutes the first species of slavery."[16] In a state of political slavery, the people of the subjugated nation are denied the right to live under a government by the consent of the governed. The day-by-day existence of each member of society may be relatively free, yet it is the government and not the people who has the ultimate authority. (2) *Civil slavery.* Civil slavery exists any time the government encroaches upon the liberties of the citizens more than is absolutely necessary for the maintenance of normal society. According to Tucker, this happens "whenever the laws of a state respect the form, or energy of the government, more than the happiness of the citizen."[17] Here, Tucker is following the principle laid down by James Madison in Federalist Paper number 43, in which Madison states, "[T]he safety and happiness of a society are the objects at which all political institutions must be sacrificed." When a government becomes more concerned with its own well-being than it is with the well-being of its citizens, a condition of civil slavery exists. Tucker also notes that civil slavery exists any time laws are unequally enforced or any time there is "inequality of rights or privileges between the subjects or citizens of the same state." (3) *Domestic slavery.* Domestic slavery is a condition in which "one man is subject to be directed by another in all his actions."[18] According to Tucker, domestic slavery combines all the disadvantages of the other forms of slavery plus all other disadvantages associated with being under the total control of another person.

It should be obvious that Tucker's efforts in opposition to slavery are much different from the rantings of the Radical Abolitionists. For one thing, Tucker does not attempt to place blame for the institution of slavery on one section or one group of people in America. He logically accepts the fact that slavery and the slave trade are part of the American experience both North and South. Although a vocal opponent of the institution, he does not attack those around him who are in possession of slaves. Most important of all, he understands that slavery can exist in many forms and that no one is ever far removed from being a slave. Certainly, there are some forms of slavery that are more tolerable than others; nevertheless, as an American, Tucker rejects all forms of slavery. This then was the crying need during the two decades prior to the War for Southern Independence as well as for our day. If, in an effort to do good by destroying domestic slavery we only set the stage for the civil slavery of all citizens, what have we accomplished? Remember, the citizens of Nazi Germany, Communist Russia, or Mao's China were civil slaves. Just because they were not bought and sold by local masters is no reason to rejoice in their condition. Would we want our children to be slaves to their state?

Tucker's appeal for the abolition of slavery in America is tempered by warnings against Radical Abolition. Tucker, being fully aware of the prejudice of his day, is an advocate of gradual emancipation and colonization. Tucker explains the need for pursuing the gradual emancipation of slaves and how they should be prepared for that freedom:

> The extirpation of slavery from the United States is a task equally arduous and momentous. To restore the blessing of liberty to near a million of oppressed individuals, who have groaned under the yoke of bondage, and to their descendants, is an object, which those who trust in Providence, will be convinced would not be unaided by the divine Author of our being, should we invoke his blessing upon our endeavours. Yet human prudence forbids that we should precipitately engage in a work of such hazard as a general and simultaneous emancipation.

> The mind of man must in some measure be formed for his future condition. The early impressions of obedience and submission, which slaves have received among us, and the no less habitual arrogance and assumption of superiority, among the whites, contribute, equally, to unfit the former for *freedom,* and the latter for *equality*. . . . Unfit for their new condition, and unwilling to return to their former laborious course, they would become the caterpillars of the earth, and the tigers of the human race.[19]

As we can see from what Tucker is writing, freeing slaves is not something to be done with little or no forethought. Preparation for life after slavery is necessary if the newly freed people are to survive as a free people. Tucker also advocates a form of compensation for slaveholders as a means of promoting the elimination of slavery. Tucker states his reasons for the necessity of compensation:

> The laws have sanctioned this species of property [slaves]. Can the laws take away the property of an individual without his own consent, or without a *just compensation*. . . . Creditors also, who have trusted their debtors upon faith of this visible property will be defrauded. If justice demands the emancipation of the slave, she also, *under these circumstances,* seems to plead for the owner and for his creditor.[20]

In the preceding discussion, we have reviewed the work of a noble Southerner and American. As we have seen, St. George Tucker was a firm advocate of the right of secession by the people of the sovereign state, an open opponent of the institution of slavery in its several different forms, and an early advocate of equality of civil liberty for all free men. Tucker, a Southerner, was not the only noted constitutional scholar who believed in the right of secession by the people of the sovereign states. Let us now proceed to look at the work of a Northerner who also shared Tucker's views.

As has already been noted, William Rawle of Pennsylvania wrote one of the first textbooks on the United States Constitution in 1825. From this work, we can ascertain how this Northerner felt about the issue of secession. Also, some Americans may find it amazing that a Northerner would be president of a Southern abolition organization. Yet, as demonstrated in preceding chapters, before the advent of the Radical Abolitionists, Northerners and Southerners worked together for the elimination of slavery. As president of the Maryland Society for Promoting the Abolition of Slavery, Rawle worked with like-minded Americans for a peaceful end of slavery. Yet, as we will see, Rawle was also a dedicated advocate of the right of secession. In Chapter 31 of his textbook on the Constitution he described how any state of the United States could legally secede from the Union. This very textbook was used at the United States Military Academy at West Point both as a textbook and as a reference book for several years.

The first edition of Rawle's book is a concise volume of 347 pages consisting of thirty-one chapters and four appendices. The year after Rawle's book was published , it was reviewed by the eminently respected Boston, Massachusetts, journal, the *North American Review*.[21] As noted, Rawle's book contained one chapter which gave unambiguous direction on how and under what circumstances a state could secede from the Union. Having been reviewed in a leading American journal in 1826, almost forty years *after* the adoption of the Federal Constitution, if secession was considered to be treasonous or un-American, certainly the political commentators of Boston would have sounded the alarm. Yet, not one word of opposition was written about Rawle's view on secession. With the exception of taking issue with Rawle's view on how the presidential election should be held, the reviewer offered much praise for Rawle's book in a cordial report. In his summation the reviewer noted, "To those, who are desirous of studying the noblest monument of human wisdom, the Constitution of the United States, we recommend the treatise of Mr. Rawle as a *safe and intelligent guide*" [emphasis added].[22] Not only was Rawle's book warmly reviewed when it first appeared in print, but twenty-eight years later, it was still being recommended. In his book, *On Civil Liberty and Self-Government,* Francis Lieber, LL.D., recommended Rawle's book (among others) to his students and former students as a guide in constitutional issues.[23] It should be noted that Rawle's book was recommended by a Boston journal thirty-four years before Southern secession and by a leading Northern jurist only seven years before Southern secession. If secession is un-American, treasonous, or a slaveholders' scheme, why did a Northern journal and a Northern jurist both recommend Rawle's book which acknowledged this right?

As to who has the right to make and unmake a government, Rawle unequivocally states, "A moral power equal to and of the same nature with that which make, alone can destroy. . . . So the people may, on the same principle, at any time alter or abolish the constitution they have formed."[24] But how can the American people "alter or abolish" a government? Is this to be a great democratic experience of the American nation? Hardly so! The act of altering or abolishing is, according to Rawle, to be done by the same power "which made" the constitution, that is, the state. "It [ratification of the Constitution] was not the simple act of a homogeneous body of men, either large or small. It was to be the act of many independent states, though in a greater degree the act of the people set in motion by those states; it was to be the act of the people of each state and not of the people at large."[25]

We find in Rawle's examination of the Constitution his theory of how the people of a state would initiate its secession from the Union. Rawle always recurs to the idea that the people within the sovereign community (that is, the state) have the right to determine their own political destiny. As Rawle states:

> The secession of a state from the Union depends on the will of the people of such state. The people alone as we have already seen, hold the power to alter their constitution. . . . Still, however, the secession must in such case be distinctly and peremptorily declared to take place on that event. . . . But in either case the people is the only moving power.[26]

True to his republican principles, Rawle demands that the people, the voters of the state, should have the final voice in the act of withdrawing from the Union. For Rawle and Tucker, self-government is the foundation of all other civil liberties. The act of acceding to a form of government or the act of seceding from a form of government is the ultimate test of self-government. In the very chapter of his book in which he discusses the right of secession, Rawle notes that the noble example of self-government given the world by America "ought never to be withdrawn while the means of preserving it remains."[27] This self-government could only be maintained by the good will and intent of the parties of the agreement. The Union as a *free association of sovereign states* cannot be enforced at the point of a bloody bayonet because force precludes volition. In his book, *Commentaries on American Law,* James Kent of New York echos Rawle's warning about how the Union is to be maintained. In discussing this subject, Kent states: "[O]n the concurrence and good will of the parts [the states], the stability of the whole [Union] depends." Kent (1827), Rawle (1825), Tucker (1803) differed greatly from Lincoln (1861) on how the Union was to be maintained. As Kent points out, the Union would be held together by the *concurrence* and *good will* of the people of the sovereign states, not by bloody bayonets. As St. George Tucker states:

> The union is in fact, as well as in theory, an association of states, or, a confederacy . . . [each state] is still a perfect state, still sovereign, still independent, and still capable, should the occasion require, to resume the exercise of its functions as such, in the most unlimited extent.[28]

The preceding has been offered as proof that secession was not considered an un-American act nor was secession a scheme invented by Southern slaveholders in an attempt to defend their slave property. Tucker and Rawle have been offered as representative men from both the South and from the North who believed in the right of secession and yet were also opposed to the institution of slavery. Yet, even before either of these men had given their views on secession Thomas Jefferson, the author of the Declaration of Independence, and James Madison, the Father of the Constitution, wrote and published the Kentucky and Virginia Resolves.

Even though these resolutions were authored by two different individuals and were then submitted to the actions of two different state legislatures, they still speak of the same principles. The tone and tenor of these resolutions are of limited federalism, State's Rights, and the ultimate right and duty of the sovereign state to judge for itself whether or not an act of the Federal government is *pursuant* to the Constitution. Then, as a sovereign entity, that state has the duty to take whatever action is required to protect the liberty of its citizens. These resolves addressed the question: Are the states subservient to the Federal government? In the Kentucky Resolution of 1798, Jefferson writes:

> *Resolved,* That the several states composing the United States of America, are not united on the principle of unlimited submission to their general government . . . they [the states] constituted a general government for special purposes, delegated to that government certain definite powers, reserving, each

> state to itself, the residuary mass of right to their own self-government; and that whensoever the general government assumes undelegated powers, its acts are un-authoritative, void, and of no force: That to this compact each state acceded as a state . . . That the government created by this compact was not made the exclusive or final judge of the extent of the powers delegated to itself . . . as in all other cases of compact among parties having no common judge, each party [state] has an equal right of judge for itself, as well of infractions, and of the mode and measure of redress.[29]

In this small portion of the Kentucky Resolve, Jefferson asserts the idea that the Federal government is the creation of the people of the sovereign states, and the people of the states have the right to judge for themselves how to respond to Federal abuse. This is what the people of the Southern states did in 1860-61 when they elected state conventions that voted to withdraw from the Union. They seceded from the Union in the same manner that they had acceded to that Union—by the action of a convention of the people of that state.

In the Virginia Resolves, James Madison made the same points as made by Jefferson. Madison writes:

> The powers of the Federal Government as resulting from the compact to which the states are parties, as limited by the plain sense and intention of the instrument constituting that compact; as no further valid than they are authorized by the grants enumerated in that compact; and that in case of a deliberate, palpable, and dangerous exercise of other powers not granted by the said compact, the States, who are the parties thereto, have the right, and are in duty bound, to interpose for arresting the progress of the evil, and liberties appertaining to them.[30]

These resolutions became the fundamental statements of the State's Rights party in American politics. Here we have two of America's paramount Founding Fathers defending the rights of "we the people" of the sovereign states against Federal abuse. But secession was more than an ideology of Southern political philosophers.

In 1803, while debating whether to purchase the Louisiana Territory, Josiah Quincy, a representative of Massachusetts, declared that his state would secede if the Louisiana Territory was added to the United States. Again, when Louisiana petitioned for admission to the Union, Quincy declared the willingness of the people of Massachusetts to secede from the Union if Louisiana was admitted to it. Now, if secession is tantamount to treason, was Representative Quincy condemned by the United States House of Representatives or the American people? Of course he was not condemned as promoting treason. The answer tells us much more about how people felt about the right of secession. In 1815, the people of New England, growing tired of the adverse effects of the War of 1812, met in convention (The Hartford Convention) to promote the secession of the New England states from the Union. The end of the war and the resumption of normal trade made secession unnecessary. If this event had not occurred, the New England states may very well have seceded from the Union some forty-five years before South Carolina found it necessary to do so. In 1835 Texas seceded from Mexico. The United States first recognized the right of Texas to secede from Mexico, then in 1845 admitted Texas into the Union. Now, if secession is such an un-American principle, why did the United States admit a state into the Union which owed its very existence to the right of secession? Again, the answer tells us how early Americans felt about the right of secession. Prior to the advent of the War for Southern Independence, the right of secession, while not something to be resorted to for light or transient reasons, was *not* viewed as treasonous or un-American.

SUMMARY

These United States of America were born as a result of a successful secession movement. The right of a people to secede from an abusive central government is enshrined in the joint Declaration of Independence adopted on July 4, 1776. Prior to the secession of the states of the South in 1861, numerous threats of secession were made by Northern states. Before the advent of the War for Southern Independence, secession, although at times considered imprudent or unwise, was not condemned as "treason." The right of secession was so enshrined in American political philosophy that the use of a textbook at West Point Military Academy which taught secession as a right of the states was never condemned. Even more shocking, the author of that book, William Rawle, was never ridiculed as promoting sedition or treason. Every Fourth of July Americans should recognize that they are celebrating America's great secession holiday.

The right and duty of "we the people" to alter or abolish any government that does not serve the happiness and safety of the people existed before the Constitution and the Declaration of Independence . "We the people" have the supreme authority to establish a government that governs by the authority of the free and unfettered consent of the people. As Rawle and Tucker, along with a host of other Founding Fathers, explained, in America this consent is given by the people of the sovereign states—each state acting for itself only. This concept of state sovereignty is indispensable to the operation of the original Constitutional Republic of 1787-88. As has been shown, the existence of these state governments predates the formation of any type of central government in the United States. Only after the defeat of the South did America repudiate this doctrine of real State's Rights. In 1803, St. George Tucker warned Americans about the threat of civil slavery if the government became the supreme authority rather than the people. According to Tucker's theory, post-Appomattox civil slavery is the legacy of all Americans.

MYTH: The idea of secession is so closely related to the defense of slavery as to make it repulsive to those who love freedom.

REALITY: Secession is nothing more than the people of each sovereign state "consenting" to the form of government they live under. As has been shown, these United States were born in the midst of the secession of thirteen colonies from Great Britain. These very same thirteen political communities, acting in their own interest, either acceded to or seceded from various forms of government, as they deemed necessary, until the adoption of the Federal Constitution. As the Constitution states, those powers not delegated to the Federal government by the states were retained by the states or the people (see the Ninth and Tenth Amendments). The right to "alter or abolish" (in the words of the Declaration of Independence) the form of government they live under was never surrendered by the people of the states as they acceded to the new Union. Therefore, that which they possessed before the adoption of the Constitution, they fully retain. The people at the local level (i.e., the state) are the supreme judge of their government, and they alone have the right to judge the limits of how they will be governed.

MYTH: Secession was just a wicked scheme by evil Southern slaveholders to protect their slave property.

REALITY: In this chapter we have looked at the life and works of two early Americans, one, St. George Tucker, a Southerner, and one, William Rawle, a Northerner. Both men worked for the elimination of slavery, and both men believed in the right of secession. How can anyone maintain that secession is a ploy of Southern slaveholders? Both Tucker and Rawle were members of the early American abolition movement; yet, unlike the Radical Abolitionists, they were highly respected members of their states. As has already been pointed out, secession was an integral part of the founding of these United States. At that time all thirteen of these states recognized slavery as legal. Those states that had the fewest slaves were the ones that were most actively involved in the nefarious slave trade. If, as many liberals contend, the secession of the Southern states must be condemned because they all recognized slavery as lawful, what can we say about the secession of the thirteen original colonies from Great Britain? Is it logical to praise the slaveholder and slave trader's secession in 1776 and condemn that same action in 1861? There is one major difference between the secessionists of 1776 and 1861: The secessionists of 1861 formed a government that categorically denied any additional importation of African slaves into the new nation being formed. Also, it should be remembered that the vast numbers of men who were to make up the rank and file of the soldiers and sailors of the Confederacy were from non-slaveholding families. How realistic is it to maintain that these men would give up the comforts of home and face death just so a rich plantation owner could live in the lap of luxury? While many Confederate leaders were slaveholders, just as many Americans were slaveholders and slave traders during the War for American Independence, many of them, such as Robert E. Lee, were practicing abolitionists before the War for Southern Independence broke out. Lee, at great cost to himself, freed his slaves several years before the War. If we are to be consistent, if we condemn the Confederacy because its first president was a slaveholder, we must also condemn the United States because its first president was also a slaveholder. If we condemn the thirteen states of the Confederate States of America because each state recognized slavery, we must also condemn the thirteen original colonies because each of them recognized slavery as well.

MYTH: The principle of secession runs counter to the American idea of civil liberty and civil rights.

REALITY: As St. George Tucker pointed out, the very foundation of civil liberty is based upon the right of self-government. The acknowledged right of the people to alter or abolish their government is an insurmountable obstacle to the abuse of civil liberties by government. Once this right has been removed, government becomes supreme, not the people. As American history teaches, the act of acceding to or seceding from one system of government into another is the American way of exerting the God-given right of self-government.

MYTH: Fighting against the Federal government is un-American. Only traitors would do such a thing.

REALITY: When it comes to resisting the abuses of the central government, Patrick Henry said it well: "The first thing I have at heart is *liberty,* the second thing is American Union."[31] As long as the Union is subservient to the cause of liberty, as Henry noted, the Union is secure. But when the Union arrogantly attempts to usurp the rightful place of liberty, it is time for the people to act. Any government that tramples upon the rights and liberties of the people must be opposed by true friends of freedom. Friends of freedom should recall the words of Patrick Henry who faced down Tories of his day when they charged him with being a traitor. Henry looked into the eyes of his accusers and boldly stated, "If this be treason, let us make the most of it." Let us take our stand with Patrick Henry—Freedom first, Union second.

CHAPTER 6

Lincoln: The Un-Emancipator

If Lincoln loved the Union, he was responsible, more than any man, for its destruction, for he consciously violated the constitution. . . . The war was not a war of slavery versus freedom; it was a war between those who preferred a federated nation to those who preferred a confederation of sovereign states. Slavery was the ink thrown into the pool to confuse the issue.

Andrew Nelson Lytle
The Virginia Quarterly Review
October 1931

No study of American slavery would be complete without a look at the mythical sixteenth president of the United States, Abraham Lincoln. It is doubtful that there is any American icon more worshiped than Lincoln. The adoration given Lincoln by modern Americans has been described as "an idolatrous religious cult wherein Abraham Lincoln is literally worshiped as a god."[1] His likeness, seated upon a marble throne as if he were the embodiment of Zeus at rest in his temple upon the Acropolis, appears more emblematic of a pagan god than a man. For many Americans, the myth of Lincoln has elevated him beyond the point of being a mere man to the position of a god. It is his name that is intoned whenever any presumed social ill needs to be resolved. Whether viewed as a Greek god or a Roman emperor-god, Lincoln, at his memorial in Washington, is the subject of adoration and reverence unlike any other of America's heroes.

Yet, the Lincoln of fact and the Lincoln of mythology are two different and distinct personalities. In examining Lincoln's views about slavery, about African-Americans, and about American liberty, we will tread down paths not often traveled by the victors of the War for Southern Independence. As demonstrated, just because an individual does not wish to go down a certain path does not mean that truth cannot be found at the end of that trail. In the following chapter a few questions regarding Lincoln and his views will be addressed: (1) How did Lincoln view African-Americans? (2)What was Lincoln's view of American slavery? (3) Did Lincoln free the slaves? and, (4)What was Lincoln's view of American liberty? Most Americans will find the answers to these questions very disturbing as their image of Abraham Lincoln is shattered and they discover the truth about the man.

Lincoln as the archenemy of slavery, promoter of equality, and friend of oppressed African-Americans is one of the most pervasive myths in modern America. Rather than being in the forefront of the advocacy of social equality for all races, Lincoln was among those who openly opposed such action. In fact, his views were more akin to those of the followers of a modern-day neo-Nazi hate group. As demonstrated in preceding chapters, the philosophy of Negro inferiority was commonly held throughout America. Even Lincoln voiced his support of this theory in the famous Lincoln-Douglas Debates of 1858:

> I will say, then, that I am not, nor ever have been, in favor of bringing about in anyway the social and political equality of the white and black races—that I am not, nor ever have been, in favor of making voters or jurors of negroes, nor of qualifying them to hold office, nor to intermarry with white people; and I will say in addition to this that there is a physical difference between the white and black races. . . . I, as much as any other man, am in favor of having the superior position assigned to the white race.[2]

In September of 1859 he had this to say about the equality of the races:

> Negro equality. Fudge! How long in the Government of a God great enough to make and maintain this universe, shall there continue knaves to vend and fools to gulp, so low a piece of demagoguism as this?[3]

Not only did Lincoln hold to the belief of Negro inferiority, he was also a proponent of removing the African-American population from America once they were freed. In his political debate with Stephen A. Douglas on the subject of slavery,

Lincoln clearly stated his ideas for the removal of freed slaves from America:

> Such separation if effected at all, must be effected by colonization. . . . [W]hat colonization most needs is a hearty will. . . . Let us be brought to believe that it is morally right, and at the same time favorable to, or at least not against, our interests to transfer the African to his native clime, and we shall find a way to do it, however great the task may be.[4]

As noted, Lincoln's views were held by the vast majority of people both in the North and the South at this time. Although most Americans today do not hold these views, there is no demand to remove Lincoln's "racist" face from every five-dollar bill. Nor is there a demand to rename schools named in honor of him because of his "racist" views, which are much different from the views of modern Americans. At the same time, all attempts to honor Southern heroes of Lincoln's day are met by wild denunciation of so-called Southern racism. A vociferous uproar is heard from the left of center establishment any time any elected official even hints at anything good about Confederate leaders (as witnessed by the liberal outcry at Sen. John Ashcroft's few nice words about some of these men). Impartial Americans should ask themselves, "Why do we respect Abraham Lincoln, who held the same racial views as most Southerners of his time, and yet denigrate Southern heroes like Robert E. Lee, Stonewall Jackson, or Jefferson Davis?"

Did Lincoln, as president of the United States, push for laws that would aid in advancing the civil rights of African-Americans in the North? First, let us look at how the North "respected" African-Americans during the War. African-Americans were successfully barred from voting in New Jersey in 1807, in Connecticut in 1814, in Rhode Island in 1822, and in Pennsylvania in 1838.[5] Add to these the state of Illinois, which, in 1862 (while its sons were pillaging the South) by an overwhelming vote of the people, passed an amendment to the state constitution declaring that "no negro or mulatto shall immigrate or settle in this state."[6] This was done after Lincoln had suggested that if the people of Illinois were fearful of Negro immigration, they could pass such a law. With the announcement of the Emancipation Proclamation, there was a general fear among Northerners that their states would be flooded with newly freed African-Americans. In response to this fear,

Lincoln sent a message to Congress in which he noted: "But why should emancipation South send free people North? And in any event cannot the North decide for itself whether to receive them?"[7] Nor was this feeling of white supremacy confined to Lincoln. Ardent Republicans Gideon Wells, Lincoln's secretary of the navy. and William Seward, Lincoln's secretary of state, both espoused this theory. Wells, referring to the taking of Indian lands during the War, was racially motivated in defending the Federal government's action against Native Americans. He stated that the Indians in Minnesota "have good land which white men want and mean to have."[8] While Lincoln was playing the race card in 1858, Seward at the same time stated, "The white man needs this continent to labor in and must have it."[9] Even Gen. William Tecumseh Sherman gave expression of his feelings about African-Americans when he stated that the reason he was fighting was "to sustain a Government capable of vindicating its just and rightful authority, independent of niggers, cotton, money, or any earthly interest."[10] These statements together with a whole host of "exclusion" laws passed by states throughout the North before, during, and after the War are proof positive that there were no feelings of good will and equality being expressed by either Lincoln or the North. Noting the prevalent racist attitude held by Northerners, English abolitionist James S. Buckingham wrote in 1842:

> This is only one among the many proofs I had witnessed of the fact, that the prejudice of color is not nearly so strong in the South as in the North. [In the South] it is not at all uncommon to see the black slaves of both sexes, shake hands with white people when they meet, and interchange friendly personal inquires; but at the North I do not remember to have witnessed this once; and neither in Boston, New York, or Philadelphia would white persons generally like to be seen shaking hands and talking familiarly with blacks in the streets.[11]

The fact is that Lincoln's opinion of African-Americans was no different from the opinion of the average American, North or South, during the nineteenth century. Lincoln was not the champion of equality that the liberal establishment has portrayed him. St. George Tucker, a Southerner who believed in the right of secession, came closer to being a defender of the civil rights of African-Americans than Lincoln did. Writing in opposition to slavery,

Tucker had this to say about laws that were passed by one social class to the disadvantage of another:

> This species of slavery also exists whenever there is an inequality of rights, or privileges, between the subjects or citizens of the same state, except such as necessarily result from the exercise of a public officer; for the pre-eminence of one class of men must be founded and erected upon the depression of another; and the measure of exaltation in the former, is that of the slavery of the latter.[12]

As we have noted, Tucker referred to the discrimination of rights between citizens of a nation as a form of "civil" slavery. At this time it should be obvious that Lincoln was no "friend of the Negro"; his view of the Negro was the same as any other American's of the nineteenth century.

If Lincoln's opinion of African-Americans was no different from that of the average American of the nineteenth century, then certainly, we are assured by the politically correct crowd, his opinion of slavery was different from that of the average nineteenth-century American. Here again, mythology and fact are at odds.

Without a doubt, Lincoln and his Republican party were opposed to slavery. But being opposed to slavery does not make one a unique creature in nineteenth-century America. After all, Robert E. Lee was opposed to slavery. Lee stated, "In this enlightened age, there are few I believe, but will acknowledge, that slavery as an institution, is a moral and political evil in any country."[13] At great personal expense, Lee freed his slaves several years before the War. On the floor of the United States Senate, Jefferson Davis had observed that slavery had a natural end. Davis stated, "[F]or its end the preparation of that race for civil liberty and social enjoyment [must be made]. . . .When the time shall arrive at which emancipation is proper, those interested will be most anxious to effect it."[14] All major biographers of Jefferson Davis agree that Davis's and his brother's slaves were better prepared for freedom than the average slave. For those who attempt to explain away Lincoln's war because of the need to end slavery, Davis stated:

> War was not necessary to the abolition of slavery. Years before the agitation began at the North and the menacing acts to the institution, there was a growing feeling all over the South for its abolition. But the abolitionists of the North, both

> by publications and speech, cemented the South and crushed the feeling in favor of emancipation. Slavery could have been blotted out without the sacrifice of brave men and without the strain which revolution always makes upon established forms of government.[15]

As has been already pointed out, Southerners had been in the forefront of the battle to end slavery. Neither Lincoln nor the Republican party held a monopoly on the idea of emancipation. They did, however, have as members of their party Radical Abolitionists who were demanding full, complete, and immediate emancipation without either compensation for slaveholders or preparation of the slaves for freedom. In this aspect only did the Republicans have a monopoly. So despised were the Radical Abolitionists that no other major political party in America would allow them leadership positions.

What was Lincoln's attitude toward slavery as it existed in the United States? Just because Radical Abolitionists found the Republican party more to their liking than any other party at the time does not mean that Lincoln was seeking the betterment of the slaves. James F. Rhodes, in his *History of the United States,* states, "Lincoln was not, however, in any sense of the word, an Abolitionist."[16] According to Rhodes, General Wadsworth said of Lincoln: "He never heard him speak of anti-slavery men otherwise than as 'radicals,' 'abolitionists'; and of the 'nigger question' he [Lincoln] frequently spoke."[17] Even more telling, Henry C. Whitney, a nineteenth-century biographer of Lincoln, in his book *On Circuit with Lincoln,* states, "He [Lincoln] had no intention of making voters of the negroes—in fact their welfare did not enter his policy at all."[18] Not only was Lincoln not an advocate of equality for African-Americans, but his views on slavery have also been overstated.

On October 13, 1858, during a debate between Lincoln and Stephen A. Douglas in Quincy, Illinois, Lincoln stated his views on several slavery-related issues. Lincoln acknowledged the difficulty of ending slavery, thus requiring a gradual system of emancipation; he acknowledged that slavery within any state was legal and could not be eliminated without the consent of that state; and, he assured his audience that he would respect the "rights of property" of the slaveholders. Lincoln stated:

> We deal with it [slavery] as with any other wrong, insofar as we can prevent its growing any larger, and so deal with it that in the *run of time* there may be *some* promise of an end to it [emphasis added]. We have a due regard to the actual presence of it amongst us, and the difficulties of getting rid of it in any satisfactory way, and all the constitutional obligations thrown about it. I suppose that in reference both to its actual existence in the nation, and to our constitutional obligations, we have no right at all to disturb it in the States where it exists, and we profess that we have no more inclination to disturb it than we have the right to do so. . . . We insist on the policy that shall restrict it to its present limits. [Then Lincoln went on to a discussion of how his party would deal with the Dred Scott case before the U.S. Supreme Court.] We do not propose that when Dred Scott has been decided to be a slave by the court, we, as a mob, will decide him to be free. We do not propose that, when any other one, or one thousand, shall be decided by that court to be slaves, we will in any violent way disturb the rights of property thus settled.[19]

Here we see Lincoln making some of the same arguments about slavery that had been made by Senators John C. Calhoun and Jefferson Davis: (1) Slavery is difficult to eliminate. (2) It has constitutional protections "thrown around it." (3) The Federal government has no right to interfere with slavery within any state. (4) The right of the property of the slaveholder must be recognized. On the issue of slavery, the major difference between Lincoln and Davis is in the limitation of the "growth" of slavery into new states. Lincoln's policy would have limited slavery to, and protected slavery within, the states where it existed. Davis and Calhoun maintained that all citizens (with their property) had a constitutional right to move into the commonly held territory of the United States. Slavery could be eliminated only when that territory became a state. Again, the leaders of the South saw the people of the state as the only agent of sovereignty and not the Federal government. This being the case, only the people of a sovereign state, not the people of a territory nor the Federal government, could abolish slavery.

Even more telling is Lincoln's views of slavery and the South. Today, it is so common to hear the South demonized because of its "refusal" to end slavery. Everything Southern is subject to defamation because of the supposed refusal of the South to free its slaves.

There are constant and incessant calls for the removal of any Southern symbol by those who have chosen to be offended by these symbols. Yet, when we look at Lincoln's view of the issue of slavery, we find him defending the Southern position. In August of 1858 Lincoln made the following statement:

> Before proceeding, let me say I think I have no prejudice against the Southern people. They are just what we would be in their situation. If slavery did not now exist among them, they would not introduce it. If it did now exist among us, we should not instantly give it up. This I believe of the masses North and South. Doubtless there are individuals on both sides who would gladly introduce slavery anew, if it were out of existence. We know that some Southern men do free their slaves, go North, and become tip-top Abolitionists; while some Northern ones go South, and become most cruel slave-masters.
>
> When Southern people tell us they are no more responsible for the origin of slavery than we, I acknowledge the fact. When it is said that the institution exists, and that it is very difficult to get rid of it in any satisfactory way, I can understand and appreciate the saying. I surely will not blame them for not doing what I should not know how to do myself. If all earthly power were given me, I should not know what to do as to the existing institution. My first impulse would be to free all the slaves, and send them to Liberia—to their own native land. But a moment's reflection would convince me that whatever of high hope (as I think there is) there may be in this in the long run, its sudden execution is impossible. If they were all landed there in a day, they would all perish in the next ten days; and there are not surplus shipping and surplus money enough in the world to carry them there in many times ten days. What then? Free them all, and keep them among us as underlings? Is it quite certain that this betters their condition? I think I would not hold one in slavery at any rate; yet the point is not clear enough to me to denounce people upon. What next? Free them, and make them politically and socially our equals? My own feelings will not admit of this; and if mine would, we well know that those of the great mass of white people will not. Whether this feeling accords with justice and sound judgement is not the sole question, if, indeed, it is any part of it. A universal feeling, whether well or ill-founded, cannot be safely disregarded. We cannot make them equals. It does seem to me that systems of gradual emancipation might be adopted; but

> for their tardiness in this, I will not undertake to judge our brethren of the South.
>
> When they remind us of their constitutional rights, I acknowledge them, not grudgingly, but fully and fairly; and I would give them any legislation for the reclaiming of their fugitives, which should not, in its stringency, be more likely to carry a free man into slavery, than our ordinary criminal laws are to hang an innocent one.[20]

The editor of the Nation Park Service's book on Lincoln, Roy E. Appleton, noted Lincoln's unchanging views on the subject of slavery. According to Appleton, Lincoln sympathized with problems faced by Southerners as they dealt with slavery. Furthermore, Appleton goes as far as stating that no evidence exists that Lincoln "ever changed position on this subject."[21] The views espoused by Abraham Lincoln in his famous debate with Senator Douglas make it clear that he was not seeking to bring about social or political equality for African-Americans. But more important, Lincoln answered the often asked question about why the so-called Civil War was being fought. In response to being denounced by leading abolitionists for not freeing the slaves early in the war, Lincoln wrote a letter to Horace Greeley of the *New York Tribune* and had it published in several newspapers. As to why he was fighting the War, Lincoln made it clear:

> I would save the Union. I would save it the shortest way under the Constitution. The sooner the national authority can be restored, the nearer the Union will be "the Union as it was." If there be those who would not save the Union unless they could at the same time save slavery, I do not agree with them. If there be those who would not save the Union unless they could at the same time destroy slavery, I do not agree with them. *My paramount object in this struggle is to save the Union, and is not either to save or to destroy slavery* [emphasis added]. If I could save the Union without freeing any slaves, I would do it; and if I could save it by freeing all the slaves, I would do it; and if I could save it by freeing some and leaving others alone, I would also do that. What I do about slavery and the colored race, I do because I believe it helps to save the Union; and what I forebear, I forebear because I do not believe it would help to save the Union.[22]

The words of Lincoln reveal a different type of person from the oft-touted champion of liberty, equality, and brotherhood. What we see is a man who held firm to the nineteenth-century concept of Negro inferiority; a man who believed that the South was correct when it asserted that it was not responsible for the institution of slavery; and a man who was willing to deal with slavery and the "colored race" in any manner to promote his political agenda (i.e., saving the Union). But, what about all those slaves that Lincoln freed? Certainly, being the godfather of freedom for millions of African-Americans would nullify any minor racist statements made by Lincoln.

The truth is that the so-called Emancipation Proclamation was not designed to free slaves. It had a three-fold purpose: (1) to be used as a propaganda ploy to influence abolitionist England and France not to recognize the Confederacy; (2) to encourage the fear of slave revolts in the South, and thus weaken the Southern armies; and (3) to placate the more radical abolitionist element of the Republican party. Very few Americans (including many teachers of history) have read the Emancipation Proclamation. Upon reading this document one will notice a few interesting points. First, the only slaves to be freed were those slaves living under the control of the Confederate government. Those parts of any Southern state that were under the control of the Federal government were left untouched by the proclamation. The words of the proclamation speak for themselves: ". . . which excepted parts are for the present left precisely as if this proclamation were never issued."[23] For example, in Louisiana, twelve parishes were unequivocally removed from the force of the proclamation. Upon the posting of Lincoln's proclamation, how many people in the Confederate States of American freed their slaves? The question itself is all that is needed to prove that Lincoln's proclamation was a bogus statement of freedom. Second, a reading of the proclamation will reveal why it was issued. Within the body of the proclamation we read why this document is being announced: "as a fit and necessary war measure for suppressing said rebellion."[24] If Lincoln's proclamation could not free any slaves in the Confederacy, what about the slaves in the Northern-controlled portions of the country? Not a one of those slaves was freed by Lincoln's vaunted proclamation. Lincoln did not free the slaves. And, to add insult to injury to the myth of the Great Emancipator, according to the proclamation, the only thing a slave state had to do to prevent this proclamation from being enforced was to cease its "rebellion" against the United States. The proclamation clearly stated who would be freed: "[A]ll persons held as slaves within any State or designated part of a State the people whereof shall then be in rebellion against the United States shall be then, thenceforward, and forever free."[25]

The story of Henry Simpson, U.S.C.T. (United States Colored Troops), will shed some light on how slaves in "loyal" areas of the South were treated. According to a document signed by Unionist W. C. Sympson, of Kentucky, "The said Henry Sympson [Simpson is spelled with either a "y" or an "i" throughout the document] was born my slave on the ___day of 1843, and continued such until entered into military Service of the United States."[26] In 1866 Symspon (a slave master) made a claim to the United States for compensation for his slave who had entered the United States military in 1864, some two years after the issuing of the famous Emancipation Proclamation. It should be noted that Symspon stated that he "was and is" a loyal citizen of the United States and therefore had all rights to claim compensation for the loss of his slave property. If Lincoln's proclamation freed the slaves in the United States, how can the slavery of Henry Simpson, U.S.C.T., two years later be explained? So secure was his master in the right of ownership of this slave that he even made an official claim for compensation from the United States for his lost property. Furthermore, this claim was made a year after the passage of the Thirteenth Amendment which outlawed slavery in America.

An examination of the life of Lincoln will demonstrate that rather than being a great liberator of men, Lincoln was the destroyer of constitutional liberty and the instigator of oppressive government in the United States. A quick look at Lincoln's record is enough to prove just how far he pushed the United States away from the goal of secure liberty. During his administration, Lincoln's government was responsible for shutting down more than three hundred newspapers. These were not all Southern newspapers; they were Northern newspapers such as the *New York World* and the *Chicago Times.* With his suspension of the right of *habeas corpus,* Lincoln trampled upon hundreds of years of Anglo-Saxon judicial and political progress. According to the laws of the United States, the legislative and not the executive branch of government has the authority to suspend the right of *habeas corpus.* This is a safeguard to prevent the establishment of executive tyranny. Lincoln succeeded in evading this safeguard. As a result of his suspension of *habeas corpus,* more than fourteen thousand civilians (Northerners) were imprisoned during the War. These civilians were then brought before military courts rather than civil courts. During Lincoln's administration, Federal censorship of the mails was introduced, and a witch hunt for "disloyal" Federal employees was initiated. All this from a man who took an oath to "protect and defend the Constitution." What good is a constitution if the most basic liberties of the people cannot be protected by it?

No doubt, the most flagrant "un-American" act committed by the Lincoln administration was the arrest and banishment of Congressman Clement L. Vallandigham. Congressman Vallandigham was an Ohio Democrat who opposed the use of force to restore the Union. As such, he led the opposition to the Lincoln administration in Congress. In February of 1863 Vallandigham spoke out against a Lincoln-backed bill. In part he stated:

> Sir, some two hundred years ago, men were burned at the stake, subjected to the horrors of the Inquisition, to all the tortures that the devilish ingenuity of man could invent—for what? For opinions on questions of religion—of man's duty and relation to his God. And now, to-day, for opinions on questions political, under a free government, in a country whose liberties were purchased by our fathers by seven years' outpouring of blood, and expenditure of treasure—we have lived to see men, the born heirs of this precious inheritance, subjected to arrest and cruel imprisonment at the caprice of a President, or a secretary, or a constable.
>
> What is it, sir, but a bill to abrogate the Constitution, to repeal all existing laws, to destroy all rights, to strike down the judiciary, and erect, upon the ruins of civil and political liberty, a stupendous superstructure of despotism.[27]

In almost prophetic language, Vallandigham continued his attack on this bill that would put into the hands of provost marshals the right to determine what is and is not a treasonable act or speech.

> Your petty provost marshals are to determine what treasonable practices are and "inquire into," detect, spy out, eavesdrop, ensnare, and then inform, report to the chief spy at Washington. These, sir, are now to be our American liberties

under your Administration. There is not a crowned head in Europe who dare venture on such an experiment. . . . Words, too—conversation or public speech—are to be adjudged "treasonable practices." Men, women, and children are to be hauled to prison for free speech. Whoever shall denounce or oppose this Administration—whoever may affirm that war will not restore the Union, and teach men the gospel of peace, may be reported and arrested, upon some old grudge, and by some ancient enemy, it may be, and imprisoned as guilty of a treasonable practice.[28]

All that Congressman Vallandigham had warned America about was eventually visited upon him. While running for governor of Ohio, Vallandigham was arrested, tried, and sentenced by the military. He was subsequently banished from the United States by the Lincoln administration.

Lincoln's flagrant disregard for constitutional liberty was so bold as to deny accused prisoners the right of counsel. Lincoln's secretary of state, William H. Seward, gave orders that prisoners were not to be allowed to secure the service of an attorney for their defense. Seward had the following letter read to the prisoners:

I am instructed, by the Secretary of State, to inform you, that the Department of State, of the United States, *will not recognize any one as an attorney for political prisoners,* and will look with distrust upon all applications for release through such channels; and that such applications *will be regarded as additional reasons for declining to release the prisoners.*[29]

In another letter on the same subject, Seward advised Lincoln's political prisoners who had engaged the assistance of lawyers "that they are expected to revoke all such engagements now existing, and avoid any hereafter."[30] Never in American history have civilians been arrested and incarcerated by the military on such a scale. Lincoln took this action in direct and palpable disregard of the Constitution. At this point one must wonder, "What kind of Union did Lincoln save?"

As sad as these events were, any American who feels a patriotic rush at the sound of the tune "The Star-spangled Banner," will forever be embarrassed by Lincoln's actions in Maryland. After the secession of the Upper South, Lincoln's government became paranoid about the possibility of Maryland seceding and joining the

Confederate States. Even though the leaders of Maryland's legislature had declared that "such fears are without just foundation,"[31] Lincoln's government ordered the arrest, in flagrant violation of every constitutional safeguard, of prominent citizens of that state.

> It will be remembered that the Mayor of the city of Baltimore, the Police Commissioners, the Marshal of Police, members of the State Legislature, and private citizens, not only of that city, but from all parts of the State, were arrested and thrown into prison, by the edict of Abraham Lincoln, and kept for months, without any warrant of law whatever.[32]

One of the citizens to be taken into custody was the grandson of the author of "The Star-spangled Banner," Francis Key Howard. It will be remembered that Francis Scott Key wrote the national anthem while a prisoner on board a British warship. The British at that time were attacking Fort McHenry. Francis Scott Key's grandson, Francis Key Howard, would also become a prisoner—a prisoner within Fort McHenry, not outside of it—a prisoner bemoaning American tyranny, not praising the United States as the "home of the free."

On the morning of September 13, 1861, Francis Key Howard was arrested on the authority of William H. Seward, secretary of state for the Lincoln administration. This was done without a warrant, and Howard was not even told of what crime he was charged. These and many other basic constitutional protections were utterly violated. Howard was taken from his home to Fort McHenry where he met newspaper publishers, members of the legislature, and other prominent citizens, all "state prisoners." Being a "state prisoner" in Fort McHenry had a special meaning to Francis Key Howard:

> When I looked out in the morning, I could not help being struck by an odd and not pleasant coincidence. On that day, forty-seven years before, my grandfather, Mr. F. S. Key, then a prisoner on a British ship, witnessed the bombardment of Fort McHenry. When, on the following morning, the hostile fleet drew off, defeated, he wrote the song so long popular throughout the country, the "Star-spangled Banner." As I stood upon the very scene of that conflict, I could not but contrast my position with his, forty-seven years before. The flag which he had then so proudly hailed, I saw waving, at the same place,

> over the victims of as vulgar and brutal a despotism as modern times have witnessed.[33]

Howard, among other political or "state prisoners," remained imprisoned for more than a year. During that time they were only allowed limited correspondence and were denied the right of consulting attorneys for their assistance. During his imprisonment, Howard gave vent to his feelings about the abuse of American civil rights:

> To have imprisoned men solely on account of their political opinions, is enough to bring eternal infamy on every individual connected with the Administration; but the manner in which we have been treated since our confinement, is, if possible, even more disgraceful to them. I should have supposed that, if the Government chose to confine citizens because their sentiments were distasteful to it, it would have contented itself with keeping them in custody, but would have put them in tolerably comfortable quarters. . . . If I had been told, twelve months ago, that the American people would ever have permitted their rulers, under any pretence whatever, to establish such a despotism as I have witnessed, I should have indignantly denied the assertion; and if I had been then told that officers of the Army would ever consent to be the instruments to carry out the behest of a vulgar dictator, I should have predicted that they would rather have stripped their epaulets from their shoulders. But we live to learn; and I have learned much in the past few months.

Fourteen months after his arrest, Francis Key Howard was released from prison. Howard and many other Marylanders had refused an early release because that release was based upon their accepting the government's charge that they were criminals. Instead, without the benefit of legal counsel, they remained in prison while denouncing the tyranny of the Lincoln administration. As Howard stated:

> Each . . . had determined at the outset to resist, to the uttermost, the dictatorship of Abraham Lincoln . . . We came out of prison as we had gone in, holding in the same just scorn and detestation the despotism under which the country was prostrate, and with a stronger resolution than ever to oppose it by every means to which, as American freemen, we had the right to resort.[34]

In his treatise on slavery, St. George Tucker described three forms of slavery: domestic slavery—the ownership of one person by another; civil slavery—the reduction of an individual's liberty by an abusive government; and political slavery—the denial by one nation of another nation's right of self-government. Although he is credited with freeing many slaves, which has been shown he did not do, Lincoln was responsible for the introduction into America of two forms of slavery which our Founding Fathers and patriots of 1776 had eliminated. With the introduction of Federal censorship of the mails, the arbitrary military arrest of civilians, the illegal suspension of *habeas corpus,* the suspension of elected legislatures, the jailing of political opponents, and the total abridgement of the First Amendment right of the press, Lincoln gave the United States its first real taste of civil slavery since the expulsion of King George's army. As commander-in-chief of the United States military, Lincoln directed the invasion and conquest of thirteen sovereign states that had allied themselves together and established the Confederate States of America. In so doing, Lincoln ushered in an age of American international conquest. The Confederacy, Cuba, Hawaii, Panama, Puerto Rico, and the Philippines have all fallen victims to the Yankee aggressor. These nations were denied their right to govern themselves as they saw fit (i.e., government by the consent of the governed), and therefore are reduced to political slavery. Rather than being the great standard-bearer for the flag of freedom, Abraham Lincoln was the purveyor of political and civil slavery.

SUMMARY

No one should ever challenge Abraham Lincoln's stated antislavery views. The record is replete with accounts of his speaking out against the evil of slavery. But in this view, Lincoln differed little from other Americans who likewise saw slavery as an evil that needed to be abolished. There were many Americans, including Southerners, who were even bolder in their efforts to end slavery than Lincoln. St. George Tucker of Virginia was an early advocate of ending slavery and *also* was one of the first Americans of prominence to question discriminatory laws against free people of color. Robert E. Lee not only ridiculed the institution of slavery but, at great personal expense to himself, freed his slaves. Nevertheless, it is Lincoln, who never freed any slaves for which he suffered pecuniary loss, and, it is Lincoln, who never sought social justice for freed slaves, who is the icon of liberty and equality in America today. Just as in every other issue that surrounds the question of slavery, common knowledge and historical fact are often at odds. Lincoln's abuse of freedom and liberty of American citizens (most of whom were Northerners) is enough to rank him as an American tyrant. His actions against Maryland alone would be sufficient to secure for him that just title. Is it any wonder that the state song of Maryland states:

> The despot's heel is on thy shore, Maryland! My Maryland!
> His torch is at thy temple door, Maryland! My Maryland!
> Avenge the patriotic gore
> That flecked the streets of Baltimore,
> And be the battle queen of yore,
> Maryland! My Maryland![35]

MYTH: Lincoln freed the slaves.

REALITY: The slaves of the United States were ultimately freed by the passage of the Thirteenth Amendment to the Constitution. Both as a candidate for office and in his first inaugural address, Lincoln stated that he would not interfere with slavery where it then existed. As shown by his own words, his view of slavery and "the colored race" was subservient to his war objectives. The Emancipation Proclamation clearly stated that the only slaves that were to be freed were those slaves within the states or portion of those states that were in "rebellion" against Federal authority. All other slaves were left as if the document had never been written. Lincoln said he freed the slaves where he had no power to do so; yet, in those areas where he did have the power to free slaves, he did not do so.

MYTH: Lincoln was a friend to African-Americans.

REALITY: Lincoln's views of African-Americans were little or no different from the views held by the majority of Americans of his day, North or South. Lincoln viewed the African in America as an inferior being who could not be trusted with an independent life within a free nation. Although this view is scoffed at today, it was commonly held during the nineteenth century, and its influence reached into every aspect of life that dealt with the issue of slavery and African-American freedom. The very words of Lincoln, "I am in favor of having the superior position assigned to the white race," would scandalize anyone advocating such a policy today. Yet, this was Lincoln's view. Some have postulated that his views on white supremacy changed just before his death. If so, there is little proof to maintain that theory. What is for sure is that Lincoln's white supremacy views were maintained by the bulk of Americans both North and South for almost hundred years after his death. Lincoln does not sound like a great benefactor of the (using one of his less offensive terms) "colored race."

MYTH: Of all of America's leaders, Abraham Lincoln had the greatest influence.

REALITY: While it is beyond doubt that Lincoln and his administration have had the most pronounced influence upon the art of government in the United States since the adoption of the Constitution, the question is of the nature of that change in government. Lincoln did enforce the authority of the Federal government throughout the Southern states, but in so doing he destroyed the concept of a Union of sovereign states. Beyond that fact, how has the nature of the Federal government changed since Lincoln?

Most people accept the idea that the South after the War was dramatically changed, but what about the change in the nation as a whole? Seventy years after the Constitution was ratified, Lincoln was elected president. During that seventy years it was not unusual at all to hear people say that "*these* United States *are*" a great republic. This was because the United States was not thought of as a single republic but as a republic of republics. In the Federalist Papers, James Madison referred to the proposed nation as a "compound republic."[36] Many other commentators have referred to the United States as a "republic of republics." As William Rawle pointed out in his textbook on the Constitution, the one unequivocal constitutional requirement for a state to be a member of the Union is that it be and remain a republic.[37] Each state (i.e., republic), uniting with its sister republics, forms a compound republic or a republic of republics—these United States of America. That concept changed after the South was denied its right to self-government at the end of the War for Southern Independence.

As a result of Lincoln's administration, much more about the United States has changed. Before Lincoln's war, the Federal government's total revenue did not exceed 2 percent of the national economic output. Now, more than 135 years after the War, the

Federal government requires revenues in the amount of at least 20 percent of the nation's economic output. Before the War, most Americans never came into contact with a Federal official unless it was at the local post office. Lincoln's government instituted drafts, high taxes, regulations, and surveillance in unparalleled proportions. Today it is impossible to do the most mundane act without coming into contact or conflict with some Federal law, regulation, or decree. Big government requires big revenues. Lincoln gave America big government. Big intrusive government is exactly what the Founding Fathers in 1776 were fighting against.

MYTH: Lincoln was elected as president and therefore had a mandate to "save the Union."

REALITY: Regardless of how many or how few votes any candidate receives, the president has only one mandate and that is to "preserve, protect, and defend the constitution of the United States."[38] We will not retrace the litany of constitutional abuses by Lincoln already cataloged in this chapter, but a review of his assault upon the Constitution proves that he did not keep his pledge to "protect and defend the constitution." Even if it is assumed that by a majority vote of the people of the United States, a president could be licensed to abuse the Constitution, Lincoln still falls short of obtaining that prerogative. In his first election, Lincoln received slightly more than 39 percent of all votes cast for president. No less that 60 percent of American voters voted for someone other than Lincoln—not too much of a "mandate." Most Americans believe that by the election for his second term as president, Lincoln was elected by an overwhelming majority of the voters. How could Americans who knew him best not vote for their emperor-god? It is true that Lincoln defeated his Democratic challenger in 1864. Yet, the vote tally is very enlightening. Out of a total vote of approximately 4,000,000 votes, Lincoln won by only 400,000 votes. The vote count was Lincoln 2,200,000, and Gen. George McClellan 1,800,000. It must be remembered that this was not a complete "American" vote count. Southerners were voting against Lincoln, not with ballots (since he was not on Southern state tickets), but with bullets (with Southern blood, sweat, and tears). If the uncounted Southern vote is added to the Northern anti-Lincoln vote, it is clear that Abraham Lincoln was a minority president—therefore, where is the mandate?

CHAPTER 7

Slavery and the Confederate States of America

The importation of negroes of the African race, from any foreign country, other than the slaveholding States or Territories of the United States of America, is hereby forbidden, and Congress is required to pass such laws as shall effectually prevent the same.

Article I, Section 9, Paragraph 1
Constitution of the Confederate
States of America

As demonstrated, to the mind of modern liberals, the Confederate States of America and the institution of slavery are synonymous. Many Americans have bought into the lie that the Southern Confederacy was created in order to maintain and expand the slavery kingdom. Yet, it was Abraham Lincoln and not Jefferson Davis who, in his inaugural address as president,[1] promised the force of government for the protection of the institution of slavery. When one contrasts how the United States Constitution dealt with the issue of the African slave trade and how the Confederate States Constitution dealt with the issue, it is hard to believe that the Confederate States of America was established to promote slavery.

In Article I, Section 9, the United States Constitution stated:

> The migration or importation of such persons, as any of the states now existing shall think proper to admit, *shall not be prohibited* by the congress prior to the year one thousand eight hundred and eight, but a tax or duty may be imposed on such importation, not exceeding ten dollars for each person [emphasis added].

Notice that according to this section of the Constitution, the importation of African slaves was protected from 1788 until 1808 or a period of twenty years. In the year 1808, the slave trade would only end if Congress passed appropriate laws ending the nefarious trade, which it subsequently did. This section of the Constitution was adopted over the objection of a majority of Southern delegates at the Constitutional Convention, who desired an unconditional termination of the trade. In a combined effort, delegates from New England and some Southern delegates managed to obtain this protection for the slave trade. The old adage that "the power to tax is the power to destroy" must have been on the minds of those who proposed this section of the Constitution. Notice that the Federal government was denied the right to tax slaves imported into the United States at more than ten dollars per slave, thus preventing Congress from taxing the slave trade out of existence. This is just another example of the Federal Constitution's protection of the slave trade.

Now, how did the Confederate Constitution treat the issue of the African slave trade? In both the Provisional Constitution of the Confederacy (March 1861 through February 1862) and the Constitution of the Confederate States (February 1862 through April 1865) the importation of African slaves from foreign countries was unequivocally prohibited. Unlike the United States Constitution, which first protected the slave trade for twenty years and then only allowed Congress at a later date to act on the issue, the Confederate Constitution completely outlawed the slave trade. Not only did the Confederate Constitution prohibit further importation of African slaves, but the Confederate Congress was required by its Constitution to pass all necessary laws to prevent said importation. Unlike the United States Constitution in which Congress was given the *option* to legislate against the slave trade twenty years after the adoption of the Constitution, the Confederate Constitution *commanded* the legislature to positively act against the slave trade.

Only one small exception to the importation of African slaves was allowed in the Confederate Constitution. The first paragraph of Section 9 stated that slaves from the slaveholding states or territories of the United States of America would be allowed into the Confederacy. Nevertheless, in the second paragraph of Section 9, Congress was given the authority to prohibit even that importation. Paragraph 2 stated:

> Congress shall also have power to prohibit the introduction of slaves from any State not a member of, or Territory not belonging to, this Confederacy.

Is it not more than just a little strange that the American Constitution that was adopted with the assistance of New England *protected* the African slave trade, whereas the Constitution that was adopted by the South unequivocally *prohibited* the African slave trade?

But how did the Confederate Constitution deal with the issue of slavery itself? In Paragraph 4 of Section 9 the Confederate Constitution stated:

> No bill of attainder, or *ex post facto* law, or law denying or impairing the right of property in negro slaves, shall be passed.

Article I, Section 9, of the Confederate Constitution comprised the limitations on the central government and therefore protection for individual civil rights. This section was analogous to the protection for civil rights found in the Bill of Rights of the Federal Constitution. The limitations of Article I, Section 9, of the Confederate Constitution were limits on the power of the Confederate government, *not* the state governments. Whereas the central government of the Confederacy was prohibited from interfering with the institution of slavery, the state governments were not so limited. It will be noted that limitations on the actions of the state governments of the Confederate States were listed in Article I, Section 10, of the Confederate Constitution. Each of the three paragraphs began with the words "No State shall." A reading of Section 10 will prove that the states of the Confederacy were not prohibited from abolishing the institution of slavery.

This section of the Confederate Constitution has provided an opportunity for many to assert that the Confederate Constitution "recognized and protected slavery." Of course, the Confederate Constitution protected slavery in the same manner that the Federal Constitution protected slavery. A review of how the United States Constitution dealt with the issue of slavery will demonstrate this point. The Federal Constitution protected the African slave trade (Article I, Section 9); it recognized the master's right in the property of his slaves (Article IV, Section 2); and it viewed the slave as only three-fifths as valuable as a white man (Article I, Section 2). Both the Constitution of the United States and the Constitution of the Confederate States recognized and protected the right of a master to his slave property. As has already been demonstrated in preceding chapters, whether it was reclaiming fugitive slaves, protecting the African slave trade, or counting slaves as less valuable than white people, the North was the leader in these actions. Furthermore, the Confederate Constitution did not protect slavery any more than Lincoln said he would do, both in his debates with Douglas and in his inaugural address. In addressing the issue of slavery within a state, Lincoln said:

> There has never been any reasonable cause for such apprehension. Indeed, the most ample evidence to the contrary has all the while existed. . . . It is found in nearly all the published speeches of him who now addresses you. I do but quote from one of those speeches when I declare that "I have no purpose, directly or indirectly, to interfere with the institution of slavery in the States where it exists."[2]

Again, the author cites Lincoln to point out that Jefferson Davis and the Confederate government were doing no more than that which Lincoln had gone on record as favoring himself. How can the Confederate government be charged with being a defender of slavery for advancing the same ideas that Abraham Lincoln advocated?

Even though the Confederate Constitution outlawed the importation of African slaves, the detractors of the Confederacy still maintain that the Southern Confederacy existed to promote slavery. Yet, the very first veto that President Jefferson Davis issued was a veto to support the letter and spirit of the Confederate constitutional prohibition against the importation of African slaves. In the body of his veto message, President Davis declared the reason he felt justified in refusing to sign the proposed bill. His recommendation that the bill not be passed was upheld by the Confederate Congress. Thus, it is hard to maintain that the Confederate States government was attempting to expand the African slave trade

> Veto Message
> Executive Department, February 28, 1861
> Montgomery, Alabama, C.S.A.
>
> Gentlemen of Congress: With sincere deference to the judgement of Congress, I have carefully considered the bill in relation to the slave trade, and to punish persons offending therein, but have not been able to approve it, and therefore do return it with a statement of my objections. The Constitution (section 7, article 1)[3] provides that the importation of African

negroes from any foreign country other than slave-holding States of the United States is hereby forbidden, and Congress is required to pass such laws as shall effectually prevent the same. The rule herein given is emphatic, and distinctly directs the legislation which shall effectually prevent the importation of African negroes. The bill before me denounces as high misdemeanor the importation of African negroes or other persons of color, either to be sold as slaves or to be held to service or labor, affixing heavy, degrading penalties on the act, if done with such intent. To that extent it accords with the requirements of the Constitution, but in the sixth section of the bill provision is made for the transfer of persons who may have been illegally imported into the Confederate States to the custody of foreign States or societies, upon condition of deportation and future freedom, and if the proposition thus to surrender them shall not be accepted, it is then made the duty of the President to cause said negroes to be sold at public outcry to the highest bidder in any one of the States where such sale shall not be inconsistent with the laws thereof. This provision seems to me to be in opposition to the policy declared in the Constitution—the prohibition of the importation of African negroes—and in derogation of its mandate to legislate for the effectuation of that object. Wherefore the bill is returned to you for further consideration, and together with objections, most respectfully submitted.

Jeff'n Davis

The preceding veto message as well as the actual words of the Confederate Constitution are historic fact. Nevertheless, sycophants of the politically correct view of the Confederate States of America still cling to the premise that the Confederacy was founded for the purpose of promoting and defending slavery. By reviewing the historical record, it is easy to establish the fact that the Confederate States of America was opposed to the African slave trade. But before the Confederacy was established, Southerners were accused of pressing forward with the "extension of slavery." From the time of the Wilmot Proviso, the North had attempted to limit the introduction of slaves into the commonly held territories of the United States. The North maintained that such movement would result in an increase in slavery in the United States. The South, on the other hand, responded by assuring the country that with the prohibition on the African slave trade, the number of slaves would remain the same regardless of where the slaves lived. For instance, if there were one million slaves residing in Virginia, the movement of one half of that number to the commonly held territories would not increase the number of slaves in the United States. The South reminded the North that the Constitution recognized and protected property in slaves and that Southerners gave their lives in the acquisition of those territories in greater numbers than the North had done. Also, if emancipation of slavery was the objective of all, then the dispersal of African-Americans over a larger area would make that eventual goal easier to obtain. Jefferson Davis stated that the movement of slaves into the territories "never did, and never could imply the addition of a single slave to the number already existing."[4] The issue for the South was a question of how its citizens would be treated by the national government. As Davis explained:

> The question was merely whether the slaveholder should be permitted to go, with his slaves, into territory (the common property of all) into which the non-slaveholder should be permitted to go with *his* property of any sort. There was no proposal nor desire on the part of the Southern States to reopen the slave-trade, which they had been foremost in suppressing, or to add to the number of slaves. It was a question of the distribution, or dispersion, of slaves, rather than the "extension of slavery." Removal is not extension. Indeed, if emancipation was the end to be desired, the dispersion of the negroes over a wider area among additional Territories, eventually to become States, and in climates unfavorable to slave-labor, instead of hindering, would have promoted this object by, diminishing the difficulties in the way of ultimate emancipation.[5]

As Davis pointed out in *The Rise and Fall of the Confederate Government,* the objection of the North to allowing slaves into the territories had more to do with reducing the influence of the South in the national government than with promoting freedom. Henry Cabot Lodge, in a letter to Sen. Thomas Pickering of Massachusetts, pointed out why the North was opposing the growth of the South. Lodge noted that with the growth of the South "the influence of *our* part of the Union must be diminished by the acquisition of more weight at the other extremity."[6] The desire to prevent the South from gaining new states in the territories, and the desire to keep the African-American population at a minimum—and not the desire for freedom—was the driving force for the North on this issue.

The South saw the attack on the issue of slavery not so much as an attempt to end slavery in the United States as much as an attempt to end Southern influence in the national government. If the North was not willing to honor a constitutional right on this point, how could the interests and rights of the South be secured on any point? It must be pointed out once again that the Constitution of the United States never authorized the Federal government to interfere with the institution of slavery, but it did impose an obligation on the Federal government to protect slavery (Article IV, Section 2), the so-called fugitive slave section. During the time of the debate over the issue of slavery in the territories, the South recognized that all of its rights, not just the right to move slave property into commonly held territories, were at risk.

Although Kansas and other territories to the west offered little hope of a Southern-style plantation system, a firm demand was maintained to keep slavery out of the territories. In the West, neither climate nor soil was favorable to the types of agriculture that necessitated the introduction of the institution of slavery. A few slaves did move with their masters into Kansas and with them many non-slaveholding Southerners. Without a strong plantation system in place, the likelihood of a new state remaining a slave state was very slim. Davis stated that the agitation surrounding the question of slavery in the territories was simply sophism to advance the cause of Northern dominance of the Federal government.

> [T]he "war-cry" was employed by the artful to inflame the minds of the less informed and less discerning; that it was adopted in utter disregard of the means by which negro emancipation might have been peaceably accomplished in the Territories, and with the sole object of obtaining sectional control and personal promotion by means of popular agitation.[7]

Thus, the Radical Abolitionists demanded immediate abolition of slavery but denied the South a chance to do what the North had done when it abolished slavery (i.e., decrease the numbers of African-Americans within its states).

If the issue of slavery in the territories was of great importance to the North, the secession of the Southern states from the Union should have been met with cries of joy. A prompt and complete end of slaves moving into the territories would have been realized once there were no more slave states in the Union. But as events around Fort Sumter would prove, the North would both refuse to allow the South equal rights in the commonly held territories of the Union and refuse to allow the South to peacefully leave the Union. At this point, Southerners began to believe that the United States Constitution could no longer protect any of their liberties. It is no wonder then that Southerners, non-slaveholders and slaveholders alike, would unite against such a perceived danger.

SUMMARY

No doubt, the most commonly held misconception about the Confederate States of America is that it was founded by slaveholders to promote and protect slavery in America. This falsehood is asserted even though the South led the nation in the founding of abolition societies and the emancipation of slaves. It has often been stated that because the states of the Confederacy were slaveholding states, they cannot be said to have been fighting for freedom. Yet, in 1776, every American state that had declared its independence from Great Britain was a "slave state." Surely, more slaves were owned in the South in comparison to the North, but then the North was much more heavily engaged in the African slave trade than the South. If, in 1861, the Confederacy is to be condemned for the institution of slavery then in existence within the South, what can be said of the United States where *both* slavery and the African slave trade existed?

As demonstrated, the very first American constitution that unequivocally outlawed the importation of African slaves into this country was the Constitution of the Confederate States of America. Confederate President Jefferson Davis's first veto as president was issued on a bill that was considered by Davis to be in conflict with the spirit and letter of the Confederate Constitution's proscription of the African slave trade. While the United States Constitution had protected the African slave trade, the Constitution of the Confederate States was unambiguous about the issue—no African slave trade.

As many Southerners noted, the Achilles heel of the Southern political movement was the issue of slavery. Therefore, this issue was politicized by the enemies of the South. This was done in order to rally support for any Northern issue that was opposed by the South. This politicization of the issue of slavery eventually led to the destruction of harmonious relations between the sections of the United States and, ultimately, war. In latter-day America, race, rather than slavery, has been used with much the same effect.

MYTH: Just as Vice President Alexander H. Stephens of the Confederacy stated, the Confederate States of America was founded on slavery.

REALITY: While speaking in Savannah, Georgia, in 1861, Stephens noted that the Republican party had elements within it that were advocating the philosophy of unconditional human equality. As shown, this was not a well-received doctrine in either the North or the South. Stephens made it clear that in the South the doctrine of abject human equality was not accepted at all. Stephens stated: "Our government [the Confederacy] is founded on exactly the opposite idea; its foundations are laid; its corner-stone rests upon the great truth that the negro is not the equal of the white man; that slavery, subordination to the superior race, is his natural and normal condition."[8] Although this view of white supremacy is infrequently expressed in this age, it was a view that was agreed upon by the vast majority of Americans both North and South during the nineteenth century. As demonstrated in Chapter 6, even Abraham Lincoln expressed the view that the white race was and should remain the superior race in the United States. As pointed out, this philosophy not only served as the foundation for domestic slavery, it also served as the main support for the African slave trade, and the exclusionary laws passed by Northern states to keep freed African-Americans out of those states. If nineteenth-century Southerners are to be condemned for holding this racial view, Northerners who held the same view must also be condemned.

MYTH: By preventing the movement of slaves into new United States territories, the North was attempting to limit the growth of slavery.

REALITY: While it is not doubtful that preventing the movement of slaves into the new territories would have limited the geography of slavery, it would not, however, have done anything to limit the number of slaves in the United States. Since the elimination of the African slave trade in 1808, the number of slaves could only have increased if the birth rate of slaves had been greater than their death rate. Therefore, the number of slaves would have remained the same regardless of how the slaves were diffused over the geography of the United States. With their strong prejudice of race, Northerners did not desire to have African-Americans in the territories that would become free states; they did not like slavery, and neither did they like African-Americans. Also, by keeping slavery and Southerners out of territories that were to become new states, Northerners could insure their control of the apparatus of the Federal government. As Lodge stated. "[T]he influence of *our* part of the Union [the North] must be diminished by the acquisition of more weight at the other extremity [the South]."[9]

MYTH: Although the fugitive slave section is part of the United States Constitution, it was only placed there to appease Southern slaveholders.

REALITY: As explained in Chapter 2, the fugitive slave portion of the United States Constitution is but a copy of the very first such law ever passed by an American political body. That act was passed by the United Colonies of New England. It was enacted for the same reason the Fugitive Slave Act was placed into the United States Constitution. Without question, the Southern states had more to gain by the adoption of this portion of the Constitution; nevertheless, every state that acceded to the Federal Constitution recognized the right of the master in his slave property and thus needed this protection. After slavery was abolished in the North, only the South was served by this portion of the Constitution; but the South had just as much right to this constitutional protection as did the New England colonies when they first wrote the Fugitive Slave Act into law. No section of the country has a right to decide which portion of the Constitution it will or will not obey. If the North no longer wanted the fugitive slave portion to be in the Constitution, there was a *constitutional* method of removing it—the amendment process. If the North could not change the Constitution by legal methods, did that give it the right to do so by illegal methods? The fugitive slave section of the United States Constitution was a legal portion of the Constitution, written by representatives of both sections of the United States, and acceded to by each state. The North is just as responsible for the fugitive slave portion of the Constitution as the South. As Abraham Lincoln himself stated, "When they [Southerners] remind us of their constitutional rights, I acknowledge them, not grudgingly, but fully and fairly; and I would give them any legislation for the reclaiming of their fugitives."[10] The North wrote the Fugitive Slave Law, and Lincoln acknowledged it as legitimate; how could anyone believe that this was a "Southern" portion of the Constitution?

MYTH: The Confederate States Constitution demanded that every state within that confederation be a slave state.

REALITY: Nowhere in the Confederate Constitution can one find a mandate that every state of the Confederacy had to maintain slavery. The Confederate Constitution, being the very epitome of a State's Rights document, left domestic institutions completely in the hands of the people of the sovereign states. What the Confederate Constitution did do was mandate that the central government not interfere with the institutions within any Confederate state. The Confederate Constitution did, however, mandate the abolition of the African slave trade and allow Congress to legislate against the importation of any slaves from any state or territory of the United States.

CHAPTER 8

The Flag of Slavery

> *The flags of the Confederacy represented the aspirations of a brave and resourceful people. . . . Their desire to live under a government based upon "the consent of the governed" should be respected.*[1]
>
> Devereaux D. Cannon
>
> *The Flags of the Confederacy*

The myth of the Confederate flag as the "flag of slavery" is, without a doubt, the most persistent and pervasive misconception in modern America. Very seldom do the agents of modern information (i.e., the liberal media) present information about the nature of the Confederate flag in an even-handed and impartial manner. Since the time of the modern civil rights movement, the Confederate flag has been inextricably linked with the most vile and degraded elements within Southern society. For example, the misuse of the Confederate flag by hate groups is quickly picked up and broadcast in newspapers and on television. Yet, when respected members of the community join with a historic organization such as the Sons of Confederate Veterans and correctly display and use the Confederate flag, the media will seldom report the appropriate use of the flag. For the average citizens, the impression they get from the media is that "only ignorant and evil people wave the Confederate flag." Is it any wonder then that people of color have difficulty in discriminating between real racists who are misusing the Confederate flag and Americans who wave the Confederate flag to express their love for their ancestors and to honor their country?

For a better understanding of the complete truth about the Confederate flag, two questions must be addressed: (1) Is the flag of the Confederate States of America the flag of slavery? and, (2) Is that flag the symbol of racism in America? Before exploring these questions, it will be necessary to give a brief overview of the use of flags in general during the nineteenth century, and also to look at what constitutes a true Confederate flag.

During the nineteenth century, flags were an essential element in the deployment of large military units. Flags were essential to unit placement, unit recognition, and unit cohesion upon the field of battle. When a battalion advanced in "line of battle," it was the regimental colors that provided the sure guide for that advancement. When the battle line was broken, it was the regimental flag that was the focal point for rallying the troops. These flags became the symbol of unit pride and, as more and more men died in defense of their flag, near adoration.

To some extent, the modern concept about flag etiquette can be traced to the use of flags in the past. For example, it is considered a disgrace to allow a state or national flag to touch the ground. This concept is related to how flags were used during battle. If, during an engagement, the color bearer was shot and his flag was dropped, the line of battle and unit cohesion would be in jeopardy, and thus the battle would be lost. Rather than allowing this tragedy to happen, a brave soldier would scoop the flag from his fallen comrade's hands and continue the advance while holding high the colors for his fellow soldiers to see and follow, thus becoming a prime target for the enemy in the process. It would be a great shame if in a large body of men there were no one who was willing to advance the colors. Today, we honor our state and nation by never allowing their flags to touch the ground, just as our forefathers did in the nineteenth century. For all armies, flags became honored emblems of valor and patriotism. At Appomattox it was not unusual to see battle-hardened men moved to tears as they surrendered their regimental flags. Stories of men rushing up to kiss the furled flag and others standing in tattered uniforms displaying the marks of many a hard-fought battle, weeping like children at the death of a beloved pet—all because of the loss of their cherished flag. What was true at Appomattox is true with all American flags, state and national. When we offer respect to these flags, we are not honoring cloth and ink. Like those brave men at Appomattox, we honor those who were willing to give their lives for their country and the principles those men held dear; this is why no true American wishes to see any flag of this nation burned or otherwise disrespected.

When discussing the Confederate flag, people often make the mistake of referring to one of the battle flags of the Confederacy as "the Confederate flag." The Confederate flag and the Confederate battle flag are not one and the same. The Confederate flag is the *official* flag of the Confederate States of America. There were three officially accepted flags adopted by the Confederate Congress which may correctly be referred to as "the Confederate flag." The three flags are known as the First, Second, and Third National Flags of the Confederacy. The First is often called "the Stars and Bars." Looking somewhat like the famous Betsy Ross American flag, the Stars and Bars displayed seven stars (later increased to thirteen) in a circle in the canton (upper left corner) and two bars of red separated by a white bar extending the distance of the fly of the flag not covered by the canton. The traditional "Rebel" flag is often incorrectly labeled as the Stars and Bars. The Second National Flag of the Confederacy consisted of a white flag with the traditional Confederate battle flag in the canton. The canton is red with a blue St. Andrew's cross (resembling an "X") bordered by white stripes and displaying thirteen white stars. This flag was adopted on May 1, 1863, in time to be draped over the coffin of Gen. Stonewall Jackson as he lay in state at the Confederate capitol in Richmond. The Third National Flag of the Confederacy was adopted on March 4, 1865. Because the Second National Flag of the Confederacy was essentially white, in the absence of a breeze the flag often resembled a white flag of surrender. This defect was corrected by Congress with the addition of a wide red outer portion to the flag. Consisting of approximately one-half the distance from the outer edge of the canton to the end of the fly, this red section eliminated the confusion caused by the mostly white Second National Flag. Thus, the current flag of the Confederate States of America is a white flag with a red canton and blue St. Andrew's cross, emblazoned with thirteen white stars, and a red bar extending the width of the flag on the outer third of the fly.

The so-called Rebel flag or battle flag was never adopted by the Congress of the Confederate States but was adopted and extensively used by the military forces of the Confederacy. Although it is the most commonly recognized flag of the South, it did not represent the government or nation of the Confederate States of America. The most commonly recognized Confederate battle flag is a rectangular red battle flag with a blue St. Andrew's cross bordered by white strips and emblazoned with thirteen white stars. This flag was more often associated with troops of the Confederate Army of Tennessee and was also used by the Confederate States Navy as a naval jack. The same flag in a square form was more often associated with the Confederate Army of Northern Virginia. Even though these are the more commonly recognized battle flags of the Confederate armies, they are by no means the only or the most numerous types of Confederate battle flags. Many Confederate battle flags, although well known by Southern and Northern troops at the time, are hardly recognized today as being associated with the Southern struggle for independence. Flags such as the battle flags of Confederate generals William D. Hardee and Leonidas Polk of the Army of Tennessee are classic examples (see photographs in this book).

In today's politically correct environment, the flag of the Confederacy is viewed as a symbol of slavery, racism, and hate. These offenses are attributed to the Confederate flag by its detractors, not its defenders. Those who attempt to promote a positive and historically correct view of the Confederate flag are often confronted with the charge that they are "defending slavery." Obviously, if what has been presented in the preceding chapters is true, the charge that the Confederate flag is the flag of slavery is simply incorrect. But, let us look into this charge of being the flag of slavery. Is there a flag in American history that could be reasonably charged with being the flag of slavery?

As has been pointed out, when the thirteen original colonies declared their independence, a vigorous and healthy system of slavery and the slave trade existed within each new state; the Constitution of these United States recognized and protected the institution of slavery in the new nation, and the flag of these United States was used by slave traders to protect their nefarious commerce. According to John R. Spears, who studied and reported on the African slave trade in the late nineteenth century, the use of the United States flag to protect slave traders provided the means by which many slave ships were allowed to continue their voyages, even though "the hold [of each slave ship] was full of sweltering, suffocating slaves."[2] It was not long before it became common knowledge among the slavers that the United States flag would protect their human cargo. In this regard Spears stated:

> Finding that our [U.S.] flag protected the slave-ship under such circumstances, the slavers made haste to get under it. Within ten years after we had by statute declared the slaver a pirate the majority of the slave-ships were not only built, but they were sailed to the coast of Africa under the American flag.
>
> There is no blacker chapter in the history of our country than that which tells how our flag became and was maintained for thirty odd years as the shield of the slaver, while those who thus degraded it—including members of every administration and Congress of the period—with loudmouthed pretence declared that they detested the trade.[3]

At the inception of both the United States and the Confederate States, slavery was a recognized legal institution. Furthermore, in 1776 the African slave trade was an important element in the North's commerce, whereas, in 1861 the Confederate States of America had unequivocally crushed that nefarious trade. With this fact in mind, how can anyone condemn the Confederate flag as being the flag of slavery while praising the United States flag as the flag of freedom? Having to yield the point that the Confederate flag is not the flag of slavery, many detractors of the South will denounce the Confederate flag as being a symbol of American racism.

The notion that all interracial relationships "down South" are based upon black/white confrontation is a cherished misconception of many in the North. This being the case in the minds of many, it only makes sense that the Confederate flag is a racist symbol. Yet, there is a flag in the United States that is a symbol of racism that is never condemned as the Confederate flag is condemned—the United States flag. As demonstrated, the United States flag is the flag of the African slave trader, and the nation it represents went to great efforts to protect both slave property and the slave trade. This alone would mark the United States flag as being just as much a symbol of racism, if not more so, than the Confederate flag. But the racist attitude of the United States in its relations with Native Americans makes more plausible the assertion of racism against the United States flag than the Confederate flag. The story has been told in many different places by many different people: the Trail of Tears, Sandy Creek, and Wounded Knee. The fundamental relationship between the Native American people and the government of the United States is one based upon a racist philosophy. Many of those who are revered for their efforts in crushing the South are the very same people who led the effort to eliminate the Native Americans.

According to the liberal view of the Yankee invasion of the South, the North was fighting for freedom and equality in America. Yet, while Yankee troops were ravaging the South during the War for Southern Independence, in 1862 they were also engaged in a campaign of genocide against the American Indians. Union general John Pope gave expression to how the "Indian problem" was to be handled when he stated, "It is my purpose to utterly exterminate the Sioux."[4] Pope planned to make a "final settlement with all these Indians." His plan was to shoot and hang as many as possible and then remove the rest from the land.[5] Here is how General Pope described the Native American population to his troops: "They are to be treated as maniacs or wild beasts, and by no means as people with whom treaties or compromise can be made."[6] Abraham Lincoln's secretary of the navy, Gideon Wells, made it clear as to what was motivating the Federal government's campaign against the Native Americans when he stated that the Indians "have good land which white men want and mean to have."[7] Imbued with the all too typical white supremacy dogma of the nineteenth century, the Lincoln administration had few if any qualms about destroying the culture and lives of the red man. The Native Americans were viewed as barbarians. Because of the Native Americans' non-materialistic values, the Federal government sought to overthrow their power and then remake the remaining native population into red copies of New Englanders. This is the same scheme that was attempted in the South after the defeat of the Southern armies.[8] The superior white class sought to impose its values and lifestyle to "change the disposition of the Indian to one more mercenary and ambitious to obtain riches, and teach him to value the position consequent upon the possession of riches."[9] Not only was the red man to be the recipient of this racist concept, but also the brown man was to be made subservient to this view. From Hawaii to the Philippines, the locally backed governments were overthrown and replaced with ones more to the liking of the "superior" people. Black Northerners, white Southerners, red Native Americans, and brown Hawaiians and Filipinos all had their local governments and culture destroyed by the all-powerful conquering

Northerners—a people who were convinced of their moral and cultural superiority over Southerners, and their racial superiority over the black, red, and brown peoples of the world.

In another attempt to discredit the Confederate flag, many liberals and misguided conservatives will insist that the institution of racial discrimination (i.e., segregation) is the product, or at least the outgrowth, of slavery. Therefore, the South and the Confederate flag represent (in their narrow-minded view) the epitome of racial discrimination in America. Of course, this view overlooks two hundred years of discriminatory laws written and enforced in the North prior to the defeat of the South in 1865. Yes, America has a long history of laws that discriminate against nonwhites. As will be recalled, a Southerner, St. George Tucker, spoke out in opposition to such laws in 1808. But it was in 1898 that the United States Supreme Court made such laws the "law of the land." In a landmark decision, *Plessey v. Ferguson,* the Federal, not the Confederate, Supreme Court approved the doctrine of separate but equal (i.e., segregation) in the United States and affirmed that anyone with at least one-eighth Negro blood was legally a Negro.[10] Although the South often gets blamed for this decision because the case originated in Louisiana, it was the Federal Supreme Court that announced the reality of segregation in America. For those who are determined to blame the South for this decision, a look at how and by whom this Supreme Court decision was made is instructive. In denying that the Fourteenth Amendment offered protection against discrimination based upon color, Justice Henry B. Brown of Minnesota, stated, "[I]n the nature of things it [the Fourteenth Amendment] could not have been intended to abolish distinctions based upon color, or to enforce social, as distinguished from political equality, or a commingling of the two races upon terms unsatisfactory to either."[11] Citing an 1849 Massachusetts law mandating separate schools for colored children as the premise for the majority ruling, Justice Brown noted that segregation in schools and society existed even "where the political rights of the colored race have been longest and most earnestly enforced."[12] Please note once again that this was the Federal Supreme Court and not a Confederate court or a Southern state court that was declaring racial discrimination (i.e., segregation) the "law of the land." Segregation became the "law of the land" in 1898 not because the South imposed its will upon the United States, but rather because a Federal Supreme Court justice from Minnesota, citing a law mandating racially segregated schools in Massachusetts, wrote a majority decision (only one judge voted against the majority decision—it was not even close) that instituted racial discrimination in America.

After the defeat of the South, during Reconstruction, the Congress of the United States established a segregated public school system for children in Washington, D.C. These schools were segregated until after the 1954 *Brown v. Topeka* Supreme Court decision which overturned *Plessey v. Ferguson.* Therefore, Dixie cannot be blamed for segregation. It should be remembered that during the middle of the twentieth century at least twenty-six out of forty-eight states in the Union at that time had laws providing for some form of segregation. Again, the author reminds the reader that there were only thirteen Confederate States of America. Thus, an equal number of border states and non-Southern states had laws promoting racial segregation as provided by the United States Supreme Court. The claim of the left that the South is to blame for the evils of slavery and racism in America cannot be substantiated by historic fact.

Few people have grasped the feelings that Southerners held for the flag of the Confederacy as did Fr. Abram J. Ryan. As a priest, he served as the religious shepherd of his community of faith. As the "poet priest" of the Confederacy, Father Ryan offered solace and hope to a defeated people. His Confederate poetry included such works as "The Land We Love," in which he touches on the loss that the South suffered, yet reminds us of the hope that remains:

Land where the victor's flag waves,
Where only the dead are the free!
Each link of the chain that enslaves,
But binds us to them and to thee.[13]

In "A Land Without Ruins" Father Ryan explains how truly poor a land is when it is not peopled with those who will risk ruin of material possessions in the defense of a noble cause:

Yes, give me a land that is blest by the dust,
And bright with the deeds of the down-trodden just. . .
Yes, give me a land with a grave in each spot,
And names in the graves that shall not be forgot . . .
And the graves of the dead with the grass overgrown
May yet form the footstool of liberty's throne.[14]

In "The Prayer of the South," Father Ryan reminds the South of its duty as a Christian society to pray not only for its loss but also for those who are responsible for that loss:

Forgive my foes—they know not what they do—
Forgive them all the tears they made me shed;
Forgive them, though my noblest sons they slew,
And bless them, though they curse my poor, dear dead.[15]

In these small excerpts of some of Father Ryan's many poems we see expressed a strong and resolute love for the Southern cause, a love that lived long after the defeat of the South. For many Southerners, his most touching work was entitled "The Conquered Banner":

Furl that Banner, for 'tis weary;
Round its staff 'tis drooping dreary;
Furl it, fold it, it is best;
For there's not a man to wave it,
And there's not a sword to save it,
And there's not one left to lave it
In the blood which heroes gave it;
And its foes now scorn and brave it;
Furl it, hide it—let it rest![16]

It may come as a surprise to many, but some sources claim that the most popular song that came out of the South during the War was not "Dixie" but "The Bonnie Blue Flag." "The Bonnie Blue Flag" was written by Harry Macarthy, a European-born entertainer who migrated to Arkansas in 1849. He premiered "The Bonnie Blue Flag" during a concert in Jackson, Mississippi, at the conclusion of the 1861 secession convention of Mississippi. Macarthy was present when the convention of the people of the state of Mississippi voted to secede from the Union. When the vote was announced, a cry of joy went up from the people around the capitol, and a blue flag with a single white star was displayed before the crowd. Macarthy was so moved by the reaction of the people of Mississippi that he wrote "The Bonnie Blue Flag." The first verse tells the story of the feelings of the people of the South:

We are a band of brothers and native to the soil,
Fighting for our Liberty with treasure, blood and toil;
And when our rights were threaten'd,
the cry rose near and far,

Hurrah for the Bonnie Blue Flag, that bears a Single Star!
Hurrah! Hurrah! for Southern Rights, Hurrah!
Hurrah for the Bonnie Blue Flag that bears a Single Star![17]

The Bonnie Blue flag became the first Confederate flag for many Southern states as each state withdrew from the Union. As time and events progressed, the single star of the Bonnie Blue flag grew to become eleven. The struggle for Southern independence was defended by many locally raised military units. Often these units of young men were sent off to war carrying a unit flag made by the mothers, wives, and daughters of those men. These flags were as varied and distinct as those seen in any army in history. Oftentimes the flags presented by the ladies would have mottoes inscribed on them. If the war was being fought to preserve slavery, the mottoes adopted by these units do not reflect that idea. An example of a few such mottoes demonstrates that these men were fighting in what they considered to be a noble struggle for freedom and justice. Here are a few such mottoes found on various Confederate battle flags:[18]

Arkansas, Company B, Fifteenth Infantry—"Let Justice Be Done though the Heavens Fall"

Florida, Company B, Third Infantry—"Any Fate But Submission"

Georgia, Company E, First Infantry—"We Yield Not to Our Country's Foes"

Louisiana, Company K, Third Infantry—"Southern Rights Inviolate"

Maryland, Company E, First Maryland Cavalry—"Hope Is Our Watchword, Truth Our Guiding Star"

Mississippi, Company C, Thirteenth Infantry—"Protector and Avenger"

North Carolina, Company E, Sixth Infantry—"In God We Trust: Victory or Death"

South Carolina, Company B, Third Infantry—"God Guide Us"

South Carolina, Company F, Fifth Infantry—"Like Our Ancestors, We Will Be Free"

Tennessee, Company H, Seventh Infantry—"The Women of Lebanon to the Lebanon Greys. Go and Fight!"

Texas, Seventeenth Infantry—"Trust in God"

Texas, Twentieth Infantry—"Our Honor and Our Rights"

Virginia, Second Infantry—"God and Our Homes"

Virginia, Thirty-Sixth Infantry—"Sic Semper Tyrannis" (Thus Ever to Tyrants)

In the literature of their spoken words, in the lyrics of their songs, and in the mottoes emblazoned upon their banners, the people of the South declared their love for home, liberty, and their flags.

After Southern defeat and Reconstruction, the North and the South came to a tacit agreement about the War, its aftermath, and Southern heroes. The South would support the national government and not again attempt secession, while the North would acknowledge the valor, honor, and courage of the members of the Confederate war effort. This *quid pro quo* arrangement meant that the North did not have to be on guard constantly against a new Southern "rebellion" and that the men of the South could always be counted on to defend American interests. The South, on the other hand, salvaged the honor of its patriots and the honor of the cause for which it fought. Thus, on the whole, after about 1880 and up until the mid-1960s, Southern heroes such as Jefferson Davis, Robert E. Lee, Stonewall Jackson, and others were considered "American" heroes. For example, during World War II the United States built several battle tanks and named them in honor of Confederate heroes such as the US M3 A1 *Lee,* a medium tank which was put into production in 1942, and the US M3 *Stuart,* a light tank which saw extensive service in North Africa. Highways, counties, and schools throughout the United States were named in honor of Robert E. Lee, Jefferson Davis, and Stonewall Jackson. The Mississippi and Alabama National Guards composed the elements of the United States Army's Dixie Division. The term "Dixie" as well as the playing of the song "Dixie" was in near universal usage during that time. As long as both parties abided by this tacit agreement, all was well. But in this age of political correctness, Big Brother has now determined that all such displays are tantamount to a hate crime. In chastising the radicals of the North for refusing to abide by the constitutional mandate of the Fugitive Slave Act, Daniel Webster correctly noted that, "A bargain cannot be broken on one side and still bind the other side."[19] Today, Southern heroes and icons have become enemies of the existing political order in the United States, and the old agreement has been broken.

Southerners are required to fight in the wars of the United States, to obey Federal laws, and to pay Federal taxes, yet, Southern heroes and symbols are the subject of ridicule and condemnation, even to the point of being banned from public display. How long should the South be expected to continue its cooperation with a nation that will not honor an agreement made while the memory of its fathers' deeds and untimely death was still strong?

SUMMARY

In the present politically correct environment of the United States, it is not uncommon to hear the Confederate flag referred to as the flag of slavery. Although there are several national flags in the world today that are recognized by reliable anti-slavery groups as flags of nations that promote slavery, nevertheless, it is still the flag of a defeated and conquered nation, the Confederate States of America, that is held up to the world as the "flag of slavery." After fifteen years of civil war in the Sudan, Muslims from the northern part of that country routinely make raids on the southern portion of it where they shoot the men and make slaves of the women and children. The slaves taken in the southern region are non-Muslim members of Christian or animist religious sects. At this writing, a slave in Sudan can be bought for as little as ninety dollars, and such slaves are routinely beaten or mutilated for the smallest of infractions. In the Sudan, for example, a six-year-old slave failed to perform a task to the liking of his master and was punished by having his index finger cut off.[20] A thirteen-year-old girl was interviewed by a member of an anti-slavery society and described her life as a modern-day African slave. Her interviewer stated, "Throughout the day, she worked in his [her master's] sorghum fields and at night in his bed. During the march [from freedom to slavery], she was raped and called a black donkey."[21] In Mauritania, slavery is as rampant as it ever was in the old days of slavery in the Upper South. Simply put, human rights abuses such as slavery and genocide are not uncommon in Africa today. Unfortunately for those suffering from such abuses, very little attention is given these oppressed individuals by the modern liberal media. This is the same liberal media that waste no effort in ridiculing and defaming the flag of the Confederate States of America. The question is, why do liberals attack the flag of a defeated nation where slavery ended more than 150 years ago, and yet seldom have the courage to speak out about human rights abuses and slavery that are rampant in Africa today? If one-half the media coverage that is given to attacking the Confederate flag were given to the abuses of human rights occurring today in Africa, those individuals now suffering as African slaves and abused citizens of various African nations would have real hope for relief from their suffering.

From chattel slavery in Africa, child labor slaves in India, to female sex slaves of Southeast Asia, slavery is still alive in the world today. This is not to mention the political and civil slavery (see St. George Tucker, Chapter 5) that is rampant in the world today. Yes, there are numerous "flags of slavery" that can be identified today, but not one slave is currently held in the Confederate States of America. Again, the author must insist: the Confederate flag is not the flag of slavery.

MYTH: The Confederate flag is a symbol of the Ku Klux Klan and other white supremacist groups and therefore should be banned.

REALITY: One of the largest parades held by the Ku Klux Klan in America was held in 1926 in Washington, D. C. Photographs demonstrate that the flag of the Klan in that parade was *not* the Confederate flag but the flag of the United States. The use of the United States flag by the Klan and other white supremacist groups is not uncommon in the United States. The largest and strongest defender of white supremacy in the South during the civil rights struggle of the mid-twentieth century was the "Citizens' Council." The logo of the Citizens' Council displays two crossed flags, a United States flag and a Confederate States flag, with the United States flag in the position of the superior flag. If the use of the Confederate flag by these groups is sufficient to cause the banning of the Confederate flag, then what must be said about the use of the United States flag by these same groups? No one should ever be willing to surrender any portion of his heritage because of the misuse of that heritage by a hate group. Remember, the same groups that misuse the Confederate flag also misuse the United States flag, the United States Constitution, the Christian cross, and the Holy Bible. Are these icons of our history and faith to be jettisoned also because of their misuse by hate groups?

MYTH: The market for slaves in the South made the African slave trade possible; therefore, the Confederate flag is the flag of the African slave trade.

REALITY: The assumption in this statement is that the only reason Yankees were involved in the African slave trade was to meet the demands of the Southern slave market. As demonstrated in Chapter 2, 94 percent of all those taken from Africa as slaves were sent somewhere other than the South. It is hard to believe that the totality of the Northern slave trade was in response to the 6 percent demand from American slave markets. Although there was a demand for slaves both from Southern and Northern slave markets, it was the planters of the West Indies and the production of sugar that were the driving forces behind the African slave trade.[22] This demand was answered by slave traders from essentially every European nation as well as New England's maritime fleet. In the year 1740, the slaving fleet of Newport, Rhode Island, alone consisted of 120 slave ships capable of carrying from 60 to 150 slaves each. By 1750, the slave-trading fleet of that city had increased by 50 additional ships capable of carrying more than 20,000 slaves to the New World each year.[23] In 1808, by an act of the Federal Congress supported by an overwhelming majority of Southern senators and congressmen, the importation of African slaves into the United States was prohibited. Nevertheless, the commercial interests of the North maintained a strong presence among the slave-trading fleets operating between Africa and the Western Hemisphere. Northerners were active in this nefarious commerce even on the eve of the War for Southern Independence as the story of the *Nightingale* demonstrates (see Chapter 4). Although the United States had declared the slave trade to be piracy and punishable by death, only one American during the entire history of the illegal African slave trade was actually executed. On February 21, 1862, Capt. Nathaniel Gordon from New York, described as a "slaver of experience," met the fate that so many other American slavers had avoided. Even as late as 1870, five years *after* the defeat of the Confederate States of America, the United States Congress was appropriating funds for continuing its efforts to suppress the African slave trade.[24] This trade did not end until after Cuba and Brazil had abolished slavery, almost twenty years after Appomattox! Slavery and the horrors of the slave trade existed long after it had been abolished in the South, yet liberals do not condemn the flag of Cuba or the flag of Brazil as "the flag of slavery." Why is this hypocrisy not condemned by those who proclaim themselves to be defenders of fairness and equal treatment?

MYTH: As a Christian society, the South should be willing to do away with any symbol, such as the Confederate flag, that insults and offends other people.

REALITY: While most Christians have no desire to be insulting or offensive to anyone, this concern for the feelings of others by no means should be taken as a willingness to ignore the commandment that instructs Christians to "honour thy father and thy mother" (Exodus 20:12 KJV). Is allowing one's ancestors to be incorrectly condemned as evil, hate-filled individuals upholding the commandment to "honour thy father and thy mother"? Is pandering to the delusions of the ignorant the most appropriate manner for promoting good will and understanding? As has been shown throughout this book, the slave trade, slavery, and racism are not the stock-in-trade of the South nor of the Confederate flag. If people choose to be offended by a Southern symbol, or if they are possessed of a Confederate flag phobia, there is little anyone, no matter how well intentioned he may be, can do to make such people less offended. Kowtowing to the ill-founded prejudices of the misguided places one in a never-ending downward spiral of historical and cultural apologies that will only end with a total debasement of a people's collective history. Christians are called upon to know the truth, for it and it alone will set one free (John 8:32). The truth about the institution of slavery and the Confederate flag should manfully and uncompromisingly be asserted.

CHAPTER 9

On the State of Slavery in Virginia

> *I was born in Mississippi, but raised in a Northern State; associations there led me to regard the Southern white man as dire foes to the Negroes, but receiving such cordial and unprejudiced association upon this floor* [Mississippi House of Representatives] *by the entire Democratic party here these tebidus [sic] suspicions have been eliminated from the bosoms of this feeble six and for them I am authorized to speak. You are our best friends. . . . This has been termed the Jeff Davis Legislature possibly because the Republicans voted for your Confederate Monument Bill. . . . . In tendering you this, we tender a grateful hand to every Democratic member, for you have shown to be our friends, not our enemies.*[1]
>
> Rep. Phillip Moore in
> (Jackson, MS) *Daily Clarion-Ledger*
> February 23, 1890

One of the chief myths about life in the United States is that the North, unlike the South, was a place that offered freedom and justice for the African-American. In this chapter we will again look at how the African-American was viewed by Northerners prior to the War for Southern Independence and what life was like for the African-American after Yankee-induced freedom. Also, we will examine the contrast between the life of modern-day African-Americans, the descendants of slaves, and the life of modern-day Africans. In this manner, we may be able to determine whether the claims of the leftist race-pimps (Al Sharpton, Jesse Jackson, et al), who are always assuring Americans that the African-American has been harmed by the actions of bygone slaveholders, are valid.

An English observer of the American political scene noted, "The federal constitution is silent about race or color . . . [but] American lawgivers arrive at the conclusion, that the United States are the property of whites. . . . There seems, in short, to be a fixed notion throughout the whole of the states, whether slave or free, that the colored is by nature a subordinate race; and that in no circumstances, can it be considered equal to the white."[2] Note that this English observer stated that this low opinion of the "colored" race was held by people in both slave *and* free states. The degraded condition of the free people of color in the North was characterized by Rep. Charles Pinckney of South Carolina as nothing less that an attempt by Northerners to rid themselves of their African-American population. In order to accomplish this goal, Pinckney stated that Northerners were "treating them [African-Americans], on every occasion with the most marked contempt."[3] Senator John Holmes of Maine recoiled at the thought of free men of color being allowed to vote and perhaps being elected to Congress. After considering the possibility of Negroes being elected to various offices, Senator Holmes stated, "Gentlemen, with all their humanity, to be obliged to sit in this Senate by a black man, would consider their rights invaded."[4] Senator Holmes's true feelings for the free people of color is displayed in his characterization of them as "a troublesome or dangerous population." In his famous debate with Daniel Webster, Sen. Robert Y. Hayne of South Carolina described the condition of life for the free people of color in the North:

> Sir, there does not exist on the face of the earth, a population so poor, so wretched, so vile, so loathsome, so utterly destitute of all the comforts, conveniences, and decencies of life, as the unfortunate blacks of Philadelphia, and New York, and Boston. Liberty has been to them the greatest of calamities, the heaviest of curses. . . . Go home, and emancipate your free Negroes. When you do that, we will listen to you with more patience.[5]

Although the South has been tarred with the stigma of white supremacy, this philosophy was a strongly held belief among some of the most noted opponents of slavery in America; men such as David Wilmot of Pennsylvania. Most Americans will remember Representative Wilmot for his famous Wilmot Proviso which attempted to prevent the movement of Southern slave property into the newly won territories from Mexico. Promoted as a great friend of the downtrodden slave, Wilmot exhibited little real concern for the well-being of the slaves. In promoting the Wilmot Proviso he was careful to note that he had "no squeamish sensitiveness upon the subject of slavery, no morbid sympathy for the slave. . . . I plead the cause and the rights of white freemen. . . . I would preserve to the free white labor a fair country, a rich inheritance, where the sons of toil, of my own race and own color, can live without disgrace which association with negro slavery brings upon free labor."[6]

New York representative Henry C. Murphy even requested strong laws to punish anyone who would bring free people of color from the South into New York. These laws would be applied "against any who shall bring the wretched beings to our Free States, there to taint the blood of the whites, or to destroy their own race by vicious courses."[7] The preceding statements were made by elected officials both of the North and the South. Thus we see that even those who were representing the so-called free states had rather strong desires to keep their society free from the influence of African-Americans. As these citations were made before the War, the next question to be answered is how African-Americans were treated after freedom.

The disenfranchisement of many white Southerners after the War and the concomitant enfranchisement of former slaves was motivated more by a desire to promote Republican control of the South and of Congress than by any deep-seated desire to promote real political equality for African-Americans. It will be remembered that while the North was enforcing suffrage for African-Americans in the South, it was at the same time excluding them not just from the ballot boxes in the North but from the Northern states themselves.[8] During Reconstruction most of the South, both black and white, was reduced to a serf-like condition of sharecropping. The freed slaves had been uprooted and removed from the only homes and families they had known by a government that had not taken the time to prepare them for freedom. The only relationship that they had known with white people was one in which they were at least valued for their abilities. That relationship was totally destroyed by the invaders of the South and replaced with a relationship in which African-Americans were viewed as pawns by the conquering Yankees. Also, the same Congress that had pushed Reconstruction on the South had established segregated schools in Washington, D.C. By 1898, the United States Supreme Court handed down a decision in *Plessey v. Ferguson* that established the so-called separate but equal provision which made segregation the law of the land. Throughout the United States the freed slaves, unprepared as they were, began their struggle toward the American goal of equality before the law. With all its faults, it was still America that held the greatest hope for achieving the goal of equal rights for all.

From the time of the elimination of slavery to the present, African-Americans have lived and worked in a nation that once only knew them as slaves. It is from this background of hardship and discrimination that many liberals now contend that reparations are owed to the descendants of former slaves. Yet, is there evidence that the descendants of America's slave population have suffered irreparable harm because of the experiences of their ancestors? What would the lifestyle of the average African-American be like if his ancestors had not been taken out of Africa? How does the lifestyle of the average Sub-Saharan African compare with the lifestyle of an African-American living in Mississippi, one of the poorest states in the Union? By answering these questions, we will have a better understanding of the conditions of life for all Africans and be able to more correctly determine whether irreparable harm has been done to the descendants of America's slave population.

A casual examination of any major daily newspaper will provide a shocking account of life in Sub-Saharan (i.e., black) Africa. By contrasting these conditions with conditions of life in the United States, we will have a basis for determining whether the descendants of America's slave population are suffering detrimental effects because of slavery or whether the results of the enslavement of their ancestors are favorably affecting their lives. Here are just a few examples of the living conditions in Africa today:

Burundi: Dysentery, cholera, and other public health diseases keep the death rate high; life expectancy at birth as of 1998 was forty-two years.

Ivory Coast: Due to political violence (in July 1999), police are empowered to shoot anyone on the streets after 6 P.M.

Rwanda: Within the past five years, thousands have died in ethnic, black-on-black civil war.

Sierra Leone: Civil war has plagued this nation for more than eight years. A common punishment for prisoners of war is to have their arms and legs hacked off. Sierra Leone holds the world's record for the shortest life expectancy—26.5 years.

Somalia: Nothing [illegible] said here; the name alone conjures up memories of starving [illegible]en and children who are subject to abuse by various black warlords.

South Africa: With more than sixty-four thousand reported rapes per year, South Africa holds the record as the rape capital of the world.

Sudan: Civil war between the Muslim North and Christian and animist South has resulted in death, starvation, and the reintroduction of chattel slavery by the Muslims.

Tanzania: Elderly women are subject to being executed as witches. Some of these killings are a result of the "skin trade" with Zambia. It is a belief on the part of some Africans that human skins provide protection from evil spirits and demons.

Zimbabwe: Twenty-five percent of this country's population is HIV positive. Africa has the distinction of having two-thirds of the world's HIV cases.

Not one nation in Sub-Saharan Africa can boast of a stable democratic government or a lifestyle anywhere close to that enjoyed by the average African-American. For example, the life expectancy at birth for the average citizen of Sub-Saharan Africa is fifty years, and the average per capita Gross National Product in 1999 was five hundred dollars per year. An African-American in Mississippi has both a longer life expectancy and a higher yearly income than his "brothers and sisters" in Africa.

Rather than looking at Sub-Saharan Africa as a whole, let us look at the following nations for life expectancy, per capita income, adult illiteracy, and infant mortality. By so doing, perhaps we can determine whether the descendants of America's slave population have suffered irreparable harm because of the legacy of slavery (a legacy their brothers and sisters in the following African nations cannot claim).

Nation	**Life Expectancy**	**Per Capita Income U.S. $**	**Adult Illiteracy**	**Infant Mortality Rate per 1000***
Angola	47	$220	no report	25
Benin	53	$380	61%	88
Botswana	46	$3,240	24%	58
Burkina Faso	44	$240	77%	99
Burundi	42	$120	53%	119

Cameroon	54	$580	25%	74
Chad	48	$200	59%	112
Congo D.R.	51	no report	40%	90
Congo, Rep.	48	$670	21%	90
Cote d'Ivoire	46	$710	54%	87
Ethiopia	43	$100	63%	115
Ghana	60	$390	30%	66
Kenya	51	$360	no report	66
Madagascar	58	$250	34	82
Malawi	42	$190	41%	138
Mali	50	$240	60%	118
Mozambique	45	$230	57%	114
Niger	53	$310	85%	115
Nigeria	53	$310	37%	81
Rwanda	41	$250	34%	124
Senegal	41	$510	64%	63
Sierra Leone	37	$130	no report	170
South Africa	63	$3,160	15%	59
Tanzania	47	$240	25%	30
Uganda	42	$320	34%	107
Zambia	42	$320	23%	82
Zimbabwe	51	$520	12%	69
Reference:				
**United States	75-80	$30,600	< 5%	7**
**United Kingdom	75-80	$22,640	< 5%	7
**Russia	65-70	$2,270	1%	18
**Ireland	75-80	$19,160	< 5%	7
**France	75-80	$23,480	< 5%	6

*The preceding values were taken from the *World Development Indicators* database, World Bank, 8/2/2000. The values for life expectancy were for the year 1998; GNP per capita income, 1999; illiteracy rates, 1999. Some of the values mentioned prior to this table will vary slightly from those given in this table due to circumstances and different dates for extracting said information. Regardless of the exact numbers, the general trend remains constant year after year in Sub-Saharan Africa.

**These figures were taken from the United Nations Development Program, Human Development Program Report, 2000.

As revealing as the above-cited information may be, it can hardly provide a genuine firsthand experience of what life is like for most Africans today. In his book, *Out of America: A Black Man Confronts Africa,* Keith B. Richburg gives a graphic account of his tour of that continent as a correspondent for the *Washington Post.* After witnessing the depth of misery that was a daily reality in Africa, after seeing for himself Africans killing and mutilating other Africans, and after learning that this *is* Africa, the Africa that by the grace of God and a slave ship he had escaped, Richburg thanked God that his ancestors had made it "out of Africa" and had thus given him the title of "American."[9] By no means did Richburg glory in the inhumanity of slavery. Nevertheless, he understood that because his people were strong enough to overcome the turmoil of enslavement, he was given a birthright that the descendants of those who remained in Africa do not enjoy. More to the point, he found nothing in Africa to induce him to surrender his American citizenship for African citizenship. Like so many of his fellow African-Americans, he too did not believe the gruesome stories about the murder and mayhem that was being reported as commonplace in Africa. Once in Africa, however, it did not take long for Richburg to realize that the mythical "Motherland," as described by so many African-American activists, did not exist. It was the contrast between the myth and the reality regarding Africa that forced Richburg to face the fact that he was an American and not an African. The unspoken message of this African myth that Richburg had to refute is that African-Americans were torn from their idyllic African home and denied the happiness of their African Valhalla by evil American slavers. But has the removal of African-Americans from the poverty, the sickness, the incessant tribal warfare, and the illiteracy that is modern-day Africa actually caused them harm?

To get a better picture of life in America as opposed to life in Africa, let us compare the preceding African statistics with those of the state of Mississippi. Since Mississippi is one of the poorest states in the Union, this will give us a minimal contrast between life in the United States for African-Americans and life in modern-day Africa. In 1991 the average life expectancy of a non-white person in Mississippi at birth was 69.6 years or almost twenty years longer than if that non-white person had been born in Sub-Saharan Africa, where the average life expectancy is approximately fifty years. In the year *1929,* a non-white person in Mississippi had a life expectancy of 51.3 years. In other words, in order to find a time when the life expectancy of an African-American in Mississippi was close to that of the average African of today, one would have to go back in time more than seventy years. Of the twenty-seven Sub-Saharan nations in the table above, the lowest infant mortality rate listed is 30 per 1,000 live births in Tanzania. The "low" of 30 is offset by a high of 170 deaths per 1,000 live births in Sierra Leone. Contrast those statistics with Mississippi's infant mortality rate of 14.5 per 1,000 live births. African-American per capita income for Mississippi stands at $11,625.[10] The highest per capita income recorded in Sub-Saharan Africa is $3,240, and a low per capita income in Ethiopia of $100. The illiteracy rate for non-whites in Mississippi is below 5 percent, whereas in Sub-Saharan Africa illiteracy rates range from a low of 12 percent in Zimbabwe, to a high of 85 percent in Niger. When Africans are compared with African-American residents of Mississippi, one of the poorest states in the Union, they fall far behind black Mississippians on every quality of life indicator. What is true about Africans living in Africa is equally true of descendants of African slaves in *any* nation in the world other than the United States of America. The legacy of slavery in America has presented African-Americans with a lifestyle and an opportunity for material advancement that makes them the envy of every non-American African in the world. How African-Americans of today can justify demanding reparation for slavery is beyond the comprehension of anyone with an ounce of common sense.

SUMMARY

Without a doubt, every new "minority" that immigrates to the United States, whether Irish, Italian, Polish, or Chinese, will face various amounts of social and political discrimination. The more dissimilar the minority is from the standard American norm of the day, the more difficult their assimilation into mainstream American culture will be. With the African-American being glaringly dissimilar in physical appearance as well as in cultural and historic background, is it any wonder that such a tortuous and protracted path had to be blazed to reach the much sought after position of equality before the law? Although many leftists find great delight in pointing out the difficulties placed before the African-American during his climb from slave to second-class citizen to the status of full citizenship, it must be remembered that it was in this country more than any other nation on earth that the dream of full citizenship and prosperity was realized by the descendants of former slaves—not Cuba, Haiti, or Brazil. Yes, the road to equality before the law was rough and difficult. But the nation that made this success possible should be celebrated for its victories and not condemned for its perceived failures. To one degree or another, every minority that has fought its way from second-class citizenship to the place of equality before the law has increased the net amount of freedom for all. Upon obtaining full citizenship, other minorities have been content to stand shoulder to shoulder with their fellow citizens. Unfortunately, because of the myth of slavery and its attending hoax, the liberal establishment has convinced many African-Americans that they should stand *on* the shoulder or neck of their fellow citizens. But let it be known that not all people of color have allowed themselves to become intoxicated on the liberals' opium of black self-pity. Men such as Ken "The Black Avenger" Hamblin inform us about the other black community in America of which they are a part. Hamblin states, "When the disgruntled hyphenated black Americans and their booster club of white liberals bemoan the racism, the poverty, the low-paying jobs—all their excuses for failure—I issue a simple challenge: Pick a better country."[11] In his book by that title (i.e., *Pick a Better Country*), Hamblin tells of his struggles as a black man and as an American. But more to the point, he tells about the country where he achieved his success. Like Richburg, Hamblin makes no demand for reparations; rather, he challenges all Americans to use the freedoms at hand to better their life and not to be possessed with false notions of a mythical African Utopia.

MYTH: After the Civil War, Southern states passed "Black Codes" to prevent African-Americans from exercising their new freedoms.

REALITY: Indeed, most Southern states did pass some form of law to regulate the new relationship between the races. By doing so, these Southern states were doing nothing more than what most Northern states had done immediately after freeing their slaves. Also, it should be remembered that at the same time the Southern states were passing these laws, many Northern states were barring African-Americans from voting and segregating black and white school children. Although most of the "Black Codes" were overturned, in 1898 the United States Supreme Court in the *Plessey v. Ferguson* decision made segregation the law of the land. Thereafter, more than twenty-six states adopted some form of separate public accommodations. These laws, both in the North and in the South, were in response to rapid social change. This is why many early abolitionists, including many leading Southern abolitionists, desired a period of time to train and prepare the slaves for freedom.

MYTH: The consequences of slavery in America have had lasting deleterious results for African-Americans today.

REALITY: No sane person would ever deny the realities of slavery. From the first passage where African tribes captured fellow Africans for the slave trade; to the middle passage where weak and sick slaves were thrown into the sea; to life on the plantations, farms, and factories of the New World; slavery was loathsome. The movement of the Irish in response to the horrors of the potato famine offers many similar cases of human abuse. With each "minority" that was pushed out of their homeland and subsequently made their way to America, there are sad stories of human atrocities. Yet each "minority" proceeded to climb the ladder of success in America. Likewise, African-Americans have had to overcome many obstacles to reach the place of equality in America, and nowhere in the world have they had as much success as they have had in America. Unlike Africans anywhere in the world, in the United States approximately 16 percent of African-Americans will earn a college degree, and approximately 20 percent will work in managerial or a professional specialty.[12] Contrast these figures with African descendants of non-slaves and ask yourself, "Who has the best lifestyle, the descendants of American slaves or the descendants of non-slave Africans?"

MYTH: Africa is the "Garden of Eden" for African-Americans, and this is where their chief loyalty should reside.

REALITY: As has been shown, the life of an African-American in Mississippi is many times more stable, free, prosperous, and healthy than the life of the average African. How anyone could continue to nurse the notion that Africa is a "Garden of Eden" and America is a place to condemn is beyond reason. With all its spots and blemishes, America is still the better choice of every "minority," not just the African-American, who has established this land as his home. If anyone doubts this fact, as Ken Hamblin is so wont to say, let him "pick a better country."

CHAPTER 10

On Jordan's Stormy Banks

On Jordan's stormy banks I stand,
And cast a wistful eye
To Canaan's fair and happy land,
Where my possessions lie.

Samuel Stennet
On Jordan's Stormy Banks

The old gospel song *On Jordan's Stormy Banks* tells the story of a pilgrim's progress through life until he is ready to cross over from the land of death and woe to a more blissful existence. Likewise, America has progressed from a land of chattel slavery in several forms with white masters, black masters, and red masters; political slavery, which ended with the recognition by Great Britain of the independence of each of the original thirteen colonies; and the dream of the end of civil slavery. Of these three forms of slavery, only chattel slavery has been destroyed in America. For the South, political slavery is as real for the thirteen Confederate states as it was for the thirteen original colonies before 1782 (before the signing of the Treaty of Paris), and for Americans in general, the unbridled force of an intrusive government is a daily reality, thus making civil slavery an all too obvious component of American life. Nevertheless, much progress has been made and much success realized by people of various "minorities" who have made America home. As has been asserted in previous chapters, all Americans are decedents of a minority group. Each group that came to this country had its own set of obstacles to overcome. No minority was welcomed to this land with bands playing and the red carpet rolled out. Each in its own way had to work and overcome various forms of discrimination and mistreatment and in so doing to make a place for themselves and their children. "No Irish need apply" was not an uncommon sign in the nineteenth century. Also, Asians were viewed with suspicion and mistrust until late in the twentieth century. For a time into the twentieth century, Asians were discriminated against in public accommodations and not allowed to vote in many Western states. Yet, each minority faced these problems without the massive aid of the government and won their liberation from many forms of civil slavery. What was true for the Irish, Polish, Chinese, and Italians was equally true for the Africans. "No Irish need apply" was simply substituted with "No Negroes need apply." The words had changed, but the tune lingered on.

Today, throughout the United States, the laws that once stood as a barrier to the upward mobility of African-Americans no longer exist. Unfortunately, several generations of African-Americans have been raised on the fable that white America is engaged in a grand conspiracy to repress them as a people. According to black reporter, Keith B. Richburg, they even have a name for the mythical anti-black conspiracy—"The Plan."[1] Richburg also points out that in Africa, a parallel conspiracy theory teaches Africans that a Western or European "Plan" is afoot to keep Africans as colonial subjects. The problem with the acceptance of these conspiracy theories by the African-American community is that it interferes with seeking the true causes of community problems. This interference results in the continuation of the problems in the African-American community. For example, today, 70 percent of African-American children are born into single-parent homes. (This phenomenon was unheard of during the age of slavery and up through the middle portion of the twentieth century.)[2] Without the stable influence of a traditional home life, is it any wonder that one out of four young black males ends up in jail? But, according to the conspiracy theory, it is the white man who is at fault—after all, it is part of "The Plan." When it is noted that more black Americans are on death row than white Americans, the rational for the problem is, it's just part of "The Plan." The Plan theory ignores the fact that African-Americans are eight times more likely to commit murder than their white counterparts. For instance, in 1992, white Americans committed just over five murders per 100,000 people, whereas African-Americans committed slightly over forty-three murders per 100,000 people.[3] Seeking to place the blame on a mythical white conspiracy for the failures of the African-American community only serves to perpetuate the root causes of these problems.

Of all the fables that are repeated, none is more accepted by American society, both black and white, than the idea that African-Americans are the victims of "hate" crimes at the hands of white Americans. On June 7, 1998, a black man was dragged to death by several white men in Jasper Texas. This hideous crime was condemned by all segments of Texas, Southern, and American society. Nevertheless, for weeks on end the nation was subjected to reoccurring accounts of this dastardly deed. By the time the men responsible were tried and convicted, few if any Americans were unaware of this sickening crime. And as usual, black civil rights activists and the liberal media spared no effort in instilling the message that white Americans, especially Southerners, were victimizing African-Americans—Jesse Jackson and other militant black activists had a heyday! Do the facts about white-on-black crime in America support this assumption? Interracial crimes are, by definition, committed by a member of one race against a member of another race. Because of liberal bias in the reporting of these crimes, most Americans believe that white Americans commit the majority of such deeds. Yet, according to the Department of Justice's National Crime Victimization Survey, the vast majority of interracial crimes are committed by black Americans against white Americans. According to a study of crime in America by the New Century Foundation: "In approximately 90 percent of the interracial crimes of violence involving blacks and whites, blacks are perpetrators and whites are victims. In terms of crime rates (calculated as the number of crimes per 100,000 population), blacks are more than 50 times more likely to attack whites than the reverse."[4] Many liberals will attempt to minimize the effects of these staggering accounts of black-on-white violence by asserting that blacks attack whites because white people are thought to have more money than blacks. But, as *The Color of Crime* report points out:

> [O]f the 1,140,670 black-on-white acts of violence reported in 1994, only 173,374 were robberies. The remaining 84.8 percent were aggravated assaults, rapes, and simple assaults, which presumably were not motivated by profit. Rape, in particular, has nothing to do with the presumed wealth of the victim. More than 30,000 white women were raped by black men in 1994, and about 5,400 black women were raped by white men. The black interracial rape rate was 38 times the white rate.[5]

As nationally syndicated columnist Samuel Francis noted, the media has a tendency toward highlighting crimes by white Americans against black Americans, while downplaying crimes by black Americans against white Americans.[6] Such was the case in Wichita, Kansas. On the night of December 15, 2000, two black brothers, Reginald and Jonathan Carr, broke into a house where five white people, three men and two women, were staying. The Carr brothers then robbed the five white people, raped the two women, lined the five up, and shot each one in the back of the head. One woman lived and identified the Carr brothers, who were subsequently arrested by the police. Now, compare the news coverage of this heinous criminal act with the coverage given to the death of the black man in Jasper, Texas. With the assistance of the liberal news media, Americans in general and African-Americans in particular are left with the impression that African-Americans are victims and white Americans are the aggressors in interracial crimes. Again, this impression only feeds the fallacy about "The Plan," which then serves to obscure the real causes of crime and other problems within the African-American community.

Because of the liberal bias in news reporting in America, most people fully accept the notion of white-on-black violence, especially when the violence is reported "down South." Yet, as demonstrated, the reverse is the case. Also, most Americans believe that hate crimes are more often committed against African-Americans by white Americans. Again, it is only because the liberal media underreport acts against white Americans by black Americans that this notion survives. For example, how many Americans know about the nineteen-year-old white man who was murdered by three black men in 1996? The reason the young white man was murdered was because he had a Confederate flag on the back of his truck. What would have been the response of the liberal media if three white men had murdered a black man because he was wearing a shirt with a picture of Malcolm X on it? Of course we know the answer to that question; all we have to do is revisit Jasper, Texas. In Columbia, South Carolina, a man returning home from a Sons of Confederate Veterans meeting was assaulted by a black man who had followed the SCV member from the meeting place to his home. Nothing of value was taken during this assault—a typical scenario of a hate crime. During a meeting of the League of the South in Sumter County, South Carolina, a drive-by shooting was reported at a barbecue where several Confederate flags were displayed. Children have been expelled from school for displaying a Confederate flag; jobs have been put in jeopardy because a worker dared to display a Confederate flag on his lunch box or car. The question the liberal media never finds time to ask is, "Who is being discriminated against here?"

With the incessant ranting by the liberal media and civil rights activists about the "flag of slavery," is it any wonder that some people incorrectly label anyone who displays the Confederate flag as an enemy of African-Americans? Yet, as demonstrated throughout this book, the South is no more nor no less responsible for the African slave trade or the institution of slavery itself than the African tribes who sold black men and women into slavery, the Yankee and other slave ship owners who brought them to this land, or those who used black labor to enrich themselves. There is condemnation enough to go around for all segments of society—white and black, African and American. It is time to admit that the Confederate flag is not the "flag of slavery and racism." Like other historical symbols, it has been misused. (Note the photograph in this book of the United States flag being carried down Pennsylvania Avenue in Washington, D.C., by the Ku Klux Klan.) Those who misuse these symbols are the ones who should be condemned, not the symbols. Even in Africa and elsewhere *today* there are many national flags that should carry the label of racism and slavery, but the Confederate flag is not one of them.

The promotion of the myth and hoax about the institution of slavery should be rejected by all Americans. As a nation, we stand on Jordan's stormy banks. We have reached the point at which we must go forward into the land of freedom, true freedom, where neither chattel slavery, civil slavery, nor political slavery will be our lot. Ahead of us is a unique opportunity to live truly free. But if we allow ourselves to be deceived by the sirens of socialism (i.e., modern liberalism), we will condemn ourselves and our posterity to the mud pits of Egyptian (Federal) slavery. The never-ceasing demands by civil rights activists for more and more involvement by the Federal government in the correction of presumed affronts is a sure formula for bigger and bigger government, less and less individual freedom, and more and more civil slavery. Virtually every minority that made America home overcame many forms of discrimination without the intrusive force of the Federal government. Nevertheless, today African-Americans are assured by the liberal media that their civil rights are a gift bestowed, guaranteed, and protected by the Federal government. Furthermore, liberals insist that civil rights cannot be secured without the watchful care of Big Brother Government. For most other minorities, government was the one agent that represented oppression and not freedom. The French Huguenots escaped the terror and tyranny of France by fleeing to America; after being pushed off their lands by the government in London, the Scottish sought freedom in the United States from the oppression of the English ruling class; the Irish, suffering from the abuse of a colonial government, found freedom in America. All of these and most other "minorities" came to America not because of the power of its government but because of the promise of freedom from an abusive government. Big Brother Government drove most "minorities" out of their former homes; *limited* government in America offered them hope for a better future.

Individuals of the African-American community today are vital members of our society. The United States Supreme Court can boast of African-American justices whose political opinions range from that of a liberal such as the late Justice Thurgood Marshall to that of a conservative such as Justice Clarence Thomas. The leader of America's last war effort was an African-American, Gen. Colin Powell. Yet we are told by the liberal media that African-Americans are not being given a fair chance to excel in America. Liberals assure us that African-Americans need the help of liberal whites to protect them and provide them with reparations for past injustices. If we are to proceed to that land of true freedom, as described by St. George Tucker, where all forms of slavery are forever abolished, we must reject the liberals' notion of a supercharged welfare state that "benevolently" provides for its people. As the quaint truism of the past states, "Any government big enough to give you everything is strong enough to take everything away from you." Let Jordan roll, and let us neither intransigently stand on her stormy banks nor retrace our steps back into *any* form of slavery. Let us cross over the river and rest in freedom's land.

SUMMARY

In the preceding work, we have taken a not so politically correct look at the issue of slavery as it occurred in America. As has been demonstrated, the institution of slavery extends into the distant past of man's history. Slavery has been a ubiquitous feature in the history of mankind. No race or ethnic group can claim to be free from the charge of enslaving its fellow man. Viking, Aztec, Zulu, and all other segments of human societies have participated in the enslavement of others. Although slavery existed in the Western Hemisphere before the Europeans arrived, and although African slavery predates slavery in the United States, modern Americans are only aware of African slavery. Nevertheless, African-Americans as well as black men in Africa owned slaves. Regardless of who owned the slaves or where slavery existed, profit was the motivating factor that kept the institution alive. When looking at the demise of slavery in America with the exception of the South, it must be kept in mind that slavery was eliminated only when it was no longer needed. Even though leading Southerners had worked for its elimination, with the advent of the Radical Abolition Movement, slavery became a national issue that transcended issues of freedom and played into the hands of political opportunists. Disavowing the South the right of dealing with the issue as the North had done, the Radical Abolitionists pushed the South into a defensive posture that ultimately led to war. Sadly for American history, only in the South and in Haiti was slavery abolished as a result of the application of armed force. The diabolical propaganda campaign waged against the South prior to the War, the extensive suffering caused by the War, and the ravages of Reconstruction after the War have made the promotion of the myths about slavery and the South possible if not predictable. Nevertheless, as we have clearly seen, the truth about the institution of slavery will destroy the myths about slavery.

Myths about Slavery

MYTH: Slavery was an institution operated by white people for the oppression of black people.

REALITY: As demonstrated in this work, slavery has deep historical roots that extend all the way back into ancient history. Slaves, both in the Old World and the New World, came in all colors and from all ethnic backgrounds. Also, it has been shown that slave masters came in all colors and from all ethnic backgrounds. In America, red men owned red and black slaves; black men owned black slaves both in the North and in the South; white men owned red, black, and white slaves. The sole reason that slavery existed was to provide a stable labor force and not to keep a certain group of people "in their place." The notion of keeping undesirable elements of society "in their place" was often advanced *after* the fact of the introduction of slavery as a rationalization for the institution.

MYTH: Slavery was a system organized by Christians.

REALITY: The notion that Christianity is somehow responsible for the introduction of slavery in the Western Hemisphere is often promoted by Black Muslims as a means of driving a wedge between African-Americans and their traditional Christian faith. As we have seen, the first movement of slaves from Africa was organized by Muslims from North Africa, the so-called Trans-Sahara slave trade. This movement preceded the Trans-Atlantic slave trade by almost five hundred years and was responsible for as many slaves taken from Africa as the Trans-Atlantic slave trade. Also, it must be remembered that today, African Muslims are routinely making slaves of Christian Africans in the Sudan. The earliest efforts to ameliorate the evils of slavery are described in the Bible. Both the Hebrews and the later Christians were given strict instruction about the care and protection of slaves. Unlike the pagans around them, the Hebrews and the Christians could own only the labor of the individual and not the complete individual. This limitation of ownership was a great first step in the final elimination of the institution of slavery.

MYTH: In America, slavery was a Southern institution.

REALITY: Slavery existed in Spanish-controlled America for more than a hundred years before it was introduced into the South. Within twenty years of its introduction in Virginia, Massachusetts had passed laws protecting the right of a master in the property of his slaves. Massachusetts also became one of the earliest colonies to become involved in the slave trade. By the time of the War for American Independence, all thirteen colonies were slaveholding colonies, and those of the North were actively engaged in the African slave trade. With the introduction of the cotton gin, cotton production became a mainstay of the planter class of the Deep South. The need for a reliable labor force in the South and the desire to remove African-Americans in the North became the motivating factors for the transfer of a large portion of Northern slaves to the South. At this time the Southern abolition movement was at its pinnacle of power, and most leading Southerners were active in promoting the abolition of slavery. With the advent of the Radical Abolitionists of the North, the cooperative efforts by the North and South in the elimination of slavery were replaced with mistrust and antagonism. Nevertheless, it should be remembered that fewer than 10 percent of Southerners owned slaves at the time of the War for Southern Independence.

MYTH: Slavery was a self-evident sin and so recognized by the Church.

REALITY: Slavery existed within the Roman Empire throughout the ministry of Jesus of Nazareth. Yet, although he and his followers condemned many acts as sinful, slavery was not condemned. Throughout the Bible, in both the Old and the New Testaments, God gave laws to regulate slavery but never condemned slavery as a sin. This is not to suggest that slavery as an institution was ever free of evil. The proposition that slavery is not a sin is not a suggestion that slavery is a desirable state. Thus, there are many good reasons to oppose slavery in its various forms, but not on the ground that it is a sin in itself. It was not until the late eighteenth century that the idea that slavery was a sin became prominent. If slavery is an odious sin, how can it be explained that for more than eighteen hundred years the Church never recognized it as such?

MYTH: Slavery existed in the North for only a very short time and had little economic impact there.

REALITY: Slavery in the North existed from approximately 1640 to 1840 or for about two hundred years. Actually, there were a few slaves in the North as late as 1850. According to R. L. Dabney, the census of 1850 recorded as many as 236 slaves in the state of New Jersey.[7] Even after Abraham Lincoln's famous Emancipation Proclamation, African-Americans were held in slavery in areas controlled by the North and were not freed until the adoption of the Thirteenth Amendment. As shown, as long as slavery was necessary for the wellbeing of a colony in the North, it was tolerated. Only after it was no longer needed was slavery eliminated. It should be remembered that even though slavery was abolished, the free people of color were not given equal rights by their liberators. Usually every effort was taken by Northern slaveholders to liquidate their slave property by selling Northern slaves to slave traders who then sold the slaves to slaveholders in the South. As for the economic effects of slavery to the North, it must be remembered that much of the wealth that was accumulated by Northerners was in one way or the other related to the African slave trade or the production and shipping of slave-grown products from the South. If it was evil for Southerners to make money from the production of slave-grown products, the same can be said about Northern factory owners and merchants who also made money on those same slave-grown products. The institution of slavery had a significant impact upon the economic wellbeing of all of the United States, and not just the South.

MYTH: The North ended slavery because it was offensive to the moral character of Northerners.

REALITY: In condemning the South because of slavery, many will assert that the North was more virtuous because it ended slavery for the good and wellbeing of the slaves. According to one of America's founding fathers, John Adams of Massachusetts, the main reason that slavery was abolished in the North was because of the increase in the number of white laborers who refused to allow competition from slave labor. Adams stated that if slavery had not been abolished, both the slaves and their slave masters would have been killed by the free white laborers.[8] The North was no different from the South when it came to the issue of slavery. As long as slavery was necessary, it was tolerated; during this time a small but growing element began working for its elimination. Nevertheless, slavery in the North was abolished only when it was no longer needed. Also, it was abolished in the North only after the bulk of the slave population could be sold, thus saving Northern slave masters the financial loss suffered by Southern slaveholders.

MYTH: The North offered the black man equality and brotherhood.

REALITY: The myth of the North as a land of freedom, equality, and brotherhood for the African-American has been exposed throughout this book. The North was the land of slavery from approximately 1640 until 1840; the land of the African slave trade from the building of the first slave ship, the *Desire,* in 1637 until as late as 1861 with the capture of the *Nightingale*; the land of discriminatory laws which prevented African-Americans from attending white schools, excluded free people of color from immigrating into the so-called free states, and excluded them from the rolls of voters. Foreigners and Americans, both Northerners and Southerners, noted the lowly condition that free people of color were assigned in the North. After traveling through the Deep South, Joseph H. Ingraham, a Yankee, made the following observation about the treatment of free people of color in the North:

> A glance at the condition of the free states of the union, as they are called, in this respect, exhibits the proofs of this condition of things. And so long as these startling anomalies [freedom without equal rights] exist—freedom without its enjoyments, equality without its social privileges—we really do not see how the people of the free states can pretend, with any show of propriety or justice, even had they the power by law and constitution, to meddle with the relations between master and slave in the slave-holding states.[9]

Ingraham was making an appeal to his Northern brethren not to be critical of the South in its dealing with the slavery issue when they could not deal fairly with the few free people of color in their own so-called free states. Once again we see a Northerner exposing the myth of the North as a land of freedom and equality for African-Americans. Even more telling is Ingraham's opinion of Northerners who insisted on interfering with Southerners who were attempting to bring the institution of slavery to an end.

> The more I see of slavery, the more firmly I am convinced that the interference of our northern friends, in the present state of their information upon the subject, will be more injurious than beneficial to the cause. The physician, like Prince Hohenloe, might as reasonably be expected to heal, with the Atlantic between himself and his patient's pulse, or to use a juster figure, an individual, wholly ignorant of a disease, might as well attempt its cure, as for northerners, however sincere their exertions, or however pure their intentions may be, under existing circumstances, to meliorate the condition of the coloured population of the south. When the chains of the slave are broken in pieces, it must be by a southern hand—and thousands of southern gentlemen are already extending their arms, ready to strike the blow.[10]

Unfortunately for the slave, the South, and America, those

thousands of Southerners who were willing to strike the blow to end slavery saw their efforts destroyed by the Radical Abolitionists of the North. Ingraham warned America about the danger of allowing the radical element of the North to push the nation into a condition far worse than that already existing. Declaring himself as being in favor of emancipation, Ingraham went on to warn of the consequences of pursing the Radical Abolitionists' plan for immediate abolition of slavery:

> Have those who advocate immediate and unconditional emancipation weighed well these several branches of inquiry on this momentous subject? It is to be feared, indeed, by their language and conduct, that they have not. They should beware, while they are denouncing the slave-holder, that they do not themselves incur a still more fearful responsibility, and make themselves answerable for jeopardizing, if not actually dissolving, the Union, and encouraging civil, perhaps servile war, with all its horrors and atrocities.[11]

These words, written by a Yankee in 1835, read more like prophecy today than when they were first written. For within twenty-five years, John Brown, the Radical Abolitionist murderer, fired the opening shots of what he hoped would be a slave uprising. Although a failure in his efforts of fomenting a servile war, he was very successful in beginning an even larger war.

MYTH: Racial discrimination and/or segregation is a legacy of Southern slavery.

REALITY: In debunking the previous myth about slavery in America, the author has already demonstrated that discrimination against free people of color has a long history both in the North and the South. As a matter of fact, in 1898, in *Plessey v. Ferguson,* the United States Supreme Court established racial discrimination (i.e., segregation) as the law of the land. In so doing, the court cited an 1845 Massachusetts law establishing separate schools for white and black children as the foundation of its decision. The majority decision for the court was written by a Federal judge from the state of Minnesota—not Mississippi. By the twentieth century, more than twenty-six states of the Union had established some form of discriminatory laws based solely on color. This represents an equal number of non-Southern states to Southern states. Racial discrimination is a legacy of the commonly held nineteenth-century white supremacy ideology. As shown, this view was held by men of both the North and the South. Whether we look at the words of Vice President Alexander Stephens of the Confederacy or President Abraham Lincoln of the United States, the plain and simple fact remains: They both believed in the nineteenth-century view of black inferiority and white supremacy.

The Hoax about Slavery

The several myths about the institution of slavery have made the acceptance of the hoax about life in America for modern African-Americans a sad reality for far too many Americans today. The hoax must be rejected.

HOAX: The lives of modern African-Americans have been irreparably damaged by the institution of slavery; therefore, various forms of government-backed entitlements and reparations are owed to African-Americans.

REALITY: While not trying to diminish the sufferings of those held in slavery, the spinning of that historic fact to foster ever-increasing demands for white guilt and government-sponsored benefits must not go unchallenged. The continuous assertion by white liberals and African-American civil rights activists that, as a group, African-Americans cannot compete in American society today because of the injustices of the past is self-debasing and utterly false. Furthermore, this hoax is used by too many in the African-American community to rationalize many failures that could be addressed and eliminated. As parents often learn, if a child is given an easy excuse for failure, more often than not he will fail. This fact has nothing to do with race; it has everything to do with human nature. White liberals and quota-blacks are not doing the African-American community a service by promoting the hoax of "slavery injustice" as a cause for present failures. The march of freedom in which each "minority" has participated has made America a land of equality before the law. The success of the struggle for freedom by the African-American community is nothing less than the continuation of the progress toward full abolition of *all* forms of slavery—chattel, civic, and political. From the bridge at Concord, Massachusetts, to the bridge at Selma, Alabama, the struggle to end government-imposed slavery continues.

Continuously repeating the hoax that African-Americans have been placed in a pathetic situation because they are descendants of slaves serves only to further the demands for more government intrusion (civil slavery) into the lives of all Americans. As has been demonstrated, nowhere in the world have Africans made more progress than in the United States of America. There are no African nations or predominately African nations which can claim a lifestyle even close to that enjoyed by America's African population. African-Americans have suffered from injustices, but so have the Irish, Polish, Asians, and most other "minorities" who immigrated to the United States. Each group, in its own way and time, overcame those injustices and made America a freer nation. The laws that once prevented African-Americans from exercising full civic freedom have been repealed; now is *not* the time to replace those laws with equally egregious laws that infringe upon the freedoms of other Americans; and, now is *not* the time, while celebrating black history, to deny Southerners (black and white) the right of celebrating Southern history. We must not be tempted by the sirens of liberalism to turn back into the wilderness of civil slavery; rather, we must cross over the River Jordan into the land of full freedom and equal opportunity and justice for all—"O who will come and go with me? I am bound for the promised land."

ADDENDUM I

Abstract On the State of Slavery in Virginia[1] St. George Tucker

While most Americans are aware of the efforts of Northern abolitionists in the promotion of the elimination of slavery, few are aware of the same efforts by notable Southerners. In a pamphlet published in 1796, St. George Tucker of Virginia identified the evils of slavery, categorized three different types of slavery, demonstrated that slavery existed in all parts of the United States, and offered a method for its elimination. As noteworthy as all this was, Tucker went even further by criticizing laws that discriminated against free people of color. This fact alone would mark St. George Tucker as an American civil libertarian 150 years before the advent of the modern civil rights movement. Yet, St. George Tucker was a Southerner, an advocate of State's Rights, and a proponent of the right of secession.

As a modern historian has noted, "Tucker's state rights understanding of the Constitution is not merely a rationalization in the defense of slavery."[2] Tucker, joined by many notable Americans such as Washington, Jefferson, Madison, and Lincoln, was an advocate of gradual emancipation and the removal of free Africans to their ancestral homeland.

The following text is a review of Tucker's views on the evils of slavery, the types of slavery, slavery as an American problem, the method for the elimination of slavery, and discrimination against free people of color.

I. The evils of slavery

> Among the blessings which the Almighty hath showered down on these states, there is a large portion of the bitterest draught that ever flowed from the cup of affliction. Whilst

America hath been the land of promise to Europeans, and their descendants, it hath been the vale of death to millions of the wretched sons of Africa. The genial light of liberty, which hath here shone with unrivalled lustre on the former, hath yielded no comfort to the latter, but to them hath proved a pillar of darkness, whilst it hath conducted the former to the most enviable state of human existence. Whilst we were offering up vows at the shrine of Liberty, and sacrificing hecatombs upon her altars; whilst we swore irreconcilable hostility to her enemies, and hurled defiance in their faces; whilst we adjured the God of Hosts to witness our resolution to live free, or die, and imprecated curses on their heads who refused to unite with us in establishing the empire of freedom; we were imposing upon our fellow men, who differ in complexion from us, a *slavery,* ten thousand times more cruel than the utmost extremity of those grievances and oppressions, of which we complained . . . such that partial system of morality which confines rights and injuries, to particular complexions; such the effect of that self-love which justifies, or condemns, not according to principle, but to the agent.

II. Types of slavery

[I]nstead of attempting a general definition of slavery; I shall, by considering it under a threefold aspect, endeavour to give a just idea of its nature.

1. [*Political slavery*] When a nation is, from any external cause, deprived of the right of being governed by its own laws such a nation may be considered as in a state of *political slavery.* Such is the state of conquered countries, and generally, of colonies, and other dependent government. . . . Subjection of one nation or people, to the will of another, constitutes the first species of slavery, which, in order to distinguish it from the other two, I have called [it] political [slavery].

2. [*Civil slavery*] Civil liberty being no other than natural liberty, so far restrained by human laws, and no farther, as is necessary and expedient for the general advantages of the public, whenever that liberty is, by the laws of the state, further restrained than is necessary and expedient for the general advantage, a state of *civil slavery* commences immediately. And this happens whenever the laws of a state respect the form, or energy of the government, more than the happiness of the citizen.

3. [*Domestic slavery*] That condition in which one man is subject to be directed by another in all his actions; and this constitutes a state of *domestic slavery*; to which state all the

incapacities and disabilities of civil slavery are incident, with the weight of other numerous calamities superadded thereto.

III. Slavery as an American problem

The first introduction of it into Virginia was by the arrival of a Dutch ship from the coast of Africa having *twenty* negroes on board, who were sold here in the year 1620. In the year 1638 we find them in Massachusetts. They were introduced into Connecticut soon after the settlement of that colony; that is to say, about the same period. Thus early had our forefathers sown the seeds of an evil, which, like a leprosy, hath descended upon their posterity with accumulated rancour, visiting the sins of the fathers upon succeeding generations.—The climate of the northern states less favourable to the constitution of the natives of Africa than the southern, proved alike unfavourable to their propagation, and to the increase of their numbers by importants. As the southern colonies advanced in population, not only importations increased there, but Nature herself, under a climate more congenial to the African constitution, assisted in multiplying the blacks in those parts, no less than in diminishing their numbers in the more rigorous climates to the north; this influence of climate, more over, contributed extremely to increase or diminish the value of the slave to the purchasers, in the different colonies. White labourers, whose constitutions were better adapted to the severe winters of the New England colonies, were there found to be preferable to the negroes, who, accustomed to the influence of an ardent sun, became almost torpid in those countries, not less adapted to give vigor to their laborious exercises, than unfavorable to the multiplication of their species. . . . The great increase of slavery in the southern, in proportion to the northern states in the union, is therefore not attributable, *solely*, to the effect of sentiment, but to natural causes; as well as those considerations of profit, which have, perhaps, an equal influence over the conduct of mankind in general, in whatever country, or under whatever climate their destiny hath placed them. What else but considerations of this nature could have influenced the merchants of the freest nation, at that time in the world, to embark in so nefarious a traffic, as that of the human race, attended, as the African slave trade has been, with the most atrocious aggravations of cruelty, perfidy, and intrigues, the objects of which have been the perpetual formentation of predatory and intestine wars? What, but similar considerations, could prevail on the government of the same country, even in these days, to patronized a commerce so diametrically opposite to the generally received maxims of that government.

IV. Method for the elimination of slavery

The extirpation of slavery from the United States is a task equally arduous and momentous. To restore the blessings of liberty to near a million of oppressed individuals, who have groaned under the yoke of bondage, and to their descendants, is an object, which those who trust in Providence, will be convinced would not be unaided by the divine Author of our being, should we invoke his blessing upon our endeavours. Yet human prudence forbids that we should precipitately engage in a work of such hazard as a general and simultaneous emancipation. The mind of man must in some measure be formed for his future condition. The early impressions of obedience and submission, which slaves have received among us, and the no less habitual arrogance and assumption of superiority, among the whites, contributes, equally, to unfit the former for *freedom,* and the latter for *equality.* . . . To discharge the [slaves] from their present condition, would be attended with an immediate general famine, in those parts of the United States, from which not all the productions of the other states, could deliver them; similar evils might reasonably be apprehended from the adoption of the measure by any one of the southern states; for in all of the proportion of slaves is too great, not to be attended with calamitous effects, if they were immediately set free. These are serious . . . obstacles to a general, simultaneous emancipation.—There are other considerations not to be disregarded. A great part of the *property* of individuals consists in *slaves.* The laws have sanctioned this species of property. Can the laws take away the property of an individual without his own consent, or without *just compensation*: Will those who do not hold slaves agree to be taxed to make this compensation? Creditors also, who have trusted their debtors upon the faith of this visible property will be defrauded. If justice demands the emancipation of the slave, she also, *under these circumstances,* seems to plead for the owner and for his creditor. . . . Must we then quit the subject, in despair of the success of any project for the amendment of their, as well as our own condition? I think not.—Strenuously as I feel my mind opposed to a simultaneous emancipation, for the reasons already mentioned, the abolition of slavery in the United

> States, and especially in that state, to which I am attached by every tie that nature and society form, is *now* my *first* and probably be my last, expiring wish. . . . The abolition of slavery may be effected without the *emancipation* of a single slave; without depriving any man of the *property* which he *possesses,* and without defrauding a creditor who has trusted him on the faith of that property. The experiment in that mode has already been begun in some of our sister states. Pennsylvania, under the auspices of the immortal Franklin, begun the work of gradual abolition of slavery in the year of 1780, by enlisting nature herself, on the side of humanity. Connecticut followed the example four years after.

V. Discrimination against free people of color

> This species of slavery also exists whenever there is an inequality of rights, or privileges, between the subjects or citizens of the same state, except such as necessarily result from the exercise of a public officer; for the pre-eminence of one class of men must be founded and erected upon the depression of another; and the measure of exaltation in the former, is that of the slavery of the latter. In all governments, however constituted, or by what description soever denominated, wherever the distinction of rank prevails, or is admitted by the constitution, this species of slavery exists. It existed in every nation, and in every government in Europe before the French revolution. It existed in the American colonies before they became independent states; and notwithstanding the maxims of equality which have been adopted in their several constitutions, it exists in most, if not all, of them, at this day, in the persons of our free negroes and mulattoes; whose civil incapacities are almost as numerous as the civil rights of our free citizens.

In the preceding texts, St. George Tucker challenged Americans to deal not only with the institution of slavery and its elimination but also with laws that discriminated against people solely on the basis of color. Note how differently Tucker and the Radical Abolitionists dealt with the issue of slavery. Tucker viewed the ownership of slaves *and* the slave trade as an American problem, not a Southern problem. Tucker, unlike the Radical Abolitionists, did not condemn the slaveholder as a sinner; rather he attempted to enlist the slaveholder as an ally in the cause of freedom. Tucker, unlike the Radical Abolitionists, understood that it would take time to prepare both the slave and white society for black freedom. Note also that Tucker, even while pursuing freedom for the slave, recognized that in the pursuit of good, bad policy should not be pursued—thus, his recognition of the rights of property for both the slaveholder and his creditor (many of whom were Northern banks). How happy would have been our national existence if we as a nation had followed Tucker's plan for the elimination of the curse of slavery from America. Even happier would we be if as a nation *today,* we would endeavor to eliminate the first two forms of slavery identified by Tucker. Regardless of the type— political slavery, civil slavery, or domestic slavery—slavery is a curse to any people and therefore must be opposed by those who believe in the God-given rights of "life, liberty, and the pursuit of happiness."

ADDENDUM II

Early Anti-Slavery Tract

The following, according to George H. Moore in *Notes on the History of Slavery in Massachusetts,* is a complete text of Judge Samuel Sewell's pamphlet written in opposition to slavery in Massachusetts. This tract was written in 1700, or approximately sixty years after slavery and the slave trade had been established in Massachusetts. Judge Sewell did not succeed in his efforts to abolish slavery and the slave trade in that state. For as Moore declares, "[Slavery and the slave trade] continued . . . long after he 'slept with his fathers.'"[1] Judge Saffins' reply to this tract can be found in Chapter 2. These two tracts by well-respected members of Massachusetts society demonstrate the difficulty faced by slaveholding societies in abolishing slavery. It was eighty years after the publication of Sewell's anti-slavery tract before Massachusetts began abolishing slavery. During this time, and for an additional forty years thereafter, it continued to be a leading member of America's slave-trading community. As was demonstrated by the United States Supreme Court in *Plessey v. Ferguson,* even though Massachusetts abolished slavery early in its history, it did not offer equal rights to its free people of color. The arguments made by Judge Sewell in opposition to slavery and by Judge Saffin in the defense of slavery echo through time. As demonstrated in Chapter 3, some of the same points debated by two of Massachusetts's judges in 1700 were being argued in 1840 by Rev. J. Blanchard and Rev. N. L. Rice in Ohio. These facts demonstrate the difficulty faced by America in the transition from chattel and civil slavery to equality before the law. Nevertheless, the transition has been made and should be a point of celebration for all Americans.

THE SELLING OF JOSEPH, A MEMORIAL[2]

By the Hon'ble Judge Sewell in New England

FORASMUCH *as* LIBERTY *is in real value next unto Life; None ought to part with it themselves, or deprive others of it, but upon most mature consideration.*

The Numerousness of Slaves at this Day in the Province, and the Uneasiness of them under their Slavery, hath put many upon thinking whether the Foundation of it be firmly and well laid; so as to sustain the Vast Weight that is built upon it. It is most certain that all Men, as they are the *Sons of Adam,* are Co-heirs, and have equal Right unto Liberty, and all other outward Comforts of Life. God *hath given the Earth [with all its commodities] unto the Sons of Adam,* Psal., 115, 16. *And hath made of one Blood all Nations of Men, for to dwell on all the face of the Earth, and hath determined the Times before appointed, and the bounds of their Habitation: That they should seek the Lord. Forasmuch then as we are the Offspring of God,* &c. *Acts* 17:26, 27,29. Now, although the Title given by the last Adam doth infinitely better Men's Estates, respecting God and themselves; and grants them a most beneficial and inviolable Lease under the Broad Seal of Heaven, who were before only Tenants at Will; yet through the Indulgence of God to our First Parents after the Fall, the outward Estate of all and every of their Children, remains the same as to one another. So that Originally, and Naturally, there is no such thing as Slavery. Joseph was rightfully no more a Slave to his Brethren, than they were to him; and they had no more Authority to *Sell* him, than they had to *Slay* him. And if *they* had nothing to do to sell him; the *Ishmaelites* bargaining with them, and paying down Twenty pieces of Silver, could not make a Title. Neither could *Potiphar* have any better Interest in him than the *Ishmaelites* had. *Gen.* 37, 20, 27, 28. For he that shall in this case plead *Alteration of Property,* seems to have forfeited a great part of his own claim to Humanity. There is no proportion between Twenty Pieces of Silver and LIBERTY. The Commodity itself is the Claimer. If *Arabian* Gold be imported in any quantities, most are afraid to meddle with it, though they might have it at easy rates; lest it should have been wrongfully taken from the Owners, it should kindle a fire to the Consumption of their whole Estate. 'Tis pity there should be more Caution used in buying a Horse, or a little lifeless dust, than there is in purchasing Men and Women: Whereas they are the Offspring of God, and their Liberty is,

Auro pretiosior Omni.

And seeing God hath said, *He that stealeth a Man, and selleth him, or if he be found in his Hand, he shall surely be put to Death.* Exod. 21, 16. This Law being of Everlasting Equity, wherein Man-Stealing is ranked among the most atrocious of Capital Crimes: What louder Cry can there be made of that Celebrated Warning.

Caveat Emptor!

And all things considered, it would conduce more to the Welfare of the Province, to have White Servants for a Term of Years, than to have Slaves for Life. Few can endure to hear of a Negro's being made free; and indeed they can seldom use their Freedom well; yet their continual aspiring after their forbidden Liberty, renders them Unwilling Servants. And there is such a disparity in their Conditions, Colour, Hair, that they can never embody with us, & grow up in orderly Families, to the Peopling of the Land; but still remain in our Body Politick as a kind of extravasat Blood. As many Negro Men as there are among us, so many empty Places are there in our Train Bands, and the places taken up of Men that might make Husbands for our Daughters. And the Sons and Daughters of *New England* would become more like *Jacob* and *Rachel,* if this Slavery were thrust quite out of Doors. Moreover it is too well known that Temptations Masters are under, to connive at the Fornication of their Slaves; lest they should be obliged to find them Wives, or pay their Fines. It seems to be practically pleaded that they might be lawless; 'tis thought much of, that the Law should have satisfaction for their Thefts, and other Immoralities; by which means, *Holiness to the Lord* is more rarely engraven upon this sort of Servitude. It is likewise most lamentable to think, how in taking Negroes out of *Africa,* and selling of them here, That which God had joined together, Men do boldly rend asunder; Men from their Country, Husbands from their Wives, Parents from their Children. How horrible is the Uncleanness, Mortality, if not Murder, that the Ships are guilty of that bring great Crouds of these miserable Men and Women. Methinks when we are bemoaning the barbarous Usage of our Friends and Kinsfolk in *Africa,* it might not be unreasonable to enquire whether we are not culpable in forcing the *Africans* to become Slaves amongst ourselves. And it may be a question whether all the Benefit received by *Negro* Slaves will balance the Account of Cash laid out upon them; and for the Redemption of our own enslaved Friends out of *Africa.* Besides all the persons and Estates that have perished there.

Obj. 1. *These Blackamores are of the Posterity of Cham, and therefore are under the curse of Slavery.* Gen. 9, 25, 26, 27.

Ans. Of all Offices, one would not beg this; viz. Uncall'd for, to be an Executioner of the Vindictive Wrath of God; the extent and duration of which is to us uncertain. If this ever was a Commission; How do we know but that it is long since out of Date? Many have found it to their Cost, that a Prophetical Denunciation of Judgement against a Person or People, would not warrant them to inflict that evil. If it would, *Hazael* might justify himself in all he did against his master, and the *Israelites* from 2 *Kings* 8, 10, 12.

But it is possible that by cursory reading, this Text may have been mistaken. For *Canaan* is the Person Cursed three times over, without the mentioning of *Cham.* Good Expositors suppose the Curse entailed on him, and that this Prophesie was accomplished in the Extirpation of the *Canaanites,* and in the Servitude of the *Gibeonites. Vide Pareum.* Whereas the Blackamores are not descended of *Canaan,* but of *Cush.* Psal. 68, 31. *Princes shall come out of Egypt* [Mizraim]. *Ethiopia* [Cush] *shall soon Stretch out her hands unto God.* Under which Names, all Africa may be comprehended; and their Promised Conversion ought to be prayed for. *Jer.* 13, 23. *Can the Ethiopian change his Skin?* This shows that Black Men are the Posterity of *Cush.* Who time out of mind have been distinguished by their Colour. And for want of the true, *Ovid* assigns a fabulous cause of it.

Sanguinetum credunt in corpora summa vocato
Ethiopum populos nigrum traxisse colorem.
Metamorph. lib. 2.

Obj. 2. *The Nigers are brought out of a Pagan Country, into places where the Gospel is preached.*

Ans. Evil must not be done, that good may come of it. The extraordinary and comprehensive Benefit accruing to the Church of God and to *Joseph* personally, did not rectify his Brethren's Sale of him.

Obj. 3. *The Africans have Wars one with another: Our Ships bring lawful Captives taken in those wars.*

Ans. For aught is known, their Wars are much as were between *Jacob's* Sons and their Brother *Joseph.* If they be between Town and Town: Provincial or National; Every War is upon one side Unjust. An Unlawful War can't make lawful Captives. And by receiving, we are in danger to promote, and partake in their Barbarous Cruelties. I am sure, if some Gentlemen should go down to the *Brewsters* to take the Air, and Fish; And a stronger Party from *Hull* should *surprise* them, and sell them for Slaves to a Ship outward bound; they would think themselves unjustly dealt with; both by Sellers and Buyers. And yet 'tis to be feared, we have no other Kind of Title to our *Nigers. There all things whatsoever ye would that men should do to you, do you even so to them: for this is the Law and Prophets.* Matt. 7, 12.

Obj. 4. Abraham *had Servants bought with his Money and born in his House.*

Ans. Until the Circumstances of *Abraham's* purchase be recorded, no Argument can be drawn from it. In the mean time, Charity obliges us to conclude, that He knew it was lawful and good.

It is Observable that the *Israelites* were strictly forbidden the buying or selling one another for Slaves. *LEVIT.* 25. 39. 46. *Jer.* 34. 8-22. And God gaged His Blessing in lieu of any loss they might conceit they suffered thereby, *Deut.* 15. 18. And since the partition Wall is broken down, inordinate Self-love should likewise be demolished. God expects that Christians should carry it to all the World, as the *Israelites* were to carry it one towards another. And for Men obstinately to persist in holding their Neighbours and Brethren under the Rigor of perpetual Bondage, seems to be no proper way of gaining Assurance that God has given them Spiritual Freedom. Our Blessed Saviour has altered the Measures of the ancient Love Song, and set it to a most Excellent New tune, which all ought to be ambitious of Learning. *Matt.* 5. 43. 44. *John* 13. 34. These *Ethiopians,* as black as they are, seeing they are the Sons and Daughters of the First *Adam,* the Brethren and Sisters of the Last ADAM, and the Offspring of God; They ought to be treated with a Respect agreeable.

Servitus perfecta voluntaria, inter Christianum & Christianum, ex parte servi patientis sape est licita, quia est necessaria; sed ex parte domini agentis, & procurando, & exercendo, vix potest esse licita; quia non convenit regula illi generali: Quacunque volueritis ut Saciant vobis homines, ita & vos sacite eis. Matt. 7. 12

Persecta servitus pence, non potest jure locum habere, nisi ex delicto gravi quod ultimun Supplicium aliquo modo meretur: quia Libertas ex naturali astimatione proxime accedit ad vitam ipsm, & eidem a multis praserri Solet.

Ames. Cas. Confe. Lib. 5. Cap. 23. Thes. 2. 3.

ADDENDUM III

Recommended Reading List

The issue of slavery in American society is so complex that no one book could completely discuss the subject. Therefore, the following list of books is offered for those desiring a more complete understanding of the issue of slavery in American history. These books are written by men of various political persuasions, but in many places the theme of each runs counter to the accepted politically correct view of the issue of slavery in America and in Africa.

Slavery in the North

1. *Notes on the History of Slavery in Massachusetts,* George H. Moore, D. Appleton and Company, New York, New York, 1866. Moore, a historian from New York, gives a no-nonsense overview of how slavery and the slave trade began and thrived in Massachusetts. A must read for anyone desiring to understand how deep-seated slavery is in American history.

2. *The Negro in Colonial New England,* Lorenzo J. Greene, Kennikat Press, Inc., Port Washington, New York, 1966. What Moore did in the nineteenth century for understanding slavery in the North, Greene has done for the twentieth century.

3. *Black Bondage in the North,* Edgar J. McManus, Syracuse University Press, Syracuse, New York, 1973. Following the path blazed by Greene, McManus demonstrates that chattel slavery and civil slavery were very common in the North.

4. *North of Slavery: The Negro in the Free States, 1790-1860,* Leon P. Litwack, The University of Chicago Press, Chicago, Illinois, 1961. The North as a land of freedom and equality is not seen in this scholar's review of African-American life in the North. This work demonstrates the second-class status (i.e., civil slavery as defined by St. George Tucker) of free people of color in the North.

Slavery in the South

1. *Roll Jordan Roll, The World the Slaves Made,* Eugene D. Genovese, Pantheon Books, Random House Inc., New York, New York, 1972. The author examines the various forces within a slave community from the master's house to the slave's cabin as very few historians have done.

2. *Life and Labor in the Old South,* Ulrich B. Phillips, Little, Brown, and Company, New York, New York, 1929. Phillips's views of slavery have drawn much criticism from liberal historians; nevertheless, he offers his readers a view of the Old South and the institution of slavery that deserves a fair reading.

3. *A Defense of Virginia and the South,* Robert L. Dabney (1867), Sprinkle Publishing Company, Harrisonburg, Virginia, republished 1977. Dabney, a Presbyterian theologian and friend of Stonewall Jackson, offers a cogent account of slavery before the War for Southern Independence.

4. *A South-Side View of Slavery; or Three Months at the South in 1854,* Nehemiah Adams, D.D. (1854), Kennikat Press, Inc., Port Washington, New York, republished in 1963. From Boston, Massachusetts, to Charleston, South Carolina, this Northerner's view of slavery and the appropriate method for its elimination is very instructive for modern Americans who have been fed a steady diet of liberal bias.

5. *The South-West by a Yankee,* Joseph H. Ingraham (1835), originally published in 1835 by Harper & Brothers, New York, New York, reprinted by Readex Microprint Corporation, 1966. In 1834, Ingraham, a Yankee from Maine, makes a trip to the "South-West" of the United States (i.e., the Natchez, Mississippi, area). During his stay there, Ingraham describes life in the Old South. His travels and experiences make him question some of his and most Northerners' views about the South and slavery.

6. *Time on the Cross: The Economics of American Negro Slavery,* Robert W. Fogel and Stanley L. Engerman, Little, Brown and Company, Boston, Massachusetts, 1974. For his work on the economics of American slavery, Fogel won the Nobel Peace Prize and the scorn of politically correct society. This work debunks liberal myths about several issues surrounding slavery such as slave breeding, overworked slaves, broken slave families, and various other forms of mistreatment of slaves by slaveholders.

African-American Slaveholders

1. *Andrew Durnford, A Black Sugar Planter in Antebellum Louisiana,* David O. Whitten, Northwestern Louisiana State University Press, Natchitoches, Louisiana, 1981. Durnford, a free man of color, in Louisiana, shatters the myth about African-Americans being the victims of slavery. Here is the story of an African-American who owns a large plantation and many slaves—none of whom are related to him.

2. *William Johnson's Natchez: The Ante-Bellum Diary of a Free Negro,* William R. Hogan and Edwin A. Davis, eds., Louisiana State University Press, Baton Rouge, Louisiana, 1993. A first-person account of the life of a free person of color in Mississippi before the War. Johnson, a businessman and slaveholder, tells how he lived and prospered in pre-war Mississippi.

3. *The Forgotten People: Cane River's Creoles of Color,* Gary Mills, Louisiana State University Press, Baton Rouge, Louisiana, 1977. Mills takes the reader on a trip to a forgotten world, the world of the free people of color who were prosperous owners of land, homes, and slaves. The South's last two companies of troops composed of free people of color resided in this area of Louisiana.

4. *Black Slaveowners, Free Black Slave Masters in South Carolina, 1790-1860,* Larry Koger, McFarland and Company, Inc., Publishers, Jefferson, North Carolina, 1985. Koger demonstrates that black slaveholders owned slaves for the same reasons white slaveholders owned them—profit. This book is a stern rebuke to those who see slavery as a white-versus-black institution.

The War for Southern Independence

1. *The South Was Right!,* James R. Kennedy and Walter D. Kennedy, Pelican Publishing Company, Gretna, Louisiana, 1994. Described as the Bible of the Neo-Confederate movement, this book refutes the many myths about the War. Myths such as the War being fought to protect slavery, the North as a land of freedom and justice, Lincoln as the freer of slaves, and many others are exposed by the authors. As the title states, the authors advance the idea that the right of secession and free government was correct in 1860-65 and is still correct in the twenty-first century.

2. *Why Not Freedom! America's Revolt Against Big Government,* James R. Kennedy and Walter D. Kennedy, Pelican Publishing Company,

Gretna, Louisiana, 1995. The consequences for all Americans of the South losing the War are reviewed. The authors contend that Robert E. Lee's surrender at Appomattox marked more than just the loss of the War for the South. It marked the end of real State's Rights and the beginning of an all-powerful Federal government. Without true State's Rights, there are no means of controlling the Federal government; its will becomes law—which is not what the Founding Fathers had in mind when they seceded from the central government in London. How this change has taken place and how it can be reversed are the major themes of this book.

3. *When in the Course of Human Events: Arguing the Case for Southern Secession,* Charles Adams, Rowman and Littlefield Publishers, Inc., New York, New York, 2000. A scholarly defense, by a non-Southerner, of the right of the Southern states (or any American state) to withdraw from the Union and form a government more pleasing to their people.

4. *Was Jefferson Davis Right?* James R. Kennedy and Walter D. Kennedy, Pelican Publishing Company, Gretna, Louisiana, 1997. The authors contend that Jefferson Davis and his Southern colleagues acted in accordance with the rights of Americans as they sought to establish a government by the consent of the governed in 1861. Moreover, Davis's life as a planter, slaveholder, soldier, and national politician displays his truly patriotic nature. His progressive views of slavery and how it should be abolished are noted in this work.

5. *A View of the Constitution of the United States: With Selected Writings,* St. George Tucker, Clyde N. Wilson, ed., Liberty Fund, Inc., Indianapolis, Indiana, 1999. St. George Tucker's views on the Constitution and slavery offer modern Americans a look into the mind of one of America's Founding Fathers. His views on slavery should be read by every American who claims to be opposed to that institution.

Miscellaneous

1. *A Debate on Slavery,* N. L. Rice, Negro University Press, New York, New York, 1969. In 1845 a debate was held in Cincinnati, Ohio, between two Presbyterian ministers on the above question. It is important to note that although today's Church does not recognize the views held by the minister who is taking the negative in this debate, those views were widely held before the mid-nineteenth century.

2. *Pick a Better Country,* Ken Hamblin, Simon and Schuster, New York, New York, 1996. Conservative radio talk-show host Ken Hamblin describes how America is the best place on earth for anyone to take control of his future. When faced with fellow African-Americans who view America as a place of black oppression and bondage, he rebukes them with the challenge, "Pick a better country"—thus the title of his first book.

3. *Out of America: A Black Man Confronts Africa,* Keith B. Richburg, Basic Books, New York, New York, 1997. A journalist gets a first-hand, up-close look at his ancestral homeland of Africa and comes away knowing he and his people are better off than any Africans in the world. His conclusion is that slavery was good for him and his people!

4. *Prince among Slaves: The True Story of an African Prince Sold in the American South,* Terry Alford, Oxford University Press, New York, New York, 1977. The author chronicles the life of Adb Rahman Ibrahima, a West African prince who, while on a slave-hunting trip, was captured by fellow Africans and sold into slavery. His story moves from Africa to Natchez, Mississippi, and back to Africa. From a prince to a slave and back to freedom, this man's story provides much information on the nature of the slave trade and slavery itself.

5. *The Suppression of the African Slave Trade to the United States of America, 1638-1870,* W. E. B. Dubois, Russell and Russell Inc., New York, New York, 1965. This noted African-American historian gives a clear picture of how the struggle to end the African slave trade was maintained. A sentinel work in the abolition of that most nefarious commerce.

6. *Twelve Years a Slave, by Solomon Northup,* Sue Eakin and Joseph Logsdon, eds., Louisiana State University Press, Baton Rouge, Louisiana, 1996. Northup begins his story in New York and explains how he was captured, taken to the South, and sold as a slave. His account covers his life as the slave of a good master and an evil master before the laws of Louisiana discover and free him.

7. *John Jasper: The Unmatched Negro Philosopher and Preacher,* William E. Hatcher, LL.D., Sprinkle Publications, Harrisonburg, Virginia, 1985. John Jasper was a slave of a Christian master. After his conversion he began to preach the gospel. One-half of his preaching career was during the time he was a slave. After the War

he continued to preach and displayed a love for his Christian master which was second only to his love for his heavenly Master. John Jasper was not politically correct!

8. *The Flags of the Confederacy: An Illustrated History,* Devereaux D. Cannon, Pelican Publishing Company, Gretna, Louisiana, 1988. In explaining the genesis and evolution of the various Confederate flags, Cannon simplifies the history and use of the Confederate flag.

9. *The Flags of Civil War South Carolina,* Glenn Dedmondt, Pelican Publishing Company, Gretna, Louisiana, 2000. For those desirous of learning more about the various battle flags of the South, this book offers a good place to begin that search.

Notes

INTRODUCTION

1. Jefferson Davis, *The Rise and Fall of the Confederate Government* (1881,William M. Coats, Publisher, Nashville, TN: 1998), Vol. I, p. 3.

2. Consistent with earlier works, *The South Was Right!, Why Not Freedom!,* and *Was Jefferson Davis Right?,* the author will refer to the War of 1861-65 by the term "War for Southern Independence." A civil war is a war in which two antagonistic factions vie for control of the central government. At no time were the people of the Confederate States of American attempting to impose their form of government upon the people of the United States of America. The Confederate government was defending itself against Northern aggression; therefore, the term "Civil War" is an insult to those brave men who fought for Southern independence, and for that reason it will not be used in this work.

CHAPTER ONE

1. O. A. Sherrard, *Freedom from Fear, The Slave and His Emancipation* (St. Martin's Press, New York, NY: 1961), p. 11.

2. James Walvin, *Slavery and the Slave Trade* (University Press of Mississippi, Jackson, MS: 1983), p. 1.

3. Ibid.

4. W. O. Blake, *The History of Slavery and the Slave Trade, Ancient and Modern* (1858, Haskell House Publishers Ltd., New York, NY: 1969), p. 24.

5. Aristotle, as cited in Walvin, p. 5. Also see Sherrard, p. 25.

6. Sherrard, p. 13.

7. Ibid., pp. 22-23.

8. William Swinton, *Outlines of the World's History* (American Book Company, New York, NY: 1902), p. 158.

9. Walvin, p. 5.

10. Tactitus, as cited in ibid., p. 9.

11. Ibid., p. 11.

12. David Brion Davis, *New York Times Review of Books,* New York, New York,

October 11, 1990, p. 37.

13. Dr. Hilary Beckles, *The Americas* (Routhledge Press, New York, NY: 1994), Vol. 41, No. 2, p. 21.

14. Rev. Richard Oastler, as cited in Michael A. Hoffman, *They Were White and They Were Slaves* (Ruffin House Publishers, Dresden, NY: 1991), p. 25.

15. Ibid.

16. Charles Shaw, *When I Was a Child* (Harper and Brothers, New York, NY: 1842), pp. 18, 20, 22.

17. Ibid., 40.

18. Blake, p. 106.

CHAPTER TWO

1. Ernest H. Pentecost, in the introduction to George F. Dow, *Slave Ships and Slaving* (1927, Cornell Maritime Press, Inc., Cambridge, MA: 1968), p. XVII.

2. Walvin, p. 28.

3. Ibid., p. 40.

4. Sherrard, p. 26.

5. Dow, p. v.

6. Sherrard, p. 26.

7. Ibid., pp. 29-30.

8. Robert L. Dabney, *A Defense of Virginia and the South* (1867, Sprinkle Publications, Harrisonburg, VA: 1977), p. 12.

9. Francis B. Simkins, *A History of the South* (Alfred A. Knopf, New York, NY: 1959), p. 116.

10. Ibid., p. 117.

11. Thomas Jefferson, as cited in Alexis de Tocqueville, *Democracy in America* (1838, The Classics in Liberty Library, New York, NY: 1992), p. 45.

12. Thomas Jefferson, *Letters and Addresses of Thomas Jefferson,* William B. Parker and Jonas Viles, eds. (National Jefferson Society, Buffalo, NY: 1903), p. 285.

13. Ibid., pp. 25-27; also see Thomas Jefferson, *Notes on the State of Virginia,* William Peden, ed. (W. W. Norton & Co., New York, NY: 1954), pp. 137-40.

14. De Tocqueville, p. 338.

15. Simkins, p. 117.

16. John S. Tilley, *The Coming of the Glory* (1949, Bill Coats, Ltd., Nashville, TN: 1995), p. 16.

17. Simkins, p. 96.

18. Ibid.

19. William Rawle, *A View of the Constitution: Secession as Taught at West Point,* Walter D. Kennedy and James R. Kennedy, eds. (1825, Old South Books, Simsboro, LA: 1993), p. 4.

20. Blake, Vol. II, p. 502.

21. Simkins, p. 117.

22. Rev. P. Fontaine, as cited in Dabney, p. 45.

23. Journal of the House of Burgesses, as cited in St. George Tucker, *A View of the Constitution of the United States: With Selected Writings,* Clyde N. Wilson, ed. (Liberty Fund, Inc., Indianapolis, IN: 1999), p. 417. All quotations from this source are by permission of the Liberty Fund, Inc.

24. Tilley, p. 17.

25. Ibid.

26. Dabney, p. 44.

27. Simkins, p. 130.

28. Ibid., p. 118.

29. Tilley, pp. 32-33.

30. Gerard C. Brandon, as cited in John K. Bettersworth, *MISSISSIPPI: A History* (The Steck Company, Austin, TX: 1959), pp. 194-95.

31. Bettersworth, p. 196.

32. Simkins, p. 105.

33. Ibid.

34. Tilley, p. 36.

35. Ibid.

36. Ibid.

37. Simkins, p. 106.

38. Tilley, p. 32.

39. Arthur H. Jennings, *The Gray Book* (The Gray Book Committee, Sons of Confederate Veterans, Hattiesburg, MS, nd), p. 4.

40. Otto Scott, *The Secret Six: John Brown and the Abolitionist Movement* (Uncommon Books, Murphys, CA: 1993), p. 73.

41. James Madison, *The Federalist No. 43,* as cited in *The Federalist, Student Edition,* Carey & McCellan eds. (Kendall-Hunt Publishing Company, Dubuque, IA: 1990), p. 228. Madison, the Father of the United States Constitution, in *The Federalist No. 43* states that all governmental institutions must be sacrificed to the safety and happiness of a society. This is the principle that motivated the Fire-Eaters. If their safety and happiness were being threatened by the Federal government, they believed they had a right as Americans to replace the Federal government with a government more pleasing to the people.

42. Bettersworth, pp. 222-26.

43. Lorenzo J. Greene, *The Negro in Colonial New England, 1620-1776* (Kennikat Press, Inc., Port Washington, NY: 1966), p. 15.

44. Gary B. Nash, "Slaves and Slaveowners in Colonial Philadelphia," *William and Mary Quarterly*, Jan. 1973, 3rd ed., Ser. 3, Vol. 30, No. 1, p. 255

45. George H. Moore, *Notes on the History of Slavery in Massachusetts* (D. Appleton and Company, New York, NY: 1866), p. 5; also see Edgar J. McManus, *Black Bondage in the North* (Syracuse University Press, Syracuse, NY: 1991), p. 2. No one can pinpoint when Negro slavery began in the North with absolute precision. What is certain is that by 1638 slaves were being bought and sold in Massachusetts. In 1626, the Dutch West India Company was making use of Negro slaves in New Netherlands.

46. Eugene D. Genovese, *Roll Jordan Roll, The World the Slaves Made* (Pantheon Books, Random House, Inc., New York, NY: 1972), p. 3.

47. McManus, p. 2.

48. Ibid., pp. 2-3.

49. David Brion Davis, *Slavery and Human Progress* (Oxford University Press, New York, NY: 1984), p. 76.

50. Greene, p. 16.

51. Moore, pp. 1-3.

52. Greene, p. 17.

53. Moore, pp. 4-5.

54. David Brion Davis, *Slavery and Human Progress,* p. 73.

55. McManus, p. 59.

56. Moore, pp. 7-8.

57. Robert W. Fogel and Stanley L. Engerman, *Time on the Cross: the Economics of American Negro Slavery* (Little, Brown and Company, Boston, MA: 1974), pp. 78-86.

58. Moore, pp. 54-55.

59. Ibid., p. 34.

60. Greene, pp. 45-46.

61. Ibid., pp. 45-46.

62. Moore, p. 234.

63. Ibid., pp. 234-37.

64. Ibid., pp. 27-28.

65. Greene, p. 18.

66. Moore, pp. 32-33.

67. Greene, p. 108.

68. Ibid., p. 109.

69. McManus, p. 59.

70. Nash, p. 225.

71. Ibid.

72. Jean R. Soderlund, *Quakers and Slavery, A Divided Spirit* (Princeton University Press, Princeton, NJ: 1985), p. 59; also see Greene, pp. 226-27.

73. Ibid.

74. Nash, p. 229.

75. Ibid., p. 232.

76. Ibid., p. 254.

77. Ibid., p. 242.

78. Dabney, pp. 42-43.

79. Moore, p. 82.

80. The author remembers as a child being told the story of the selling of Joseph. This storytelling took place in Mississippi in 1956 by the author's fifth-grade teacher.

81. Moore, p. 253.

82. Judge John Saffin, "A Brief and Candid Answer to a Late Printed Sheet, Entitled, The Selling of Joseph," as cited in Moore, pp. 251-56.

83. Abraham Lincoln, as cited in *The Lincoln-Douglas Debates of 1858,* R. W. Johannsen, ed. (Oxford University Press, New York, NY: 1965), pp. 162-63.

84. Mike Tuggle, "Slave Reparations vs. History," *Southern Events,* Vol. 7, No. 1, p. 6.

85. Robert H. Bork, *Slouching toward Gomorrah* (Regan Books, New York, NY: 1996).

86. Jared Taylor, *Paved with Good Intentions* (Carroll & Graf Publishers, Inc., New York, NY: 1992), p. 298.

87. Francis W. Springer, *War for What* (Bill Coats Ltd., Nashville, TN: 1990), p. 9.

88. Taylor, p. 297.

89. Herbert B. Gutman, *The Black Family in Slavery and Freedom, 1750-1925* (Vintage Books, New York, NY: 1977), p. 32. Also see Fogel and Engerman, p. 49.

CHAPTER THREE

1. N. L. Rice, D.D., *A Debate on Slavery* (1846, Wm. H. Moore & Co., Negro University Press, a Division of Greenwood Publishing Corp., New York, NY: 1969), p. 33.

2. J. Steven Wilkins, *America: The First 350 Years* (Covenant Publications, Monroe, LA: 1988), pp. 140-50.

3. Rice, p. 25.

4. Rice, pp. 24-41.

5. Ibid., p. 257.

6. Ibid., p. 255.

7. R. L. Dabney, *Discussions, Secular* (1897, Sprinkle Publications, Harrisonburg, VA: 1979), Vol. IV, p. 569.

8. Ibid., pp. 498-505, 470-75, 280.

9. Rice, p. 33.

10. John Hopkins, as quoted in G. M. Wharton, ed., *Scriptural, Ecclesiastical, and Historical View of Slavery* (1864, republished by Columbia Press, Tulsa, Oklahoma, nd), p. 4.

11. Ibid., p. 5.

12. Ibid., p. 6.

13. Ibid., p. 50.

14. George Fitzhugh, *Sociology for the South, or the Failure of Free Society* (Burt Franklin Publisher, New York, NY: nd), p. 206.

15. Joseph R. Wilson, in a letter to George T. Jackson, et al., Augusta, Georgia, January 8, 1861. *Documenting the American South.* University of North Carolina at Chapel Hill Libraries.

16. Rice, pp. 470-82. The preceding was taken in part from Dr. Rice's sixteenth and final speech on the subject "Is Slave-Holding in Itself Sinful." For the full text of both Dr. Rice's and Rev. Blanchard's debate, see Rice, *A Debate on Slavery* (1846, Wm. H. Moore & Co., Negro University Press, A Division of Greenwood Publishing Corp., New York, 1969).

17. Dr. Joseph R. Wilson, *Mutual Relation of Master and Slaves as Taught in the Bible.* Sermon preached in the First Presbyterian Church, Augusta, Georgia, January 6, 1861. Taken from web site: http://metalab.unc.edu/docSouth/wilson.htm/.

18. Simkins, p. 159.

19. William E. Hatcher, *John Jasper, The Unmatched Negro Philosopher and Preacher* (Sprinkle Publications, Harrisonburg, VA: 1985), pp. 97-98.

20. Ibid., pp. 28-29.

21. James R. Kennedy and Walter D. Kennedy, *Was Jefferson Davis Right?* (Pelican Publishing Company, Gretna, LA: 1998), p. 40.

22. *Twelve Years a Slave, by Solomon Northup,* Sue Eakin and Joseph Logsdon, eds. (Louisiana State University Press, Baton Rouge, LA: 1996), pp. 227-44, 265.

CHAPTER FOUR

1. Genovese, p. 9.

2. Ulrich B. Phillips, *Life and Labor in the Old South* (Grosset and Dunlop, New York, NY: 1929), p. 214.

3. Cotton Mather, as cited in Moore, p. 31.

4. John Adams, as cited in Greene, pp. 113, 322.

5. Alexis de Tocqueville, as cited in ibid.

6. Moore, p. 11.

7. Greene, p. 47.

8. Daniel P. Mannix, *Black Cargoes* (The Viking Press, New York, NY: 1962), p. 162.

9. Nash, p. 225.

10. Dow, p. 295.

11. Ibid.

12. Dow, p. 295.

13. Greene, pp. 20-21.

14. Dow, p. 296.

15. Ibid.

16. W. E. B. Dubois, *The Suppression of the African Slave Trade to the United States of America 1638-1870* (Russell and Russell Inc., New York, NY: 1965), pp. 162-63, 298.

17. Moore, pp. 18-19.

18. Dow, p. 297.

19. De Tocqueville, p. 340.

20. Michael Chevalier, *Society Manners and Politics in the United States* (1839, Augustus M. Kelly, Publishers, New York, NY: 1966), p. IV.

21. Ibid., pp. 360-61.

22. Ibid., p. 362.

23. Ibid.

24. McManus, p. 180.

25. New Jersey Assembly Acts, as cited in ibid.

26. Acts and Laws of Connecticut, 1784, as cited in ibid.

27. McManus, p. 181.

28. Fitzhugh, pp. 261-62.

29. McManus, p. 182.

30. De Tocqueville, p. 347.

31. Ibid., p. 348.

32. McManus, p. 192.

33. *William Johnson's Natchez, The Ante-Bellum Diary of a Free Negro,* William R. Hogan and Edwin A. Davis, eds. (Louisiana State University Press, Baton Rouge, LA: 1993), p. 2.

34. Woodrow Wilson, *Epochs of American History: Division and Reunion, 1829-1909* (Longmans, Green, and Company, New York, NY: 1910), pp. 125-26.

35. John Randolph, as cited in Russell Kirk, *John Randolph of Roanoke, A Study in American Politics* (Liberty Press, Indianapolis, IN: 1978), p. 46.

36. Kirk, p. 188.

37. John Randolph, as cited in ibid., p. 159.

38. Edmund Burke, "Speech on Conciliation with the Colonies" in *The Norton Anthology of English Literature,* Third Edition (W. W. Norton and Company, New York, NY: 1974), Vol. I, p. 2356.

39. James Kent, *Commentaries on American Law* (1827, Da Capo Press, New York, NY: 1971), Vol. I, p. 186.

40. Mannix, p. 205.

41. Kirk, p. 189.

42. Genovese, p. 5.

43. Ibid., p. 6.

44. Mark M. Smith, *Debating Slavery, Economy and Society in the Antebellum American South* (Cambridge University Press, Cambridge, UK: 1998), p. 4.

45. Ibid., p. 46.

46. *SLAVE NARRATIVES: A FOLK HISTORY OF SLAVERY IN THE UNITED STATES FROM INTERVIEWS WITH FORMER SLAVES,* the Alabama Narratives, Vol. I, p. 224.

47. Ibid., Oklahoma Narratives, Vol. VII, p. 296.

48. Ibid., Alabama Narratives, Vol., I, p. 215.

49. Ibid., Texas Narratives, Vol. IV, p. 296.

50. Kate Stone, *Brokenburn: The Journal of Kate Stone, 1861-1868* (Louisiana State University Press, Baton Rouge, LA: 1955), p. 139.

51. Oliver Hering in letter to Mary Helen Hering Middleton, copy of letter in author's possession.

52. Mary Helen Hering Middleton in letter to Oliver Hering, copy of letter in author's possession.

53. Belinda Hurmence, ed., *Before Freedom, When I Just Can Remember* (John F. Blair, Publisher, Winston-Salem, NC: 1989), pp. XII-XIII.

54. Jefferson Davis, p. 6.

55. McManus, p. 111.

56. Phillips, pp. 162, 197.

57. "Toby," as cited in James R. Kennedy and Walter D. Kennedy, *The South Was Right!* (Pelican Publishing Company, Gretna, LA: 1994), p. 98.

58. Smith, p. 15. Another way to understand slave ownership in the Old South is to look at the number of white families who owned slaves as opposed to the number of white families who did not own slaves. In 1860, out of 1.5 million households, 385,000 households, or about 25 percent

of the households in Dixie, owned slaves. Regardless of how one looks at the issue, more people in the South did not own slaves than did own slaves. A similar situation existed in the North with both slavery and the African slave trade; that is, the few partook of the institutions of slavery and the slave trade, while the many did not do so.

59. Rita Moore Krouse, "The Germantown Store," *North Louisiana Historical Association Journal,* Winter 1977, Vol. VIII, No. 2, p. 56.

60. Ibid., p. 57.

61. Ibid., p. 61.

62. Phillips, p. 211.

63. Woodrow Wilson, p. 127.

64. Phillips, p. 211, and Woodrow Wilson, p. 127.

65. Charles Eliot Norton, *Letters of Charles Eliot Norton* (Houghton Mifflin, Boston, MA: 1913), Vol. I, p. 121.

66. Louis F. Tasistro, *Random Shots and Southern Breezes* (Harper and Brothers, New York, NY: 1842), Vol. II, p. 13.

67. Solomon Northup, as cited in Eakin and Logsdon, p. 74.

68. Ibid., p. 62.

69. Phillips, p. 217.

70. John William Deforest, as cited in David C. Edmonds, *Yankee Autumn in Acadiana* (The Acadiana Press, Lafayette, LA: 1979), p. 62.

71. Larry Koger, *Black Slaveowners, Free Black Slave Masters in South Carolina, 1790-1860* (McFarland and Company, Inc., Publishers, Jefferson, NC: 1985), pp. 28-29.

72. Ibid., p. 31.

73. Ibid., p. 18.

74. Ibid., p. xiii.

75. Ibid., p. 1.

76. Ibid.

77. Gary B. Mills, *The Forgotten People, Cane River's Creoles of Color* (Louisiana State University Press, Baton Rouge, LA: 1977), p. 178.

78. Gary B. Mills, "Patriotism Frustrated: The Native Guards of Confederate Natchitoches," *Louisiana History,* Lafayette, LA, Vol. 18, Fall 1977, pp. 437-38.

79. Mills, *The Forgotten People,* p. 110.

80. Koger, p. 2.

81. David O. Whitten, *Andrew Durnford, A Black Sugar Planter in Antebellum Louisiana* (Northwestern Louisiana State University Press, Natchitoches, LA: 1981), p. 11.

82. Ibid.

83. Andrew Durnford, as cited in Whitten, p. 31.

84. Ibid., p. 32.

85. Ibid., p. 34.

86. Ibid., p. 35.

87. Ibid., p. 37.

88 John W. Haley, as cited in *The Rebel Yell and the Yankee Hurrah,* Ruth L. Silliker, ed. (Down East Book, Camden, ME: 1985), p. 116. John W. Haley was a private in the Seventeenth Maine Infantry. He made these comments during the summer offensive in Northern Virginia in 1864. It is of interest to note that this Yankee understood that slavery required a more extensive commitment on the part of the Southern plantation owner to his slaves than that of a Northern factory owner to his laborers.

89. William Johnson, Sr., as cited in Hogan and Davis, p. 15.

90. Ibid.

91. Ibid., p. 16.

92. Ibid., p. 17.

93. William Johnson's diary has been edited by William R. Hogan and Edwin A. Davis and republished by the Louisiana State University Press. As republished, Johnson's diary is just under eight hundred pages in length. For those who only wish to view the Old South as a society of white people enjoying the fruits of black oppression, Johnson's diary will be a disappointment.

94. Hogan and Davis, p. 35.

95. Ibid., p. 347.

96. Ibid., p. 523.

97. Ibid., p. 36.

98. Simkins, p. 127.

99. Ibid.

100. Ibid.

101. Frederick Law Olmsted, *A Journey in the Sea-Board States* (Mason Brothers, New York, NY: 1859), p. 17.

102. Abraham Lincoln, as cited in Beverly B. Mumford, *Virginia's Attitude Toward Slavery and Secession* (L. H. Jenkins, Inc., Richmond, VA: 1915), p. 173.

103. For a more complete look at the blatant racist attitude of the North during the early part of the nineteenth century, see Kennedy and Kennedy, *The South Was Right!,* pp. 53-58.

104. For a detailed and touching account of a Northern free man of color

who was kidnapped and sold into slavery, see the story of Solomon Northup in Eakin and Logsdon.

CHAPTER FIVE

1. Bettersworth, p. 214.

2. Moore, p. 2.

3. The idea that the states were the originators of, and the power behind, the movement for American independence is examined in Kennedy and Kennedy, *Was Jefferson Davis Right?*, pp. 258-59.

4. Article II of the Articles of Confederation states: "Each state retains its sovereignty, freedom, and independence, and every power, jurisdiction and right, which is not by this Confederation expressly delegated to the United States in Congress assembled." The people who wrote and ratified these Articles clearly understood that they were members of thirteen sovereign states.

5. Clyde N. Wilson, p. xv.

6. St. George Tucker, as cited in Clyde N. Wilson, pp. 23, 24.

7. In modern America, the idea of consent is often relegated to the principle of voting. That is to say, Americans give their consent by voting for or against their political leaders. While an important aspect in representative government, the right to vote is not what the Founding Fathers were demanding when they signed their names to the Declaration of Independence. Furthermore, not only do Americans have the right to consent to their government, but also to radically change that form of government to their liking as is stated in the Declaration of Independence.

8. St. George Tucker, as cited in Clyde N. Wilson, p. 27.

9. Ibid.

10. Ibid., p. 28.

11. Ibid., pp. 86-87.

12. Ibid., p. 403.

13. Clyde N. Wilson, p. 402.

14. St. George Tucker, as cited in Clyde N. Wilson, p. 403.

15. Ibid., pp. 405-6.

16. Ibid., p. 407.

17. Ibid, p. 408.

18. Ibid., p. 409.

19. Ibid., pp. 434-435.

20. Ibid, p. 434.

21. *North American Review* (1826: AMS Press, Inc., New York, NY: 1965), Vol. XXII, pp. 446-51.

22. Ibid., p. 450.

23. Francis Lieber, *On Civil Liberty and Self-Government* (J. B. Lippincott and Company, Philadelphia, PA: 1853), p. 270.

24. Ibid, p. 12.

25. Ibid, p. 13.

26. Ibid., pp. 295-96.

27. Ibid., p. 300.

28. St. George Tucker, as cited in Jesse T. Carpenter, *The South as a Conscious Minority* (The New York University Press, New York, NY: 1930), p. 202.

29. Thomas Jefferson, as cited in Kennedy and Kennedy, *Was Jefferson Davis Right?,* p. 282.

30. James Madison, as cited in ibid., p. 284.

31. Patrick Henry, as cited in Herbert J. Storing, *What the Anti-Federalists Were For* (The University of Chicago Press, Chicago and London: 1981), p. 24.

CHAPTER SIX

1. Greg Loren Durand, *America's Caesar, Abraham Lincoln and the Birth of a Modern Empire* (Crown Rights Book Company, Wiggins, MS: 1999), p. 207.

2. Abraham Lincoln, as cited in Johannsen, pp. 162-63.

3. Abraham Lincoln, as cited in *The Collected Works of Abraham Lincoln,* Ray P. Basler, ed. (Rutgers University Press, New Brunswick, NJ: 1953), Vol. II, p. 399.

4. Abraham Lincoln, as cited in Johannsen, pp. 162-63.

5. McManus, p. 184.

6. Mumford, p. 172.

7. Ibid., p. 173.

8. David A. Nichols, *Lincoln and the Indians* (University of Missouri Press, Columbia: 1978), p. 87.

9. William H. Seward, as cited in Mildred L. Rutherford, *Truths of History* (M. L. Rutherford, Athens, GA: 1907), p. 92.

10. William Sherman, as cited in the *Official Records: War of the Rebellion,* Vol. XXX, pt. IV, p. 235.

11. J. S. Buckingham, *The Slave States of America* (1842, Negro University Press, New York, NY: 1968), Vol. II, p. 112.

12. St. George Tucker, as cited in Clyde N. Wilson, p. 408.

13. Robert E. Lee, as cited in Douglas S. Freeman, *R. E. Lee* (Charles Scribner's Sons, New York, NY: 1947), Vol. I, p. 372.

14. Jefferson Davis, as cited in Robert McElory, *Jefferson Davis, The*

Unreal and the Real (Harper and Brothers Publishers, New York, NY: 1937), Vol. I, p. 104.

15. Ibid.

16. James F. Rhodes, *History of the United States* (The MacMillian Company, New York, NY: 1920), Vol. II, p. 325.

17. Ibid.

18. Henry C. Whitney, as cited in Charles L. C. Minor, *The Real Lincoln* (1904, Sprinkle Publications, Harrisonburg, VA: 1992), p. 11.

19. Abraham Lincoln, as cited in *Abraham Lincoln From His Own Words and Contemporary Accounts,* Roy E. Appleman, ed. (National Park Service Source Book Two, Washington, DC: 1956), p. 19.

20. Ibid., pp. 20-21.

21. Ibid.

22. Ibid., p. 29.

23. Emancipation Proclamation, as cited in Jennings, p. 9.

24. Ibid.

25. Ibid.

26. W. C. Sympson, "Legacy of Slavery," *The United States Civil War Center Newsletter,* Vol. 5, No. 1, March 2000, p. 6.

27. Clement L. Vallandigham, *The Record of Honorable C. L. Vallandigham* (1863, J. Walter and Company, Columbus, OH, republished by Johnson Graphics, Decatur, MI: nd), 2nd ed., p. 209.

28. Ibid., pp. 215-16.

29. Ibid., p. 221.

30. Ibid.

31. An address to the people of Maryland, John A. Marshall, *American Bastile* (1881, Crown Rights Book Company, Wiggins, MS: 1998), p. 643.

32. Ibid., p. 642.

33. Francis Key Howard, as cited in ibid., pp. 645-46.

34. Ibid., p. 711.

35. Written by James Ryder Randall, 1861, adopted as the state song in 1939 as enacted by Chapter 451, Acts of 1939; Code State Government Article, sec. 13-307, Maryland State Archives.

36. James Madison, as cited in *The Federalist,* George W. Carey and James McClellan, eds. (Kendall/Hunt Publishing Company, Dubuque, IA: 1990), p. 268.

37. Rawle, p. 234.

38. Article II, Section I, United States Constitution.

CHAPTER SEVEN

1. For the text of President Davis's two inaugural addresses, see Kennedy and Kennedy, *The South Was Right!,* pp. 321-26.

2. This quotation is taken from Lincoln's first inaugural address in 1861. In 1860, at the Republican Convention, Lincoln stated that ". . . the maintenance innovate of the rights of the States, and especially the right of each State to . . . control its own domestic institution . . . exclusively, is essential to that balance of power on which the perfection and endurance of our political fabric depends." J. D. Randall and David H. Donald, *The Civil War and Reconstruction* (D. C. Heath & Co., Lexington, MA: 1969), p. 370.

3. Provisional Constitution of the Confederate States of America. This constitution was superseded by the Constitution of the Confederate States of America on February 22, 1862. The same provision limiting the African slave trade in the provisional constitution was incorporated into the final Confederate constitution.

4. Jefferson Davis, p. 7.

5. Ibid.

6. Ibid., p. 12.

7. Ibid., p. 30.

8. Alexander H. Stephens, as cited in *The Confederate Cause and Conduct in the War Between the States,* Hunter McGuire and George Christian, eds. (1907, Boonton Bookshop, Boonton, NJ: 1994), p. 179.

9. Jefferson Davis, p. 12.

10 Appleman, p. 21

CHAPTER EIGHT

1. Devereaux D. Cannon, *The Flags of the Confederacy* (Pelican Publishing Company, Gretna, LA: 1988), p. 73.

2. John R. Spears, "The Slave-Trade in America," *Scribner's Magazine,* July 1900, Vol. III, No. 1, p. 456.

3. Ibid.

4. Nichols, p. 87.

5. Ibid., p. 95.

6. Ibid., p. 87.

7. Ibid., p. 97.

8. For a more complete look at the campaign of cultural genocide against the South after the War, see Kennedy and Kennedy, *The South Was Right!,* Chapter 13.

9. Nichols, p. 180.

10. Forrest McDonald, *A Constitutional History of the United States* (Robert

E. Krieger Publishing Company, Malabar, FL: 1986), p. 153.

11. Justice Henry B. Brown, as cited in ibid.

12. Ibid.

13. Abram J. Ryan, *POEMS: Patriotic, Religious, Miscellaneous* (D. L. Brill Publishing Company, Mobile, AL: 1894), p. 74.

14. Ibid., p. 60.

15. Ibid., p. 64.

16. Ibid., p. 111.

17. Bettersworth, p. 234.

18. Early in the War, it was not unusual for a flag to be presented to an infantry company (approximately one hundred men and officers). As the war progressed, many of these companies and their flags were incorporated into a regiment. Many company flags then became regimental flags. Also, these units were organized around an all-volunteer force; therefore, each of these regiments was designated as a "volunteer" regiment.

19. Daniel Webster, *The Great Triumvirate, Webster, Clay, and Calhoun,* Merrill D. Peterson, ed. (Oxford University Press, New York, NY: 1987), p. 483.

20. Walter E. Williams, "Black Slavery Is Alive and Well," *Southern Partisan,* Vol. XX, 3rd Quarter 2000, p. 42.

21. Ibid.

22. Spears, p. 9.

23. Ibid.

24. Ibid. Also see Dubois, p. 298.

CHAPTER NINE

1. Representative Moore, *Daily Clarion-Ledger,* Jackson, MS, February 23, 1890.

2. William Chambers, as cited in Leon P. Litwack, *North of Slavery: The Negro in the Free States, 1790-1860* (The University of Chicago Press, Chicago, IL: 1961), pp. 30-31.

3. Ibid., p. 36.

4. Senator John Holmes, as cited in ibid., p. 37.

5. Senator Robert Y. Hayne, as cited in ibid., p. 39.

6. David Wilmot, as cited in ibid., p. 47.

7. Representative Henry C. Murphy, as cited in ibid.

8. Kennedy and Kennedy, *The South Was Right!,* p. 57.

9. Keith B. Richburg, *Out of America, A Black Man Confronts Africa* (Basic Books, New York, NY: 1997), p. xiv.

10. U.S. Census Bureau, *1990 Median Household Income by Race and State.* Prepared by: Income Statistics Branch/HHES Division, U.S. Department

of Commerce, Washington, DC.

11. Ken Hamblin, *Pick a Better Country* (Simon and Schuster, New York, NY: 1996), p. 249.

12. *Profile of the Country's African American Population,* U.S. Department of Commerce, Economic and Statistics Administration, Bureau of the Census.

CHAPTER TEN

1. Richburg, pp. 145-46.

2. Walter Williams, "Blacks Need an Equal Chance," *The News-Star,* Monroe, LA, April 6, 2001, p. 13-A.

3. Samuel Francis, "The Truth about Guns and Race," *The Southern Partisan,* 2nd Quarter 1994, p. 48.

4. *The Color of Crime* (New Century Foundation, Oakton, VA: 1999), p. 2.

5. Ibid., p. 3.

6. Samuel Francis, "Hate crimes against whites blacked out by media," *SF Online,* columns@samfrancis.net, January 16, 2001.

7. Dabney, *A Defense of Virginia and the South,* p. 85.

8. John Adams, as cited in Greene, pp. 113, 322.

9. Joseph H. Ingraham, *The South-West by a Yankee* (Harper and Brothers, New York, NY: 1835), reprinted by Readex Microprint Corporation, 1966, Vol. II, p. 269.

10. Ibid., pp. 265-66.

11. Ibid., p. 270.

ADDENDUM I

1. For a complete text of this pamphlet, see Clyde N. Wilson, pp. 402-47.

2. Ibid., p. 402.

ADDENDUM II

1. Moore, p. 87.

2. Ibid., pp. 83-87. This tract is reproduced as closely as possible to the way it was written in 1700. Therefore, some words and style of writing may appear somewhat unusual.

Bibliography

Adams, Charles, *When in the Course of Human Events, Arguing the Case for Southern Secession,* Rowman & Littlefield Publishers, Inc., New York, New York, 2000.

Adams, Nehemiah D., *A South-Side View of Slavery; or Three Months at the South in 1854,* Kennikat Press, Inc., Port Washington, New York, 1963.

Alford, Terry, *Prince among Slaves: The True Story of an African Prince Sold in the American South,* Oxford University Press, New York, New York, 1977.

Appleman, Roy E., Ed., *Abraham Lincoln From His Own Words and Contemporary Accounts,* National Park Service Source Book Two, Washington, D.C., 1956.

Bettersworth, John K., *MISSISSIPPI: A History,* The Steck Company, Austin, Texas, 1959.

Blake, W. O., *The History of Slavery and the Slave Trade, Ancient and Modern,* Haskell House Publishers Ltd., New York, New York, 1969.

Buckingham, J. S., *The Slave States of America,* Negro University Press, New York, New York, 1968.

Chevalier, Michael, *Society and Manners & Politics in the United States,* Augustus M. Kelly, Publishers, New York, New York, 1966.

Curry, J. L. M., *Confederate Military History,* The Archive Society, Harrisburg, Pennsylvania, 1994.

Dabney, Robert L., *A Defense of Virginia and the South,* Sprinkle Publications, Harrisonburg, Virginia, 1977.

Dabney, Robert L., *Discussions, Secular,* Sprinkle Publications, Harrisonburg, Virginia, 1979.

Davis, David B., *Slavery and Human Progress,* Oxford University Press, New York, New York, 1984.

Davis, Jefferson F., *The Rise and Fall of the Confederate Government,* William M. Coats, Publisher, Nashville, Tennessee, 1998.

De Tocqueville, Alexis, *Democracy in America,* Mayer and Lerner, Eds., Harper and Row, New York, New York, 1966.

Dow, George F., *Slave Ships and Slaving,* Kennikat Press, Inc., Port Washington, New York, 1969.

Dubois, W. E. B., *The Suppression of the African Slave-Trade to the United States of America 1638-1870,* Russell and Russell Inc., New York, New York, 1965.

Duncan, Christopher M., *The Anti-Federalists and Early American Political Thought,* Northern Illinois University Press, DeKalb, Illinois, 1995.

Durand, Greg L., *American Caesar, Abraham Lincoln and the Birth of a Modern Empire,* Crown Rights Publishing Company, Wiggins, Mississippi, 1999.

Eakin, Sue and Joseph Logsdon, Eds., *Twelve Years a Slave, by Solomon Northup,* Louisiana State University Press, Baton Rouge, Louisiana, 1996.

Edmonds, David C., *Yankee Autumn in Acadiana,* The Acadiana Press, Lafayette, LA, 1979.

Fitzhugh, George, *Sociology for the South, or the Failure of Free Society,* Burt Franklin Publisher, New York, New York, nd.

Fogel, Robert W. and Engerman, Stanley L., *Time on the Cross: the Economics of American Negro Slavery,* Little, Brown and Company, Boston, Massachusetts, 1974.

Freeman, Douglas, S., *R. E. Lee,* Charles Scribner's Sons, New York, New York, 1947.

Genovese, Eugene D., *Roll Jordan Roll, The World the Slaves Made,* Pantheon Books, Random House Inc., New York, New York, 1972.

Greene, Lorenzo J., *The Negro in Colonial New England, 1620-1776* Kennikat Press, Inc., Port Washington, New York, 1966.

Hamblin, Ken, *Pick a Better Country,* Simon and Schuster, New York, New York, 1996.

Hatcher, William E., *John Jasper, The Unmatched Negro Philosopher and Preacher,* Sprinkle Publications, Harrisonburg, Virginia, 1985.

Hoffman, Michael A., *They Were White and They Were Slaves,* Ruffin House Publishers, Dresden, New York, 1991.

Hogan, William R., and Davis, Edwin A., Eds., *William Johnson's Natchez, The Ante-Bellum Diary of a Free Negro,* Louisiana State University Press, Baton Rouge, Louisiana, 1993.

Hurmence, Belinda, Ed., *Before Freedom, When I Just Can Remember,* John F. Blair Publisher, Winston-Salem, North Carolina, 1989.

Jefferson, Thomas, *Notes on the State of Virginia,* William Peden, Ed., W. W. Norton & Co., New York, New York, 1954.

Johannsen, R. W., Ed., *The Lincoln-Douglas Debates of 1858,* Oxford University Press, New York, New York, 1965.

Kennedy, James R. and Walter D., *The South Was Right!,* Pelican Publishing Company, Gretna, Louisiana, 1994.

Kennedy, James R. and Walter D., *Was Jefferson Davis Right?,* Pelican Publishing Company, Gretna, Louisiana, 1998.

Kennedy, James R. and Walter D., *Why Not Freedom! America's Revolt Against Big Government,* Pelican Publishing Company, Gretna, Louisiana, 1995.

Kent, James, *Commentaries on American Law,* Da Capo Press, New York, New York, 1971.

Kirk, Russell, *John Randolph of Roanoke, A Study in American Politics,* Liberty Press, Indianapolis, Indiana, 1978.

Koger, Larry, *Black Slaveowners, Free Black Slave Masters in South Carolina, 1790-1860,* McFarland and Company, Inc., Publishers, Jefferson, North Carolina, 1985.

Lieber, Francis, *On Civil Liberty and Self-Government,* J. B. Lippincott and Company, Philadelphia, Pennsylvania, 1853.

Litwack, Leon P., *North of Slavery: The Negro in the Free States, 1790-1860,* The University of Chicago Press, Chicago, Illinois, 1961.

Mannix, Daniel P., *Black Cargoes,* The Viking Press, New York, New York, 1962.

Marshall, John A., *American Bastile,* Crown Rights Publishing Company, Wiggins, Mississippi, 1998.

McDonald, Forrest, *A Constitutional History of the United States,* Robert E. Krieger Publishing Company, Malabar, Florida, 1986.

McElory, Robert, *Jefferson Davis, The Unreal and the Real,* Harper and Brothers Publishers, New York, New York, 1937.

McKitrick, Eric L., Ed., *Slavery Defended: The View of the Old South,* Prentice-Hall, Inc., Englewood Cliffs, New Jersey, 1963.

McManus, Edgar J., *Black Bondage in the North,* Syracuse University Press, Syracuse, New York, 1973.

Mills, Gary, *The Forgotten People, Cane River's Creoles of Color,* Louisiana State University Press, Baton Rouge, Louisiana, 1977.

Minor, Charles L. C., *The Real Lincoln,* Sprinkle Publications, Harrisonburg, Virginia, 1992.

Moore, George H., *Notes on the History of Slavery in Massachusetts,* D. Appleton and Company, New York, New York, 1866.

Mumford, Beverly B., *Virginia's Attitude Toward Slavery and Secession,* L. H. Jenkins, Inc., Richmond, Virginia, 1915.

Nichols, David A., *Lincoln and the Indians,* University of Missouri Press, Columbia, Missouri, 1978.

Nicholson, James W., *Stories of Dixie,* Claitor's Book Store Publishing Division, Baton Rouge, Louisiana, 1966.

Parker, William B., and Viles, Jonas, Eds., *Letters and Addresses of Thomas Jefferson,* National Jefferson Society, Buffalo, New York, 1903.

Phillips, Ulrich B., *Life and Labor in the Old South,* Grosset and Dunlop, New York, New York, 1929.

Rawle, William, *A View of the Constitution: Secession as Taught at West Point,* Walter D. Kennedy and James R. Kennedy, Eds., Old South Books, Simsboro, Louisiana, 1993.

Rice, N. L., *A Debate on Slavery,* Negro University Press, New York, New York, 1969.

Richburg, Keith B., *Out of America: A Black Man Confronts Africa,* Basic Books, New York, New York, 1997.

Scott, Otto, *The Secret Six,* Times Books, New York, New York, 1979.

Simkins, Francis B., *A History of the South,* Alfred A. Knopf, New York, New York, 1959.

Sherrard, O. A., *Freedom from Fear, The Slave and His Emancipation,* St. Martin's Press, New York, New York, 1961.

Smith, Mark M., *Debating Slavery, Economy and Society in the Antebellum American South,* Cambridge University Press, Cambridge, U.K., 1998.

Soderlund, Jean R., *Quakers and Slavery, A Divided Spirit,* Princeton University Press, Princeton, New Jersey, 1985.

Swinton, William, *Outlines of the World's History,* American Book Company, New York, New York, 1902.

Tilley, John S., *The Coming of the Glory,* Bill Coats Ltd., Nashville, Tennessee, 1995.

Tucker, St. George, *A View of the Constitution of the United States: With Selected Writings,* Clyde N. Wilson, Ed., Liberty Fund, Indianapolis, IN, 1999.

Vallandigham, Clement L., *The Record of Honorable C. L. Vallandigham,* 1863, J. Walker and Company, Columbus, Ohio, republished by Johnson Graphic, Decatur, Michigan, nd.

Walvin, James, *Slavery and the Slave Trade,* University Press of Mississippi, Jackson, Mississippi, 1983.

Wharton, G. M., Ed., *Scriptural, Ecclesiastical, and Historical View of Slavery,* 1864, republished by Columbia Press, Tulsa, Oklahoma, nd.

Whipple, Edwin P., Ed., *The Great Speeches and Orations of Daniel Webster,* Little, Brown, & Co., Boston, Massachusetts, 1894.

Whitten, David O., *Andrew Durnford, A Black Sugar Planter in Antebellum Louisiana,* Northwestern Louisiana State University Press, Natchitoches, Louisiana, 1981.

Wilson, Woodrow, *Epochs of American History: Division and Reunion, 1829-1909,* Longmans, Green, and Company, New York, New York, 1910.

Wilkins, J. Steve and Wilson, Douglas, *Southern Slavery As It Was,* Canon Press, Moscow, Iowa, 1996.

Index

abolitionist(s):
- changing view of slavery, 32, 37, 42, 64, 65, 96-98, 101, 113
- critics of gradual emancipation, 78-88, 168, 189, 220
- emergence of movement, 31-34, 65, 67, 69, 71, 78, 110
- encouraging civil war, 232
- lack of biblical authority, 79-80, 83
- Lincoln's opposition, 166, 168, 170-71
- modern-day, 35, 93, 116, 121, 125, 136, 206
- Northern, 28, 52, 72, 160
- Republican Party, 172
- Southern, 28, 29, 32, 114, 148, 149, 152, 153, 160, 167
- unpopularity, 17, 168
- view of the South, 32, 36, 70-75, 88, 89, 113, 141, 227, 229

Adams, John, 50, 54, 103, 136, 230

Africa, 21, 205-22, 225, 227
- living conditions in, 214-218, 220
- natives/sons of, 148, 151
- as origin of slaves, 18, 64, 65, 104, 105, 117, 121, 137, 199
- "The Plan" (of Western domination) in, 222
- slave removal/return to: 27, 110, 170
- slavery/genocide in, 28, 221, 228, 206-7

African (Negro) inferiority, 25, 27-35, 60, 107-8, 112, 134, 137, 211-13

African slave trade (see slave trade)

African-American(s):
- as compared to native Africans, 214-19, 220
- as members of American society, 226
- as slaveowners, 62, 91, 125-33, 135, 138-39, 227
- as victims of discrimination, 211-14, 218-20, 223-24, 231-33
- as victims of slavery, 13, 61-63, 227-30
- and Abraham Lincoln, 163-68, 171-72, 179-81
- and crime, 233-35
- and discrimination, 211-14, 219-20, 232-33
- and reparations, 92, 233-34
- and the Southern Baptist Convention, 89-90
- and U.S. territories, 188-89, 191-92
- free born and slave, 101-39

Alabama, 39, 119, 186, 205, 234

American Indians (see Native Americans)

Appomattox, 147, 159, 196, 208

Arkansas, 203, 204

Articles of Confederation, 48, 143, 147, 148

Baptist church(es), 89, 95

Battle Flag of the Confederacy, between 144-45

Bettersworth, John K., 141

"Black Avenger" (see Hamblin, Ken)

"Black Codes," 219

Blanchard, J., 70-72, 86

Bonnie Blue flag, 204

"The Bonnie Blue Flag" (song), 203-4

Brown, John, 33, 34, 232

Calhoun, John C., 114, 169

California, 38, 39, 110

Charleston, 123, 127, 128
chattel slavery, 132, 207, 215, 221, 225
civil slavery, 145, 146, 151, 152, 159, 178, 207, 221, 222, 225, 234
Confederate flag, 62, 135, 195-209, 225
as "flag of slavery," 195, 198, 206-7
as symbol of racism, 195, 199, 201-2, 207, 209
as symbol of slave trade, 199, 207-8
Confederate States Constitution, 183-93
and the slave trade, 184-85, 187, 188
and slavery, 185-86, 189-90, 193
Connecticut, 45, 47, 50, 53, 87, 104, 107, 108, 126, 165
Cuba, 22, 24, 44, 105, 178, 208, 219

Dabney, Robert L., Rev., 24, 55, 71
Davis, Jefferson, 67, 96, 120, 136, 165, 167, 169, 183, 186, 188, 190, 205
Declaration of Independence, 30, 47, 52, 142, 143, 145, 156, 158, 159
De Tocqueville, Alexis, 27, 103, 106-7, 111
Dixie (place), 21, 64, 66, 105, 112, 202
"Dixie" (song), 203, 205
domestic slavery, 152, 178, 191
Dow, George W., 22
Durnford, Andrew, 128-29, 133

Engerman, Stanley L., 45
Emancipation Proclamation, 136, 165, 172, 173, 179, 229

Fire-Eaters, 37-40
First National Flag, between 144-45
Florida, 204
Fogel, Robert W., 45, 91
Franklin, Benjamin, 40-41, 104, 144
Franklin, Josiah, 40-41, 104
free man of color, 124, 128, 132, 133
free people of color, 47, 101, 106, 108-12, 125, 126-33, 137, 138, 178, 212, 213, 229, 231, 232
Fugitive Slave Law, 48, 49, 136, 192, 193

Garrison, William Lloyd, 34, 35
Genovese, Eugene D., 41, 101
Georgia, 30, 31, 191, 204
Greene, Lorenzo J., 42, 50

Hamblin, Ken, 92, 219, 220
Hardee, William D., 198
"Hate crimes," 223
Henry, Patrick, 36, 149, 161
Hopkins, Bishop John H., 55, 82-83, 88, 96, 99
Howard, Francis Key, 176-77

Ibrahima, Abd Rahman, between 144-45
Illinois, 78, 110, 165, 168
Indiana, 78
Ireland, 216
Irish, 16, 50, 129, 218, 220, 221, 222, 226, 234

Jasper, John, 90
Jefferson, Thomas, 29-30, 36, 66, 96, 149, 156
Johnson, William, 130-33

Kansas, 34, 189, 224
Kent, James, 116, 155
Kentucky, 25, 74, 76, 156, 157, 173
Kentucky and Virginia Resolves, 156, 157
Key, Francis Scott, 176
Ku Klux Klan, between 144-45, 207, 225

Lee, Robert E., 50, 66, 96, 136, 160, 165, 167, 178, 205
Leflore, Greenwood, between 144-45
"legacy of slavery," 61-63, 215-18
Lieber, Francis, 154
Lincoln, Abraham, 176, 181, 233
civil slavery, 136, 173, 178, 180
constitutional right of slavery, 168-70
destruction of the Union, 146, 148, 156, 163, 173-75, 180-83
dictatorship, 177
freeing the slaves, 164, 170-73, 178, 179
equality of the races, 60, 136, 163-72, 178-80, 186, 191, 223
freedom of press, 173
gradual emancipation, 164, 168-70
mandate to save the Union, 181
Native Americans, 200
Negro colonization, 27, 149, 165, 170
protection of the institution of slavery, 183
rights of slaveholders, 170-71, 183, 186, 192
slave revolt, 30, 172
slavery, 27, 30, 163-64, 167-72, 178

war objective, 171
worshiped, 163
Louisiana, 90, 93, 94, 98, 99, 122, 125, 126, 127, 128, 129, 130, 133, 138, 157-58, 173, 201, 204

Maine, 105, 212
Malmaison, between 144-45
Maryland, 25, 28, 99, 106, 127, 144, 154, 175-77, 179, 204
Massachusetts, 41-50, 53, 54, 55, 60, 78, 90, 94, 102, 103, 104, 105-6, 107, 108, 112, 116, 130, 141, 154, 157, 158, 188, 201, 202, 228, 230, 232
McManus, Edgar J., 111, 121
Minnesota, 166, 201, 202, 233
Mississippi, 12, 32-33, 37-40, 67, 89, 110, 128, 130-33, 141, 203, 204, 205, 211, 214, 215, 217-18, 220, 232
Moore, George H., 42, 43, 44, 54, 105, 141

Native American(s), 16, 19, 22, 41, 42, 50, 64, 65, 102, 104, 166, 199, 200
Native American slavery (see slavery)
New England, 23, 30, 32-33, 42-50, 53-54, 66, 71, 88, 94, 98, 99, 102, 103,104, 106, 107, 108, 158, 184, 185, 192, 208
New Hampshire, 24, 53, 105
New Jersey, 53, 87, 108, 109, 166, 230
New Orleans, 128, 129
New York, 41, 42, 48, 50, 53, 87, 98, 105, 107, 108, 110, 124, 126, 127, 128, 155, 166, 208, 212, 213
Nightingale, between 144-45, 105, 208, 230
North American Review, 154
North Carolina, 106, 121, 144, 204
Northup, Solomon, 124-25

Ohio, 55, 69, 70, 71, 77, 78, 84, 96, 110, 117, 136, 174, 175
Olmsted, Frederick L., 134

Pennsylvania, 28, 50, 51, 52, 53, 82, 87, 108, 129, 144, 154, 165, 212, 225
Phillips, Ulrich B., 101, 121, 123, 125
"The Plan" (of white supremacy), 222-24
political slavery, 151, 178, 221, 225
Polk, Leonidas, 198

Radical Abolitionism, 66, 78, 79, 80-83, 87-88, 122, 125, 136, 172, 227, 232
abuse of the South, 35, 36 death blow to early emancipation, 32, 40, 64, 65, 67, 98
non-biblical view of slavery, 69, 70, 83, 88, 96, 98
Radical Abolitionists, 31-37, 64-67, 101, 160
abuse of the South, 125, 152, 153
adverse reaction, 28, 33, 34, 35, 36, 64, 113, 116, 125, 136, 229, 232
efforts to incite slave insurrection, 30
negative reaction in the South, 32, 79, 80, 189, 227
unite with the Republican Party, 168, 172
view of slavery as sin, 71, 78, 82, 83, 87, 97
Randolph, John, 24, 114, 116, 117
Rawle, William, 28, 144, between 144-45, 153-56, 159-60, 180
Rhode Island, 50, 53, 104, 165, 208
Rice, N. L., Rev., 55, 69-88, 96, 136
Richburg, Keith B., 217, 219, 222
Roots, 91, 102, 123
Ryan, Fr. Abram J., 202-3

Saffin, Judge John, 54-60, 78
secession, 37, 141-61, 176, 190, 204, 205
Second National Flag, between 144-45
segregation (racial), 201-2, 219-20, 232-33
Sewell, Judge Samuel, 54, 55
Sherrard, O. A., 14
Simkins, Francis B., 24, 28, 33, 133, 136
slave(s):
beating (whipping), 45-46, 132-33
breeding, 44-45
emancipation, 28, 36, 37, 53, 70, 79, 109, 166
importation, 29, 30, 32, 51-52, 104, 108-9, 117, 137, 208
manumission, 15, 24, 130-32
uprising (servile insurrection), 33, 40
slave narratives, 91, 120
slave trade:
African, 19, 21, 23, 30, 32, 41, 52, 64, 66, 73, 91, 104, 115, 116, 117, 135, 138, 143, 149, 183-87, 190, 191, 193, 208, 228
American, 23, 24, 52, 66, 91, 104-5, 143, 208
Arab, 18
New England, 66, 104

Northern, 104-6, 208
Southern, 183-87, 190, 193
Trans-Atlantic, 18, 21-22, 64, 104, 105, 228
Trans-Sahara, 18, 228
Sub-Sahara, 18, 19, 64, 214-18
slavery:
abolition of, 14, 25, 27, 28, 30, 32, 35, 36, 37, 51, 53, 55, 64, 67, 69-99, 103, 108, 109, 111, 112, 113, 114, 115, 144, 149, 152, 154, 160, 167, 189, 190, 193, 228-29, 232, 233
African, 21-24, 30, 41, 43, 52, 55-60, 101-39, 115, 117, 135, 150, 151
ancient, 13-19
and the Bible, 54-60, 69-88, 89, 93-99, 105, 228, 229
and Christianity, 14-16, 19, 46, 49, 54-60, 69-99, 102, 125, 203, 206, 209, 215, 228
and the Confederacy, 183-209
and Lincoln (see Lincoln, Abraham)
and paternalism, 113-25
and religion, 14, 18-19, 54, 69-99, 102, 103, 228-29
and secession, 141-61
as sin, 69-99
defending, 34-35, 54, 71, 79, 114, 116, 134-35, 198
child, 17-18
hoax about, 233
in the New World, 21-67
in the North, 40-60, 91, 102-12, 134-38, 229-30
in the South, 23-40, 65-67, 91, 98-99, 102-33, 228-29
Jewish (Hebrew), 55-60, 81-82, 84, 94, 228
modern-day, 63, 206-7
myths, 227-28
Native American, 21-22, 41, 43, 47, 50, 104
proto, 16, 17
public versus private, 14
reparations, 92, 214, 218, 219, 226, 233
white, 16-18, 46, 50, 51, 65
Sons of Confederate Veterans, 195, 224
South Carolina, 24, 30, 90, 103, 106, 120, 123, 126, 127, 128, 130, 138, 158, 204, 212, 224
Southern Baptist(s), 88-93, 95
Southern Baptist Convention, 88-96
Racial Reconciliation Resolution, 89-96
State's Rights, 114, 115, 141, 146, 149, 156, 157, 159, 193
Stephens, Alexander, 191, 233

Tennessee, 198, 205
Texas, 119, 158, 204, 205, 223-24
Third National Flag, between 144-45
Tilley, John S., 32, 35
Time on the Cross, 91
Tucker, St. George, 50, 67, 115, 144, between 144-45, 148-53, 156, 159, 160, 161, 166, 178, 201, 207, 226

Uncle Tom's Cabin, 45, 91, 102, 123
Underground Railroad, 137-38
United Colonies of New England, 48, 192
United States Constitution, 24, 25, 39, 40, 48, 49, 144, 153, 183, 184, 185, 190, 192
Unusual Confederate flags, between 144-45

Vallandigham, Clement L., 174-75
Vermont, 24, 55, 82, 96, 99
Virginia, 28-30, 44, 46, 48, 55, 62, 67, 71, 80, 91, 104, 105, 110, 115, 127, 129, 144, 149, 156, 157, 163, 178, 188, 205, 228

Wanderer, The, 208
War for Southern Independence:
and abolition, 70
and invading Union army, 34, 200
and myth of slavery, 133, 142, 163, 211
and secession, 158, 180
and slavery/slave trade, 15, 41, 52, 53, 96, 102, 104, 105, 121, 127, 136, 141, 152, 160, 208, 229
cause and effects of, 95
Whitney, Eli, 31, 64
Wilson, Clyde N., 144, 149